Puerto Rico

Off the Beaten Path®

Help Us Keep This Guide Up to Date

Every effort has been made by the authors and editors to make this guide as accurate and useful as possible. However, many things can change after a guide is published—establishments close, phone numbers change, and facilities come under new management, etc.

We would love to hear from you concerning your experiences with this guide and how you feel it could be improved and kept up to date. While we may not be able to respond to all comments and suggestions, we'll take them to heart and we'll also make certain to share them with the authors. Please send your comments and suggestions to the following address:

The Globe Pequot Press
Reader Response/Editorial Department
P.O. Box 480
Guilford, CT 06437

Or you may e-mail us at:
editorial@GlobePequot.com

Thanks for your input, and happy travels!

OFF THE BEATEN PATH® SERIES

Puerto Rico

THIRD EDITION

by Tina Cohen
and John Marino

The
Globe
Pequot
Press

GUILFORD, CONNECTICUT

Details listed in this guidebook were confirmed at press time. We recommend, however, that you contact establishments before traveling to obtain current information.

Text design by Laura Augustine
Maps created by Equator Graphics © The Globe Pequot Press
Illustrations by Carole Drong

ISSN 1536-9455
ISBN 0-7627-2771-3

Manufactured in the United States of America
Third Edition/First Printing

Acknowledgments

Puerto Rico became part of my life when I got to know people who had grown up there and had maintained close ties with the island. Over the years, my family has visited the island many times and established more connections with Puerto Ricans, both there and on the mainland. It is this group of aficionados—my family and friends for whom the island is an important place—I have to thank the most. Sharing this place has been a privilege and distinct pleasure.

Two Puerto Ricans who generously answered questions, made suggestions, and provided intellectual backbone deserve special acknowledgment: Carlos Santiago and Martín Espada, both living in Amherst, Massachusetts. ¡Muchisimas gracias!

No book is ever written in a vacuum, and so this project was given nurturance and sustenance in many places: by colleagues at Deerfield Academy; friends who took great notes on their trips or listened to mine; and pen pals who lent their expertise by answering questions through their on-line Web sites. Specifically, Judy Leach and Jim Starke at http://enchantedisle.com helped with Vieques and Culebra, and Marcos and Emily Androcini at http://rinconadventure.com helped with the Rincon area. I also wish to thank the staff who worked with Michael Giessler in his office at La Calenta Guest House and Realty in Old San Juan. Lastly, I must thank the islanders who always make us feel welcome; their "mi casa es su casa" hospitality truly gives us a second home. ¡Saludos!

—Tina Cohen

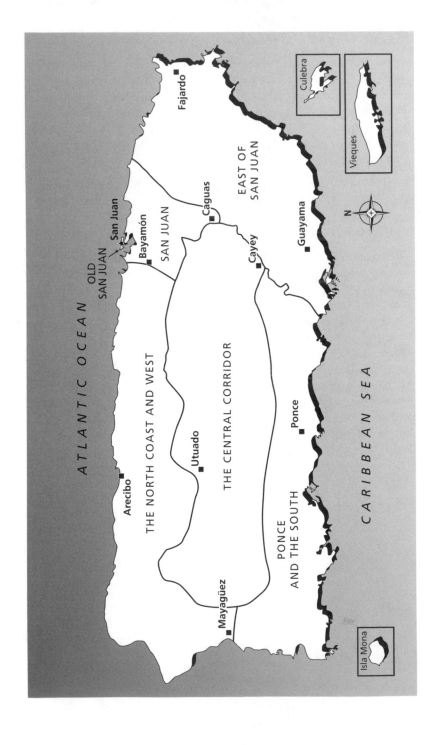

ATLANTIC OCEAN

Culebra

Vieques

N

Fajardo

EAST OF
SAN JUAN

San Juan

Caguas

OLD
SAN JUAN

Bayamón

SAN JUAN

Cayey

Guayama

Arecibo

THE NORTH COAST AND WEST

Utuado

THE CENTRAL CORRIDOR

Ponce

CARIBBEAN SEA

Mayagüez

PONCE
AND THE SOUTH

Isla Mona

Contents

Introduction viii

Old San Juan 1

Metropolitan San Juan 27

East of San Juan 53

Ponce and the South................................... 89

The North Coast and West.............................. 125

The Central Corridor 153

Index... 173

About the Authors..................................... 183

Introduction

Geography

Puerto Rico is the easternmost island of the Greater Antilles, a designation it shares as part of a chain of islands that includes Cuba, Jamaica, and Hispaniola. Its north shore is washed by the Atlantic Ocean, its south by the Caribbean Sea. At 35 miles long by 100 miles wide, it is roughly the size of Connecticut. The island's geographic diversity makes for a dramatic landscape. Karst hills of exposed rock undulate in the northwestern quadrant of the island; this limestone area also includes a vast series of caves. The *Cordillera Central* (central corridor) of mountains running down the island is full of jagged peaks. Its hillsides hold coffee plantations and steep, twisting roads. North and south, it levels to flat coastal plains cultivated in sugarcane, pineapples, and citrus groves. Rain forests of both primary and secondary growth have a dramatic presence as well as remarkable dry forests. Beaches are found in pockets around the island, ranging from rocky to sandy, white-sand to black.

Climate

The temperature averages around 82 degrees Fahrenheit year-round. It's slightly cooler in the mountains, most noticeably at night. Trade winds from the northeast and steady breezes moderate the heat and high humidity on the coast. Although air conditioners are routinely available, they are often unnecessary.

Hurricanes and drought are the two natural disasters Puerto Rico periodically faces. Hurricanes occur most commonly between June and November, the island's rainy season. If you're planning a visit to Culebra or Vieques, be aware that some hotels and inns close during September and October, in part due to the threat of bad weather that could lead to emergency conditions.

People

Puerto Rico's people reflect a rich mixture of Indian, African, and European roots. The earliest residents of the island were the Archaics, Arawaks, Taínos, and Caribs. The tribes found common ground defending their island in the early sixteenth century against the Spaniards, who enslaved the Indians and used their labor to mine the island's rivers for gold and silver.

It was the cultivation of sugarcane, a labor-intensive crop, that brought the next wave of outsiders. By 1518, West Africans arrived and were sold by Portuguese and Dutch slave traders.

During the nineteenth century, as other Caribbean islands claimed independence, Puerto Rico welcomed displaced Europeans and freed slaves. In 1873 slavery was abolished, and by 1897 the island had the right to self-government. In 1898 war was declared on Spain by the United States, and Puerto Rico was claimed as an American possession.

Even though Puerto Rico has been defined for hundreds of years as a "possession," islanders are clearly their own people with their own culture, influenced by their Spanish, Taíno, and African roots. Taíno symbols are a common motif in artwork. The most popular music is Latin, a hybrid with African roots and influences from the United States, the Dominican Republic, and Cuba. Architecture contains elements of styles both Spanish and African. Religion mixes Catholic and Yoruba (West African) beliefs and practices. Islanders favor the use of Spanish over English, although they usually speak both, sometimes combined as Spanglish.

Cuisine

Like almost everything else in Puerto Rican culture, Puerto Rican cuisine, most often called *comida criolla,* draws on the island's Taíno, African, and Spanish roots. Since the 1950s, the United States has had some influence as well. From the Taínos came yuca (cassava), *yautia* (taro root), corn, *ñame* (yam), peanuts, lima beans, black-eyed peas, and fruits growing wild such as guava, soursop, and pineapple. Spaniards introduced garlic, onions, eggplant, cilantro, and chickpeas. From their Latin American exploration, they also brought potatoes, papaya, avocado, cocoa, and coconuts. With African slaves came *plátanos* (plantains), *batata* (sweet potato),

Traditional Flavor

Ajilimojili *is the sauce to use with fried fish,* tostones *(fried plantains), grilled meat, or vegetables.*

For one cup:

4 garlic cloves, peeled
10 sweet chili peppers, seeded
1 tsp. black pepper
1 tsp. salt
½ cup olive oil
½ cup lime juice

Mix all ingredients in a blender. Store in a closed container in the refrigerator. Variations include using malt vinegar or lemon juice instead of lime.

INTRODUCTION

okra, and breadfruit. The American mainland interaction has added salads and fast foods and substituted healthier oils for the heavy use of lard.

Surrounded by water, the island's cuisine includes a lot of locally caught fish. Sea bass, red snapper, and shellfish, including *camerones* (shrimp) and *congrejos* (crab), are popular. *Bacalao* (salt codfish), shipped from colder climes, is also very common.

Poultry is probably the most popular main course on the island, and a traditional dish is *arroz con pollo,* chicken rubbed with a blend of garlic, onion, oregano, salt, and pepper and then sautéed and left to cook in a stew of onions, peppers, beer, garlic, chili peppers, and rice. *Lechón asado,* roasted suckling pig, is the national dish of Puerto Rico and is festively presented at holidays and family occasions. Roadside stands across the island offer this as a specialty year-round.

Island Life

The Puerto Rican government has created ways for islanders and visitors to enjoy special places around the island. There are parks with facil-

Public Beaches

Escambrón, *Puerta de Tierra, San Juan*

Carolina, *Route 37, Carolina*

Isla Verde, *Route 187, Isla Verde*

Luquillo, *Highway 3, Luquillo*

Seven Seas, *Route 987, Fajardo*

Flamenco, *Route 251, Culebra*

Sun Bay, *Route 997, Vieques*

Punta Santiago, *Highway 3, Humacao*

Punta Guilarte, *Highway 3, Arroyo*

El Tuque, *Highway 2, Ponce*

Caña Gorda, *Route 333, Guánica*

Playa Santa, *Route 325, Salinas*

Boquerón, *Route 101, Boquerón*

Añasco, *Route 410, Añasco*

Rincón, *Route 413, Rincón*

Crash Boat, *Route 458, Aguadilla*

Guajataca, *Route 446, Quebradillas*

Los Tubos, *Route 686, Manatí*

Cerro Gordo, *Route 690, Vega Baja*

ities at beaches and at other important natural areas. *Paradores* (small hotels) and restaurants provide a true local experience, and camping and *centros vacacionales* (vacation centers) offer affordable lodging.

Although Puerto Rican law defines all beaches on the island as public property, getting to or using some can be problematic. **Balnearios** are the answer. At these designated beaches around the island, the facilities include a parking lot, changing rooms with showers and lockers, lavatories, refreshment stands, picnic tables, and lifeguards. A $2.00 fee is charged for parking. Weekdays are quiet, weekends are busy. During the winter, *balnearios* are open from 9:00 A.M. to 5:00 P.M.; in the summer, they close at 6:00 P.M. The facilities close on Mondays, but beaches may still be visited. When a holiday falls on a Monday, *balnearios* are open and then closed that Tuesday. Call the Department of Sports and Recreation at (787) 728–5668 for information.

There are twenty *reservas forestales* (public forest areas) administered by the Department of Natural and Environmental Resources. They feature picnic areas, nature exhibits, and hiking trails and are open from 8:00 A.M. to 5:00 P.M. Tuesday through Sunday. Camping is allowed in some of the locations. Required camping permits must be obtained either by mail or in person at the department's offices in San Juan. Call (787) 724–3724 for details. Camping is permitted in the Caribbean National Forest at El Yunque, but you must secure a permit at the Catalina Work Center, located on Route 191 in the park. Because there are no facilities, everything must be packed in and out. For information, call (787) 888–1880.

Forests and Beaches With Camping

Bosque Susua, *Sabana Grande*	**Bosque Toro Negro,** *Orocovis*
Bosque Cambalache, *Arecibo*	**Balneario Playa Sun Bay,** *Vieques*
Bosque Monte Guilarte, *Adjuntas* (*cabins also available*)	**Balneario Playa de Cerro Gordo,** *Vega Baja*
Balneario Seven Seas, *Fajardo*	**Bosque Estatal de Toro Negro,** *Adjuntas*
Bosque Carite, *Cayey*	
Bosque Rio Abajo, *Utuado*	**Balneario Playa Flamenco,** *Culebra*
Isla de Mona, *Cabo Rojo*	**Balneario Punta Guilarte,** *Arroyo*
Bosque Guajataca, *Isabela*	**Lago Lucchetti Wildlife Refuge,** *Yauco*

Vacation Centers

There are five vacation centers sponsored by the Puerto Rican government. *Cabañas* (cabins) can be rented starting at $65 per night. The *centros vacacionales* are located in Añasco, Arroyo, Boquerón, Humacao, and Maricao. All are beach-oriented except for Maricao, set in the interior's mountains. Facilities are available for a minimum of two nights and maximum of four during the summer; in the winter, weekly rentals are permitted. The cabins and villas can sleep six, and the group must be considered a family unit. Accommodations include a very basic bathroom, kitchen, and bedrooms. Sheets, towels, and pillows must be brought, although their rental may be arranged ahead. Centers provide recreational facilities such as pools and basketball courts. Reservations must be made in advance but not more than ninety days ahead. Call the reservations office at the Compañía de Parques Nacionales, (787) 622–5200.

Inns and Guest Houses

Spending time in some of the island's prettiest and culturally significant spots is made easier by the provision of *paradores* and *mesones gastronómicos,* small inns and guest houses with restaurants featuring local ingredients and island cuisine. These are both sponsored by the Puerto Rico Tourism Company, (787) 721–2400. *Paradores* cost about $100 per night and are cheaper during the off-season. Reservations may be made by calling toll-free from the United States (800–443–0266), or on the island (800–981–7575). More information can be found on the Web sites www.gotopuertorico.com and www.prtourism.com. Accommodations and services vary, but each has a distinct personality and local identity. The restaurants offer dependably good food and often host area musicians on weekend nights.

Taxis and Buses

Puerto Rico has two bus systems: AMA (Metropolitan Bus Authority, 787–250–6064) and Metrobus (787–763–4141). Bus stops are marked with signs, PARADA or PARADA DE GUAGUAS. There are two routes visitors to San Juan commonly use. A5 takes you between Old San Juan and Isla Verde. B21 goes between Condado and Old San Juan, including Plaza las Américas. On Sundays and holidays, almost no buses run.

Holidays in Puerto Rico

The following holidays are observed throughout Puerto Rico:

New Year's Day, January 1

Three Kings Day, January 6

Martin Luther King's Birthday, third Monday in January

Eugenio Maria de Hostos' Birthday, second Monday in January

Presidents' Day, third Monday in February

Emancipation Day, March 22

Jose de Diego's Birthday, third Monday in April

Memorial Day, last Monday in May

Independence Day (U.S.), July 4

Luis Muñoz Rivera's Birthday, third Monday in July

Commonwealth Constitution Day, July 25

Jose Celso Barbosa's Birthday, July 27

Labor Day, first Monday in September

Columbus Day, second Monday in October

Veterans Day, November 11

Puerto Rico Discovery Day, November 19

Thanksgiving, fourth Thursday in November

Christmas, December 25

On the following days, all businesses are closed:

Good Friday

Easter

Mother's Day, second Sunday in May

Father's Day, third Sunday in June

Because there is no islandwide bus or train service, *públicos* transport passengers from town to town outside the metropolitan area. Check at the airport or Plaza Colón in Old San Juan for the vans; their destinations are noted on signs on the windshield. They generally travel to main plazas, so to customize a stop, talk to the driver and expect to pay extra. Because of the number of stops these vehicles make, travel is slow and timing unpredictable, but prices are cheap.

Taxis have posted rates for rides from the airport to Isla Verde ($8.00), Condado, Ocean Park, or Miramar ($12.00), and Old San Juan ($16.00). Extra charges apply for baggage and pickup service. In the city, you can catch a cab most easily from outside one of the hotels. After 10:00 P.M., there is a surcharge.

A good strategy is to ride the bus during the day and take a taxi at night.

Travel Information

The Puerto Rico Tourism Company (800–866–7827; www.gotopuerto rico.com) publishes a free magazine, *Que Pasa,* and *Go to Puerto Rico Travel Planner,* a series of helpful brochures. The tourism company's main offices are by the waterfront in Old San Juan: at La Casita (787–722–1709), open 8:30 A.M. to 8:00 P.M. Monday through Wednesday, 8:30 A.M to 5:00 P.M. Thursday and Friday, and 9:00 A.M. to 8:00 P.M. Saturday and Sunday; and in the La Princesa building (787–721–2400), open 9:00 A.M. to 4:00 P.M. Monday through Friday.

On the island, look for the free magazine *Bienvenidos,* published by the Puerto Rico Hotel and Tourism Association (www.enjoypuertorico. com). This publication is offered at hotels, guest houses, and inns. The association also publishes *Places to Go* magazine.

The *San Juan Star* is Puerto Rico's newspaper that appears in both English and Spanish. The Thursday edition lists weekend events. Other daily newspapers include *El Nuevo Día, El Vocero,* and *Primera Hora.*

Some visitors to Puerto Rico spend the majority of their time on the grounds of their hotel or the sun-drenched beach beside it. That just makes it all the easier to get off the beaten path and experience firsthand the charms of the place that Puerto Ricans call *la isla del encanto,* "the enchanted island."

Old San Juan

O ld San Juan is a seven-block, mile-square city wedged between the San Juan Bay and the Atlantic Ocean and connected to the rest of San Juan by a narrow strip of land named *Puerta de Tierra* (land gateway). San Juan, which is what all the locals call this historic zone, is the oldest city under the U.S. flag and the second oldest European settlement in all of the Americas. It began life in 1521 when Spanish settlers decided, over the objections of governor Juan Ponce de León, to leave their mosquito-plagued settlement in present-day Caparra for the peninsula that rises up as it narrows to split the calm bay waters from the strong Atlantic currents.

The breezy weather, which no doubt lured the first Spanish settlers, is still here today. Old San Juan, also known as the Old City, is an open, sunlit neighborhood of cleanly built Spanish colonial buildings with high ceilings and pastel-colored facades.

There's a reason writers call Old San Juan a living museum, and it has to do with the fortresses and mansions, monuments and churches, and other reminders found here of Puerto Rico's long and dramatic history. The island's recorded past dates back to Columbus's second voyage, a 1493 venture to colonize the New World. Although much less well-known than his 1492 journey of discovery, Columbus's second voyage was no less harrowing and infinitely more complicated, as it comprised seventeen ships and 1,200 men, including criminals, cartographers, astronomers, and common laborers.

Old San Juan is where you'll find some of the finest examples of sixteenth- and seventeenth-century Spanish colonial architecture in the Western Hemisphere. Many nineteenth- and early twentieth-century buildings also have been restored. Narrow stone streets, which climb from the bay to high ground overlooking the Atlantic, run through the city. Most of these streets still sport *adoquines,* the bluish chunks of slag brought here from Spain as ship's ballast. The streets are lined with colonial churches, residences, and mansions—all painted in pastel colors and many with wooden balconies.

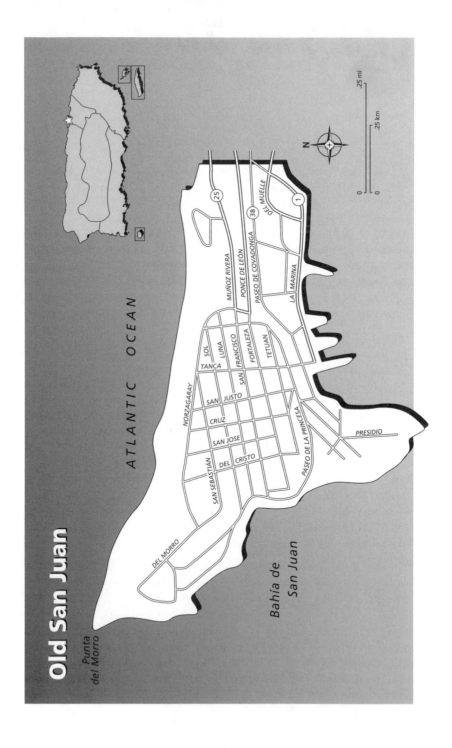

Old San Juan

Punta del Morro

ATLANTIC OCEAN

Bahía de San Juan

.25 mi
.25 km

N

DEL MUELLE
LA MARINA
PASEO DE COVADONGA
PONCE DE LEÓN
MUÑOZ RIVERA
SOL
LUNA
TANCA
SAN FRANCISCO
FORTALEZA
TETUAN
NORZAGARAY
SAN JUSTO
CRUZ
SAN JOSE
DEL CRISTO
SAN SEBASTIAN
PASEO DE LA PRINCESA
PRESIDIO
DEL MORRO

25
38
1

OLD SAN JUAN

Although it has a long history, San Juan is still very much a part of contemporary Puerto Rican life. It is a center of culture and art. There are fine examples of Spanish colonial and 1930s architecture. Galleries feature the best of current Puerto Rican art, and several museums offer traveling exhibits of all sorts. At night Old San Juan's clubs, restaurants, and theaters draw in visitors, while during the day its vibrant commercial sector and waterfront district do the same.

The Waterfront and Fortaleza

Visitors who come by bus or water or who take the lower route via Fernandez Juncos Avenue will enter Old San Juan by the waterfront district. The city's transportation hub, *Covadonga,* is at the corner of Covadonga and Harding, where you'll find a bus station, public parking, a stand for the free trolley, and a taxi stop. It's right across the street from the busiest cruise ship piers.

If you want to tour Old San Juan without walking its streets, some of which are hilly, you can hop the free trolley that starts at the Covadonga parking area and the La Puntilla parking area off the Paseo de la Princesa. Due to the congested streets, the thirty-minute ride will be at a leisurely pace, and you are free to get on and off the trolleys as often as you like.

For a taste of the island, check out the exhibit and rum tasting at *Casa Don Q* (787–977–1720), where you'll get to sample a variety of Don Q (*Don* is pronounced with a long *o* and the Q is *coo*) from the Serrales family of Ponce. This quality rum is not as well known as Bacardi outside Puerto Rico, and some of the ones you can taste and buy here are currently not exported. From October to April, it's open 11:00 A.M. to 8:00 P.M. Friday through Tuesday, 9:00 A.M. to 6:00 P.M. Wednesday; from May to September, 9:00 A.M. to 6:00 P.M. daily except Thursdays.

For tourist information, cross the street to visit La Casita at Plaza de la Dársena (787–722–1709). The yellow "little house" built in 1937, is now an office for the Puerto Rico Tourism Company. Rum tasting is also offered here as cruise passengers disembark on the waterfront. Open 8:30 A.M. to 8:00 P.M. Monday through Wednesday, 8:30 A.M. to 5:00 P.M. Thursday and Friday, and 9:00 A.M. to 8:00 P.M. Saturday and Sunday. Out on the plaza, vendors offer handmade crafts, food, and beverages. A popular snack is *piraguas,* shaved ice cones flavored with a tropical fruit syrup. On weekends, free concerts are often provided on an adjacent stage. The first Saturday of every month, prominent Puerto Rican artisans display their work outdoors from 6:00 to 8:00 P.M.

Behind La Casita, a point of land—La Puntilla—juts out into the bay with a parking area and several historic buildings. If you walk down Puntilla Street, you come first to La Aduana, the Old Spanish Customs House. Continuing on, you arrive at *El Arsenal* (787–724–5949). This was once a Spanish naval station and the last place vacated when the Spanish conceded the island to the United States in 1898. Today it houses exhibits sponsored by the Puerto Rican Institute of Culture; open 8:30 A.M. to 4:00 P.M. Monday through Friday.

With your back to the bay, across from La Casita is *Plaza de Hostos,* a small park with cement tables under shady trees. Locals, usually seasoned seniors, gather to play games of dominoes. Stop to relax and watch the players slap their pieces down as onlookers kibitz. Across the way, on Recinto Sur Avenue, is the original *Banco Popular* building, a restored Art Deco building from the mid-1930s. Its surrounding plaza, *Plazoleta*

Old Spanish Customs House

OLD SAN JUAN

Rafael Carrión Pacheco, is named for one of the bank's founders. In the bank's lobby, you can take the elevator to the third floor where an exhibit space holds changing shows of Puerto Rican art Tuesday through Sunday from 10:00 A.M. to 5:00 P.M. (787–722–7388). The strange and playful statue of a mysterious creature located outside is by local artist Jorge Zeno.

At the corner of Recinto Sur and San Justo is **Carli Cafe Concierto** (787–725–4927), a lively restaurant hosted by talented pianist Carli Muñoz, who played with the Beach Boys from 1971 to 1981. Carli attracts guest musicians who are visiting San Juan, providing quality sounds daily except Monday, when the restaurant is closed. Tables are available outside on the *plazoleta*, a popular location for combining good food, music, and people-watching.

Recinto Sur, the avenue that runs parallel to the waterfront, is known for its long string of restaurants. **Yukiyu Sushi Bar and Teppan-Yaki** (311 Recinto Sur; 787–721–0653) is Puerto Rico's most famous sushi place. Those who aren't sushi fans can also find satisfaction here. **Lupi's Mexican Grill and Sports Cantina** (313 Recinto Sur; 787–722–1874) is a Tex-Mex restaurant and sports bar famous for margaritas and fajitas. At 315 Recinto Sur is a new restaurant, **Ají** (787–723–3514), serving creative Caribbean cuisine daily for lunch and dinner. **Viet Nam Palace Seafood Restaurant** (332 Recinto Sur; 787–723–7539) is worth a look for midpriced entrees.

If a peaceful, scenic stroll is what you want, head west along the waterfront on **Paseo de la Princesa.** You can walk along the bay all the way to El Morro on the opposite side of the city if you wish. Just west of La Casita, you will come to a fountain and a statue, **Raíces (Roots),** by Luis Sanguino, which celebrates the island's diverse cultural origins. Also located on the promenade is **La Princesa,** an 1837 colonial building once used as a jail, reputedly one of the most feared in the Caribbean, and now the headquarters of the **Puerto Rico Tourism Company** (787–721–2400; www.gotopuertorico.com). On the first floor, art exhibits are open to the public Monday through Friday from 9:00 A.M. to noon and 1:00 to 4:00 P.M. Behind the building, along the east side, the vestiges of prison cells can be seen.

TOP ANNUAL EVENTS

Noches Galerias, first Tuesday of the month, September through December and February through May, at local art galleries and museums

Three Kings Day, January 6 on Calle Fortaleza

Fiesta de Calle San Sebastian, third week of January

Artisans Fair of Puerto Rico Tourism Company, late July

San Juan Bautista Day, June 23

Puerto Rican Music Festival, last week of November

5

The Raíces fountain

Continuing west, the city wall—*la muralla*—is to your right. Admire the endurance of these sandstone blocks that have stood strong since being constructed between 1539 and 1641. In places, the wall measures up to 20 feet thick. If you hadn't thought of San Juan's past, *la muralla* is a vivid reminder that the city began as a Spanish fortress for protecting the colony. Puerto Rico was the first and last place Spanish ships visited during trips between the New World and Spain; supplies, men, and precious metals all passed through here. Naturally, this *puerto rico* (rich port) attracted interest from other acquisitive European powers. La Fortaleza looms above *la muralla* in this southwest part of the old city. Walk far enough along the paseo to see the **Puerta de San Juan,** one of the six original gates through the wall. Here is where new arrivals disembarked from ships to enter the settlement. Walking up the short street in front, they arrived at the Catedral de San Juan and gave thanks for a safe passage.

After going through the gate, turn right on Recinto Oeste and view **La Fortaleza** (787–721–7000, ext. 2358; www.fortaleza.govpr.org), the first fort built between 1533 and 1540, which was quickly replaced by more strategically located fortresses such as Casa Blanca and El Morro. This complex has the distinction of serving as the oldest governor's mansion in continuous use in the Americas. You can tour La Fortaleza weekdays except holidays from 9:00 A.M. to 3:30 P.M. Ask at the visitor center for times of tours in English. Occupied twice by foreign powers, the fort briefly had the British flag over it in 1598 and the Dutch in 1625. The building was expanded between 1800 and 1846 and includes beautiful gardens. The governor occupying La Fortaleza since the 2000 election is Sila Calderón, the first woman to hold that position in Puerto Rico. Having also served as mayor of San Juan, Calderón announced in May 2003 her intentions to retire from politics after her term as governor ends.

Walking down *Fortaleza* Street offers many great opportunities for dining and shopping in the old city. Heading east from La Fortaleza, you'll stroll past many esteemed establishments. *Café la Violeta,* (56 Fortaleza; 787-723-6804) is a nice place to take a break. There's piano music in the pleasant main room Thursday through Saturday nights from 9:00 P.M. to 2:00 A.M. At 101 Fortaleza is *Pareo* (787-724 6284), a store with colorful apparel for women. The art gallery of *Frank Meisler Sculptures* (787-722-7698) showcases his intricate small metal works. *La Calle,* at 105 Fortaleza, is a small shopping "mall" of stores crammed with Puerto Rican goodies. The first you enter, *Olé* (787-724-2445), has an interesting selection of art prints, marionettes, santos, Panama hats, musical instruments, jewelry, and more. *Máscaras de Puerto Rico* (787-725-1306) features masks and hammocks. Across the street is *Barrachina Village* (104 Fortaleza; 787-725-8239 or 800-515-3582; www.barrachina.com). A plaque outside notes that this is where the piña colada was created. In the restaurant's bar, you can ask for a sample of this tropical concoction of coconut creme, pineapple juice, and rum. The setting is a verdant patio with parrots and turtles, a cool escape from the city heat. Stores around the complex offer fine jewelry, perfume, liquor, and island art.

Upstairs at 152 Fortaleza is a famous showroom and cafe, *Butterfly People* (787-723-2432; www.butterflypeople.com), long a fixture in Old San Juan. The gallery of mounted butterflies is full of artful arrangements that are stunning with their detail and iridescent colors. Purchases can be packed and shipped. The cafe serves light lunch fare

Taxis in San Juan

G ood places to pick up a taxi in Old San Juan are around Covadonga, across the street at the cruise-ship piers, and next door at the Wyndham. There are standing areas on Plaza de Armas and on the southern end of Plaza Colón, along Tanca Street. Almost everywhere in the metro area can be reached for $16, and most places for significantly less.

Trivia

Casa Blanca was built as a home for Juan Ponce de León, but he died without ever seeing it, perishing in what is now the state of Florida while searching for the Fountain of Youth. According to Taíno lore, the fountain he was seeking was actually located in Puerto Rico: the rejuvenating hot springs of Coamo.

from 11:00 A.M. to 6:00 P.M.; the store's hours are 10:00 A.M. to 6:00 P.M. Downstairs is **Saminá** (787-723-1027), a great place to shop for women's summer apparel with colorful batik designs.

Puerto Rican Art and Crafts (204 Fortaleza; 787-725-5596; www.puertoricanart-crafts.com) has a great variety of tiles, ceramics, jewelry with Taíno designs, metal and wood sculpture, santos, and hammocks. Open Monday through Friday 9:00 A.M. to 6:00 P.M., Saturday noon to 5:00 P.M. **Traditions,** another gift store featuring artisans' work is at 251 Fortaleza (787-725-0181). **Café Tabac** (262 Fortaleza; 787-725-6785) is a club with live jazz Thursday through Sunday evenings during the winter months. Men's clothing is the specialty at **Clubman** (268 Fortaleza; 787-724-5631). Stop in for a guayabera, the traditional dress shirt for Puerto Rican men (especially before the advent of air-conditioned offices), worn tieless and spiffed up with narrow tucks down the front.

The **Gallery Cafe** (305 Fortaleza; 787-725-8676) is a California-style bistro with salads and sandwiches. Check out the live music featured Wednesday through Saturday nights; it's a happening place. A good place to stay in the center of Old San Juan action is **Hotel Milano** (307 Fortaleza; 787-729-9050; www.hotelmilanopr.com). Opened in 1999, it has four floors with thirty rooms. The rooms aren't overly large but are clean and attractive. Continental breakfast is included. Up on the roof, there's a restaurant with a nice view, **Panorama Terrace Bar and Latin Grill** (787-729-9050), serving Puerto Rican dishes. Open noon to 10:00 P.M. Monday through Thursday, noon to 11:30 P.M. Friday and Saturday, and 2:00 to 10:30 P.M. Sunday.

At 311 Fortaleza, **Trois Cent Onze,** named in French for the address "311," serves food from the south of France and has an extensive wine selection. Open Tuesday through Saturday 5:30 to 10:30 P.M. and Sunday noon to 10:00 P.M. Check the schedule of live music. **Moondance** (315 Fortaleza; 787-723-0249) is an interesting store to browse for jewelry, art, and clothing from around the world. **Sala** (317 Fortaleza; 787-724-4797) is a new restaurant with live music and an ample dance floor. Open Tuesday through Saturday, 6:00 P.M. to 2:00 A.M., with music Wednesday through Saturday nights. Specialties include *mofongo*, ceviche, and calamari.

At 319 Fortaleza, on the corner of **Callejón de la Capilla,** is a house with two museums. The *Casa de Callejón* holds the *Museo de la Farmacia* (the Pharmacy Museum), with its exhibit of containers labeled with the herbs once used. Upstairs is the *Museo de la Familia del Siglo XIX* (the Museum of the Nineteenth-Century Family). Opened in 2002, this restored house showcases how a well-off Puerto Rican family would have lived. A tour guide, fluent in Spanish and English, explains the rooms and furnishings. Run by the Institute of Puerto Rican Culture (787–977–2700), a small fee is charged. Open Tuesday through Saturday 9:00 A.M. to noon and 1:00 to 4:00 P.M.

Down the alley Callejón de la Capilla is one of the newest attractions in Old San Juan, the *Nuyorican Café* (787–977–1276). A menu of moderately priced criollo dishes is available, but the big draw here is the music, featuring an array of styles like salsa, jazz, and folk. Open Tuesday through Sunday from 7:00 P.M., with live bands nightly. College students are big fans of this space and often put on shows of their own in the alley, sharing street theater, drumming, and poetry.

La Querencia (320 Fortaleza; 787–723–0357) offers respite with its comfortable elegance. The decor and creative dishes served here will make you think you're in Spain. Aris and Jaime Descals are hands-on owners, making you feel as if you've been invited into their home for the evening. One front room is being converted to a space for live guitar music and poetry readings; the other front room holds the Grand Jury Bar. Open Tuesday through Saturday 6:00 P.M. to midnight. *Restaurant Siglo XX* (355 Fortaleza; 787–723–3321) is a Spanish-style *panaderia,* a combination deli-bakery. Open for breakfast, lunch, and dinner with straightforward food at good prices. The exotic *Restaurante Tantra* (356 Fortaleza; 787–977–8141), serves gourmet Indian food and offers belly dancing on Friday and Saturday after 9:00 P.M. Open daily, noon to 11:00 P.M., later on weekends. At 358 Fortaleza, *Bossa Nova* offers Brazilian cuisine and music Tuesday through Sunday from 6:00 P.M. to midnight (787–722–0093).

The next three restaurants on the block all have "buzz." Owned by a local family, they offer high-impact ambience, innovative food emphasizing fresh ingredients, and a "see and be seen" allure. Beginning with the opening of *The Parrot Club* (787–725–7370; www.parrotclub.com) the area began to be referred to by some as "SoFo," a nod to SoHo, New York's neighborhood with trendy bars and bistros. This lively restaurant at 363 Fortaleza boasts bright Caribbean colors. The long bar is an inviting place to try the house specialty, Passion Parrot, a drink using *puncha* (passion fruit juice). The menu's Spanglish is a tip-off to the blending of culinary influences that create *nuevo latino* cuisine. Open daily, weekdays starting at 11:30 A.M. and weekends at noon. On Tuesday, Thursday, and Saturday nights, starting around 9:00 P.M., there's live Cuban jazz or salsa. A patio at the back offers a dimmer, quieter space.

Across the street at 366 Fortaleza is *Dragonfly* (787–977–3886), an especially hot little place these days. Described by many as resembling a bordello or opulent opium den with its exotic red decor, it fits into a narrow space ten small tables, one large one, and a crowded bar. Asian fusion is the cuisine and is inventive in transforming traditional Puerto Rican dishes. Open Monday through Saturday from 6:00 P.M. to midnight. One caveat: The music is house techno pumped up with a heavy bass. The vibes are youthful and glitzy, but possibly not for everyone. Next door is *Aguaviva* (364 Fortaleza; 787–722–0665), featuring raw seafood such as oysters, ceviche, and sushi Latin-style. The cool, euro-chic decor and patrons may remind you as much of Barcelona as New York. Open Tuesday through Saturday from 6:00 P.M. to midnight.

At the corner of Fortaleza and O'Donell Streets is the *Haitian Gallery* (367 Fortaleza; 787–725–0986), a fun store full of bright, primitive-style paintings, carved wood, and other handicrafts primarily from Haiti but representing, as in many stores, crafts from all over Latin America. Next door is a great little restaurant, *Café Puerto Rico* (208 O'Donell; 787–724–2281), with salads, *mofongo,* and lots more. *Wheels for Fun,* at 204 O'Donell, rents scooters or bicycles by the hour or day (787–725–2782).

O'Donell Street is the western edge of *Plaza Colón.* On the southeast edge on Fortaleza (at the corner of Norzagaray) is *Teatro Tapia* (787–722–0407), built in 1832. One of the oldest theaters in the Americas, it continues to be used as the setting for plays, operas, ballets, and other shows. Named for the writer and dramatist Alejandro Tapia y Rivera,

Bacardi Rum Factory

*T*he Catano ferry is the best way to go to the *Bacardi Rum Factory* (787–788–8400; www.bacardi.com). When you disembark, take a público (about $2.00 per person in a shared van) to the "Cathedral of Rum," as the distillery is dubbed. The free guided tours, tastings, and chance to shop for souvenirs are offered Monday through Saturday from 8:30 A.M. to 4:30 P.M. Some suggest you'll enjoy the tour more if you sample first instead of waiting until the end.

the theater was recently restored. Check for events being offered. Across the street from the theater is *El Casino,* a nineteenth-century social club for San Juan's elite, now used by Puerto Rico's Department of State.

Right around the corner heading toward the waterfront are two nice restaurants. For a fancy gourmet French meal, try *La Chaumiere* (367 Tetuán; 787–722–3330). At 359 Tetuán, *Café Zaguan* (787–724–3476) provides friendly service and simple food. Lunch is sandwiches; dinner is Mexican fare. With outdoor seating available, this could be a good place to take a break. Check for live rock on Friday nights.

If you want to get out on the bay, *Bahía San Juan,* there are several different ways to be waterborne. A ferry that runs across to Cataño boards at Pier #2, slightly west of the Covadonga parking. The *Acua Expreso* (787–788–1155) costs 50 cents each way and leaves every half hour from 6:00 A.M. to 9:00 P.M. Another ferry runs across the bay to *Hato Rey,* the section of San Juan with both art galleries and financial institutions. You can also head out onboard one of the cruise boats that ply the bay. **La Rumba** (787–375–5211) is a 65-foot boat that leaves from Pier #1 for eighty-minute trips twice a day. Evenings feature a nightclub scene with a bar and DJ. *Anticipation Harbor Cruises* (787–725–3500) goes out evenings for a one-hour party cruise with bar, music, and dancing. Other boats offer outings; check at the pier.

Norzagaray, San Sebastián, and the Fortresses

O n Plaza Colón's northeast corner looms *Castillo de San Cristóbal,* one of two fortresses on the Atlantic side of the old city. What began in 1634 as a small fortification spread to a complex on twenty-seven acres by its completion in the 1780s. Built as a defense against attacks by land, strategic units are connected by a maze of moats and tunnels. The view from *La Garita del Diablo* (Devil's Sentry Box) lets you look out over the surging water below. The U.S. National Park Service runs San Cristóbal and offers a video presentation and guided tours. Open daily, 9:00 A.M. to 5:00 P.M. (787–729–6960). A small admission fee is charged; one ticket admits bearer to San Cristóbal and El Morro.

Walk along the waterfront west on Norzagaray Avenue toward El Morro. You'll pass the subtle entrance to *The Gallery Inn* at 204 Norzagaray (787–722–1808; www.thegalleryinn.com). Your tip-off may be sighting some stony-faced heads staring back at you; they're the work of innkeeper and sculptor Jan D'Esopo. Jan and her husband, Hector Gandía, have

Devil's Sentry Box, San Cristóbal

created an incredibly eclectic, rambling guest house decorated with art, birds, plants, and antiques. With a clientele that includes many artists and musicians, the mix is lively. In the four connected houses, Jan offers twenty-two rooms with a variety of accommodations. There are great views from here to the water and the city, and terraces offer space to enjoy them, whether at continental breakfast or with an evening drink. Catered meals can be arranged in the sumptuous dining area.

As you head to the northwest corner of Old San Juan, you'll walk along more of the city's wall and above one of the poorest neighborhoods, La Perla. It was this slum that anthropologist Oscar Lewis wrote about in 1965 in his book *La Vida,* in which he described generations of some of its families with the now controversial label "the culture of poverty." La Perla is best observed at this distance, as it has been the location of street crime. Changes are appearing in the neighborhood's upkeep; while some neglected or storm-damaged buildings continue to deteriorate, others are being renovated and boast satellite dishes and pools.

West of La Perla is the ***Cementerio de San Juan.*** This cemetery can be reached by descending to it on a road accessible from the grounds of El Morro. There are works of art in the carved stones, and among those interred are important Puerto Ricans, including Jose de Diego and the father of the independence movement, Pedro Albizu Campos. The rotunda-topped chapel was built in 1863. Plan any sightseeing here for daytime hours.

El Castillo San Felipe del Morro, the fort whose shortened name, *El Morro,* means "headland," sits impressively at the edge of a huge rolling expanse of lawn. Built in 1540 to ward off attacks by sea, the fort over time underwent expansion and renovations, and was the largest Spanish fortress in the Americas. Sir Francis Drake led an unsuccessful assault on El Morro in 1584 when the British hoped to intercept New World gold being stored before transport to Spain. The National Park Service has a video presentation, tours, a gift shop, and a museum. The same ticket provides admittance to El Morro and San Cristóbal. Open daily, 9:00 A.M. to 5:00 P.M. (787–729–6960). The lawn is a popular place to picnic and fly kites.

Besides the venerable military vestiges of the city, this neighborhood also houses some of the best museums and cafes in San Juan. If you want a segue between sights, take a break on San Sebastián Street, famous for its restaurants and bars. On the corner of Cristo, at 100 San Sebastián, is *Nono's* (787–725–7819). With a great jukebox and lots of locals, this is one of the best places to sit and enjoy a cold beer. Try the Puerto Rican brew, Medalla. Some like it with a slice of lime. The second floor has balconies and pool tables. Or visit *El Patio de Sam* (787–723–1149) at 102 San Sebastián. This place is known more for its drinks than its food, but the burgers are considered the best around. Open daily, 11:00 A.M. to midnight.

At 104 San Sebastián is *El Boquerón* (787–721–3942), a bar open every day after 5:00 P.M. *Amadeus* (787–722–8635) is a well-respected restaurant at 106 San Sebastián. This trendy place features changing exhibits of art and Latin fusion cuisine. Open Monday for dinner from 6:00 P.M., Tuesday through Sunday for lunch and dinner, noon to 1:00 A.M.

Hijos de Borinquén, on the corner of San José Street, is a lively little bar with acoustic music that starts after 10:00 P.M. Down San José are several places worth looking at for night action. There's *Krugger's* (52 San Jose; 787–723–2474), a bar open Tuesday through Sunday nights. Across the street is *La Cubanita* (51 San Jose; 787–725–8837). Back on San Sebastián, at the corner or a little side street, Plaza del Mercado, is *Café San Sebastián* (787–772–9660) with food, a bar, and pool tables. Next door at 9 Plaza del Mercado is a new restaurant and bar called *Baires* (787–977–7126), which offers "sensual cuisine." Check *El Quínque* at 114 San Sebastián for live music.

A fairly new upscale restaurant with buzz is *Barú* (150 San Sebastián; 787–977–5442), where Latin and Mediterranean flavors combine in exciting creations like shrimp kabobs with yucca *mofongo.* Open daily except Monday from 5:00 P.M. to 3:00 A.M. For live music at night, the place to be is next door at *La Rumba* (152 San Sebastián; 787–725–4407). It's a mecca for fans of all ages of salsa, rumba, and Cuban jazz. There's no cover; a bar in front staves off thirst; and you can dance up a storm in the open space fronting the stage. (This is a place where to fit in you need to know the dance steps.) Bands start around 10:00 P.M., Thursday through Sunday.

Other bars in the area include *Café Seda* (157 San Sebastián; 787–725–4814) and *Aqui Se Puede,* at the corner of San Justo (787–724–4448). This little neighborhood bar is welcoming; its name translates to "Here You Can," and may refer to how comfortable you'll be while chilling to salsa and merengue on the sound system and quaffing cold *cervezas.*

With a street like that, don't get distracted from the cultural opportunities that await you here. The *Plaza de San José* is a pleasant space enjoyed by artists working in this area as well as tourists and residents. Tables serviced by the San Sebastián cafes add to the conviviality. A statue of Juan Ponce de León stands here, the product of melting down and recasting British cannonballs captured after the Brits' invasion attempt in 1797.

At Plaza de San José, you can visit two small museums housed in the Casa de los Contrafuertes at 101 San Sebastián. Built in the eighteenth century, it is considered the oldest house in Old San Juan. Its name translates to "House of Strong Buttresses," a reference to the architectural detail of its facade. Located here are the *Museo Pablo Casals* (787–723–9185), illustrating the career and accomplishments of cellist Pablo Casals, and the *Museo de Nuestra Raíz Africana* (Museum of Our African Roots; 787–724–0700). Both are important exhibits of sources of Puerto Rican pride. Museo Pablo Casals pays tribute to the great musician whose mother was Puerto Rican, spent the last years of his life on Puerto Rico, and for whom world peace and human rights were as important as his art (see box). Museo de Nuestra Raíz Africana honors the culture brought to the island with slaves from West Africa and looks at the tribulations they endured in their sojourn. Both are open Tuesday through Saturday, 8:30 A.M. to noon and 1:00 to 4:00 P.M. There is a small admission fee. Because of minimal staffing, either museum may adjust its schedule, leaving a handwritten sign noting the time to return.

Also at the Plaza is the *Iglesia de San José.* Built in the 1530s, it is the second oldest church and one of only a few of Gothic architecture in the Americas. Of note inside is a fifteenth-century altar from Cádiz, a wooden crucifix given by Juan Ponce de León, and the remains of the great Puerto Rican artist Jose Campeche. The church has been closed temporarily for restoration work but is due to reopen in 2004. Next door is the *Convento de los Dominicos* (98 Norzagaray), the Dominican convent built in 1523. Now home to a bookstore, crafts gallery, and gift shop run by the Instituto de Cultura Puertorriqueña (the Institute of Puerto Rican Culture), it's open Monday through Saturday 9:00 A.M. to 5:00 P.M. (787–721–6866).

Pablo Casals, A Special Puerto Rican

*P*ablo Casals is considered the world's greatest cellist and influential teacher as well as a composer and conductor. Born in 1876 near Barcelona in Spain, his mother came from Mayagüez, Puerto Rico. In 1937, unwilling to live under the fascist dictatorship of the Franco regime, Casals relocated to the French Pyrenees. When World War II ended and Franco remained in power, the musician refused to perform in any country that acknowledged Franco.

In 1955, Casals met Marta Montanez, a Puerto Rican whose mother was also from Mayagüez. They moved to Puerto Rico, where Casals supported an annual festival of classical music similar to one he had founded in France. His leadership was also sought to begin a music conservatory and a Puerto Rico symphony orchestra. The first Casals Festival was held in San Juan in 1957, the same year Casals married Marta. They lived in the Condado district, but later built a beachfront house in Isla Verde, where Casals enjoyed long walks on the beach. As the airport on Isla Verde expanded, the couple moved to Río Piedras, near the university.

In the last years of his life, Casals gained international respect for his humanitarian work on behalf of political refugees and for speaking out against human rights abuses. He was nominated for the Nobel Prize for Peace in 1958 and was honored by the United Nations.

In October 1973 Casals was stricken with a heart attack while playing dominoes with friends. He died a few days later. Although initially buried in Puerto Rico, his body was returned to Spain in 1979, as he wished, when Franco no longer ruled and democracy had been restored. A farewell ceremony was held at the San Juan Cathedral. The Museo Pablo Casals was later established in Old San Juan to showcase his talent, accomplishments, and contributions to the world. The annual Casals Festival marks the importance for islanders of a tradition, embodied in Casals himself, of quality musicianship, stirring performances, and the passion that music can express.

San Sebastián Festival

Fiesta de la Calle San Sebastián is a lot like Mardi Gras in New Orleans. Picture exuberance, Latin-style. Thousands come to Old San Juan during the third week of January to celebrate the good life with street music, dancing, art, and food, all centered around San Sebastián. The festival begins with a parade of marchers wearing oversized masks lampooning characters from Puerto Rico lore. This world-class party is an intoxicating experience for all the senses.

Between Plaza de San José and El Morro is another plaza, the **Plaza del Quinto Centenario,** with its tall granite and terra-cotta pillar. **Totem Telurico,** by artist Jaime Suarez, was erected for the quincentennial of Christopher Columbus's voyage to the Americas. With recognition of indigenous people as the island's first settlers, Columbus is no longer, popularly and inaccurately, credited with "discovering" Puerto Rico.

Close by is the **Escuela de Artes Plasticas** (787–725–8120), a school for the visual arts. It is housed in the former insane asylum, a connection artists may or may not appreciate. Another building here is the **San Juan Art Students League.** Between it and the Quincentennial Plaza is an underground garage, **Parking Ballajá.** The former home for the poor, Asilo de Beneficencia, built in the 1840s, is now headquarters for the **Instituto de Cultura Puertorriqueña** (787–724–5949). The institute, which features interesting changing exhibits in several galleries, is open Tuesday through Sunday from 10:00 A.M. to 4:00 P.M. Admission is free. Parque de Beneficencia is across the street.

Across Beneficencia Street stands the largest barracks built by the Spanish in the Americas, **Cuartel de Ballajá.** Dating from 1867, today it houses the **Museo de las Américas,** with two permanent exhibits of note. One presents popular culture and art from the continents of North and South America and the Caribbean islands; the other examines the culture of western Africa and its legacy in Puerto Rican life. Open Tuesday through Friday, 10:00 A.M. to 4:00 P.M. and weekends 11:00 A.M.to 5:00 P.M. Admission is free.

Casa Blanca (1 San Sebastián; 787–725–1454), built in 1521, was intended by the family of Juan Ponce de Léon to be his home, but he died in Florida while searching for the elusive Fountain of Youth, so only his descendants got to live here. The home's construction was significant in marking the development of the area as residential as well as a fortified defense. And indeed, to visit it now is to enter the most serene and peaceful place in all of Old San Juan. Although some of the grounds and several outbuildings are currently closed for renovations, the house is open Tuesday through Saturday from 9:00 A.M. to noon and 1:00 to 4:00 P.M. Until 1967, Casa Blanca was the oldest continuously occupied residence in the Americas. A self-guided tour with background from a helpful, bilingual staff member gives you an idea of early colonial life here, laden with its Spanish influences. If you're lucky, your visit will include overhearing an eloquent aria sung by the security guard as he patrols the grounds. The man and his music are famous in the neighborhood, and are really the frosting on the cake. A small admission charge gets you into the house; visiting the garden is free and highly recommended.

Cristo Street

oing south down Cristo from San Sebastián, you head toward the Catedral de San Juan, passing by a few secular places worth noting. What's a city without a good little ice-cream place? You can enjoy frozen treats at **Ben and Jerry's** (61 Cristo; 787–977–6882). Fans of this small-scale quality ice-cream chain love the incongruity of its Vermont trappings in the tropics. At 107 Cristo is a workshop, **Mi Pequeño San Juan** (My Small San Juan), referring to the fact that what is created here are miniature ceramic reproductions of various houses and storefronts from around Old San Juan, painted as brightly as the originals, and personalized to your request. Also for sale are tiles and other artwork (787–977–1636). Next door, another artisan's showroom worth seeing is that of **Monolo Diaz**. Known for his carved and painted wood, he has wall hangings and furniture for sale.

Il Perugino (787–722–5481), a restaurant at 105 Cristo, has been proclaimed the best Italian restaurant on the island year after year. Located in a restored 200-year-old home, dinners are pricey but memorable. Dinner is served nightly from 6:30 to 11:00 P.M. At 103 Cristo is **Don Pablo's,** a famous, grungy local bar that attracts young people. Next door at 101 Cristo is **El Batey,** another well-known hole-in-the-wall hangout. Even if you don't go in, take a look at the decor, which features business cards.

Across the street is the luxurious **Hotel El Convento** and its three classy restaurants (100 Cristo; 787–723–9020, 800–468–2779; www.elconvento.com). Opened in 1651, it was a Carmelite convent until 1903, and was then used variously as a flophouse, dance hall, and garage for garbage trucks. In 1962 a one-hundred-room hotel was opened in the rehabilitated space. The current owners have reduced the number of rooms to fifty-seven and have redone the hotel with high-end outfitting. There is a terrace where continental breakfast is served in the morning and a spread of wine and cheese is available in the evening. On the rooftop, a row of lounge chairs lines the edge of a small swimming pool and hot tub. Late at night, it's the perfect get-away for relaxing. The sparkling lights around you—stars overhead, ship traffic in the bay—are dazzling.

The hotel's restaurants include *El Picoteo Tapas Bar* (787–643–1597), which serves pitchers of sangria and more than eighty varieties of tapas Tuesday through Sunday for lunch and dinner. *Patio del Níspero* (787–723–9260), with lovely outdoor seating, serves lunch daily. *Café Bohemio* (787–723–9200) is a chic bistro in marble and mahogany. Offering lunch and dinner, it segues into a live music venue when the kitchen closes, after 9:00 P.M. on Thursday, Friday, and Saturday.

Across from El Convento on Cristo is the *Catedral de San Juan* (787–722–0861), the oldest cathedral in the Americas. Originally built in 1521 but destroyed by a hurricane, it was rebuilt in 1529. Three restorations have resulted in its present structure, dating from 1852. This is the final resting place of Juan Ponce de León, Puerto Rico's first governor. Open daily 8:30 A.M. to 4:00 P.M.

The small square across the street is the *Parque de las Monjas* (Park of the Nuns). The *Museo del Niño* (Childrens' Museum) is on the square's west side at 150 Cristo (787–722–3791). The interactive exhibits will feel like play, but your kids are sure to learn something too. Open Wednesday through Friday 9:30 A.M. to 5:00 P.M. and weekends 12:30 to 5:00 P.M. The museum is popular with school groups on weekdays. Admission is charged.

An interesting convergence occurs in this small section of the city: tributes to women important in the history of San Juan and the island. If you take the street on the southern side of this park dedicated to nuns, one block west, you'll arrive at the *Museo Felisa Rincón de Gautier* (787–723–1897) at the corner of Recinto Oeste and Caleta San Juan. This was the home of San Juan's beloved mayor Doña Felisa from 1946 to 1968. Open Monday through Friday 9:00 A.M. to 4:00 P.M.; admission is free. Doña Felisa is credited with creating the original Legal Aid Society to provide free representation for those unable to afford lawyers. Other innovative programs she began included day care for young children (a precursor to Head Start) and centers offering services for the elderly. Another former mayor of San Juan, now Puerto Rico's first woman governor, Sila Calderón, currently lives within reach here in nearby La Fortaleza. One block up Recinto Oeste to the north is the *Plazuela de la Rogativa* with its sculpture, **La Rogativa.** This statue of an archbishop accompanied by women bearing torches acknowledges the role they played as they marched through the streets of San Juan in

San Juan Cathedral

1797 as British ships offshore threatened the city. Hoping that a *rogativa* (religious procession) would strengthen their defense, they boldly held torches high and clanged bells. The women's action saved the day. Observing the commotion, the British believed reinforcements had arrived from the island's interior and General Abercrombie ordered a retreat. This sculpture was installed in 1971 by Australian artist Lindsay Daen in honor of his wife's Puerto Rican mother.

Across from the park, at the bottom of Caleta las Monjas, is a guest house called **La Caleta** (11 Caleta las Monjas; 787–725–5347; www.thecaleta.com). Situated in a quiet nook of this picturesque neighborhood, the apartments offer kitchenettes and comfortable furnishings;

Gallery Nights

*I*f you're in Old San Juan on the first Tuesday of the month, from February through May or September through December, you can partake in an evening of open houses and receptions in art galleries, Noches de Galerias. At least twenty galleries invite visitors to see their exhibits and enjoy refreshments between 6:00 and 9:00 P.M. Sometimes live music or theater is offered as well. It's a great occasion to browse the collections, stroll the streets, and conclude with a late dinner.

some have balconies with great views overlooking the bay. There are sixteen apartments with different combinations and affordable rates to choose from. Michael Gissler and his friendly staff are available on-site, but you'll feel like a local resident rather than a renter when you stay here.

Back on Cristo heading south, you enter the zone of high-end shopping for clothes, art, and souvenirs. Some of the names will be familiar to you as labels available everywhere. Discounts and no sales tax (except on jewelry) may entice you, but the locally owned stores and food establishments are what make the street browse-worthy. Two stores side-by-side could make the whole family happy. At 154 Cristo is **El Galpón** (787–725–3945), with a great display of Puerto Rican crafts, cigars, Panama hats, *guayaberas,* marionettes, masks—it's all here and of good quality. There's also **Spicy Caribee** (787–725–4690), tastefully displaying ingredients you can take home for the Caribbean flavors you'll miss. A selection of cards and small prints makes good souvenirs as well.

Kamel Art Gallery (156 Cristo; 787–722–1455), is a bead lover's heaven. Bracelets, earrings, necklaces, and purses—all exquisitely beaded—are the specialty here, plus Persian rugs and other exotic items. Speaking of exotic, the menu next door at **La Ostra Cosa** (787–722–2672) may appeal to you if you're wondering where to get a meal billed as an aphrodisiac. The setting in a lovely courtyard looks respectable, but the chef has mischief on his mind, promoting the sensual qualities (and practically guaranteeing the results) of the specialty, *ostra* (oysters).

At 200 Cristo is **Galería Fosil Arte** (787–725–4252; www.fosilarte.com), selling—yes!—art made from fossils. **Chef Marisoll Creative Cuisine** (202 Cristo; 787–725–7454), showcases the work of Marisoll Hernandez, Puerto Rico's first female executive chef and winner of many culinary awards. Open Tuesday through Sunday for lunch and dinner;

reservations are required. *Maria's,* at 204 Cristo (787–721–1678), provides beverages for every occasion; blender drinks, sangria, and Medalla are among the choices. The *batidas* (fresh fruit frappes) are famous. *Atlas Art,* housed in a building that's more than 300 years old, features fine art by Puerto Ricans, ranging from antique *santos* to modern bronzes by Angel Botello. It's located at 208 Cristo (787–723–9987 or 888–24–ATLAS; www.atlasgalleries.com) and open daily. Across the street at 207 Cristo is *Galería Palomas* (787–724–8904). At 209 Cristo is *Boveda,* a store with an assortment of artsy jewelry, clothing, and decorations, open Monday through Saturday 10:00 A.M. to 8:00 P.M.

The last block of Cristo is closed to traffic and makes for a quieter setting as you wind down this walk. *La Casa de las Casitas and Handcraft* (250 Cristo; 787–723–2276) has a good selection of crafts from around Latin America. Across the street at 255 Cristo is a small museum, *Casa del Libro* (House of the Book). Admission is free to see this collection of more than 5,000 manuscripts. You can appreciate the city's history here in a restored eighteenth-century house with items such as a document signed by Spain's king and queen, Ferdinand and Isabela. Open Tuesday through Friday 12:30 to 4:30 P.M. (787–723–0354).

The street ends at *Capilla del Cristo,* (Chapel of Christ). The tiny chapel draws people there to give thanks for miracles (see sidebar), and you can see the *milagros* they've left if you visit on Tuesdays between 9:30 A.M. and 3:00 P.M., when the gate is opened to admit visitors. Next to the chapel is *Parque de las Palomas* (Park of the Pigeons). It's a charming place with a lovely view of the bay, sometimes bustling with

Chapel of Christ

*T*his chapel celebrates miracles. It is a tiny outdoor sanctuary adjacent to the Parque de las Palomas at the end of Cristo Street. Built where it is, one explanation has it that the chapel prevents people and animals from falling over the edge of the city wall. In the eighteenth century, as the story goes, one rider in a horse race was carried down Cristo by his runaway steed. Both he and the horse fell over the edge. Although some records indicate he died, the popular conclusion is that he miraculously survived. Hence the chapel was built, in 1753, to commemorate Christ's intercession in the saving of a life. Over the years, believers have placed milagros, tiny silver replicas of body parts, on the altar in thanks for miracles of healing in their own lives. The fence admitting visitors is open on Tuesdays only, 9:30 A.M. to 3:00 P.M.

visits by children with parents or teachers in tow. If you enjoy pigeons or have kids with you who will, this park lets you indulge. Hundreds roost here, are tame enough to land on visitors, and gratefully accept the snacks of seeds you can purchase. Perhaps a prayer next door first will work as protection from the aerial droppings pigeons are famous for. Relax! With all the scenery, it's a great place to kick back.

Plaza de Armas and Surrounding Streets

P laza de Armas is the main square of the old city. Laid out by the Spanish in the sixteenth century and used over the years as a market and military grounds, it continues to play a role for residents who now consider it a place to relax. It is dominated by a fountain with four statues representing the seasons of the year in a knock-off of classical Roman sculpture. A kiosk sells refreshments, and there are tables in a gazebo.

On the north side of the plaza, on San Francisco Street, is the *Alcadía,* or City Hall (787–724–7171). Completed in 1789 to resemble Madrid's, it boasts turrets, balconies, and an inner courtyard. Open 9:00 A.M. to 5:00 P.M. Monday through Friday. Several other government buildings from the nineteenth century line the square along the western edge on San Jose Street.

Farther down is the new *Hotel Plaza de Armas* (202 San Jose; 787–722–9191; www.ihphoteles.com). Opened in January 2003 in a proudly restored building, it has fifty-one rooms. The ones facing the plaza have balconies. Continental breakfast is included; rooms have various arrangements to accommodate different needs. The hotel is polished and modern but also has some old-world charm.

Across the plaza on the eastern edge along Cruz Street is a friendly *Pueblo* supermarket (201 Cruz; 787–725–4839) full of helpful supplies and possible souvenirs. The array of island rum sells at a good price. Of interest are a coffee section, tropical fruit juices (many like the Puerto Rican Lotus brand of pineapple), and dried herbs and spices. Different snacks (like *plátano* chips), candies, and cookies are fun to try, and you can stock up on bottled water in gallon jugs if needed.

As you explore the streets around the plaza, you'll find a variety of interesting shops, galleries, guest houses, and restaurants.

La Mallorquina (207 San Justo; 787–722–3261) is a formal restaurant that's more than 150 years old. As they serve classic *comida criolla*, the waiters look stiff in their long white aprons, but they warm up as they answer questions. *Asopao* is the house specialty, done here as a shrimp stew. *Cafe Manolin* (258 San Justo; 787–723–9743) is a traditional San Juan restaurant with food at good prices.

One block west, *Club Lazer* (251 Cruz; 787–721–4479; www.clublazer. com) is a popular nightclub for the young. There's loud music, psychedelic lighting, a vibrating dance floor, and a rooftop deck for cooling off. *Divino Bacadito* (252 Cruz; 787–977–0042; www.divinobocadito. com) is a Spanish restaurant run by two ex-pats who brought their food and music from southern Spain with them. They offer flamenco dancing on Sunday, lessons on Wednesday, music nightly; closed Monday and Tuesday.

Two galleries on San Jose are worth a visit: *Galería Mora* (54 San Jose; 787–721–3454), with paintings described as "magical realism," and *Taller Galería En Blanco* (107 San Jose; 787–721–2646). *Hecho a Mano* (250 San Jose; 787–722–0203) offers handmade crafts.

Cafetería Los Amigos (253 San Jose) is just south of Plaza de Armas. Eating breakfast or lunch at this unpretentious luncheonette lets you mingle with the locals and enjoy simple food, good prices, and a *joie de vivre*. Closed Sundays. Next door, *Cronopolis Bookstore* (255 San Jose; 787–724–1815) is one of those places that inspires you to grab something off the shelf you must read. An intelligent selection of books in both Spanish and English is beautifully displayed, and there's great recorded music as well. *La Fonda El Jibarito* (280 Sol; 787–725–8375) offers *cocina criolla* in no-frills surroundings. This place comes with a certain *cachet*.

Luna is a multi-faceted street. Here you'll find *The Steam Works* (205 Luna; 787–725–4993), a gay bathhouse and La Cochera Parking Garage, between Cruz and San Justo. There are also many different art galleries and studios on this street including *Sin Titulo Galería de Arte Contemporaneo* (157 Luna; 787–723–7502), *DMR Gallery* (204 Luna; 787–722–4181), featuring handcrafted furniture, and *Galeria Arte Luna* (357 Luna; 787–725–8720).

Over on San Francisco, you'll find plenty to keep you busy. *La Casa del Peru* (257 San Francisco; 787–725–5754) is a fun excursion for browsing great arts and crafts from Peru. The furniture may be too clunky for the plane ride home, but there's lots of stuff here that's portable. *La Bombanera* (259 San Francisco; 787–722–0658) is an institution in the city. Fresh-squeezed *jugo de china* (orange juice) and a warm pastry from the bakery with *café con leche* (dark Puerto Rican coffee with steamed milk)—that's a breakfast! Open daily from 7:30 A.M. to 5:00 P.M.

Cafetería Mallorca (300 San Francisco; 787–724–4607) is similar to La Bombanera and reassuring in its fifties time-warp. Any meal is good here, and affordable. There's counter seating as well as tables. Waiters are efficient but busy. Closed Sunday. Nearby is *Galería Arte Espinal* (304 San Francisco; 787–723–1197).

Arepas y Mucho Mas (366 San Francisco; 787–724–7776) is a little cafe with Venezuelan *arepas,* South America's version of a corn tortilla, and a variety that ranges from breakfast to supper. Also here is *Jah Rastafari Store* (787–725–5432), a friendly place showcasing Bob Marley and Haile Selassie as heroes of the Rastafarians from Jamaica. You'll find posters, T-shirts, accessories, and a great selection of reggae and dub music. *Café Berlin* (407 San Francisco; 787–722–5205) features honest bread, delicious pastries, and healthy food thanks to Ernst, the German who runs it. You can grab a good sandwich here.

Conclude your tour of Old San Juan on Tetuán at *Galería Wilfredo Labiosa* (200 Tetuán; 787–721–2848), a respected art gallery, and *Gopal* (201 Tetuán; 787–724–0229) is a vegetarian restaurant run by a Hare Krishna family. The restaurant is attractive, the food energizing and affordable.

The recently restored *Santa Ana Chapel* on the corner of Tetuán and Cruz was historically an important stop for seafaring visitors.

Casa de Ramón Power y Giralt (155 Tetuán; 787–722–5834; www.fideicomiso.org) is the headquarters for the *Conservation Trust of Puerto Rico,* which oversees sites on the island such as Hacienda Buena Vista and Cabezas de San Juan. The building is a beautifully restored eighteenth-century home. Exhibits include Taíno artifacts and stuffed birds, plus a gift shop. Open Tuesday through Saturday 10:00 A.M. to 4:00 P.M.

PLACES TO STAY IN OLD SAN JUAN

THE WATERFRONT AND FORTALEZA

Wyndham Old San Juan
Hotel and Casino
100 Brumbaugh
(787) 721–5100 or
(800) 996 3426
www.wyndham.com

PLAZA DE ARMAS AND SURROUNDING STREETS

Guest House Old San Juan
205 Tanca
(787) 722–5436

PLACES TO EAT IN OLD SAN JUAN

THE WATERFRONT AND FORTALEZA

Al Dente Ristorante
Italiano
309 Recomtp Sir
(787) 723–7303

Dársena
Wyndham Old San Juan
Hotel and Casino
100 Brumbaugh
(787) 721–5100

Hard Rock Cafe
253 Recinto Sur
(787) 724–7625

NORZAGARAY, SAN SEBASTIAN, AND THE FORTRESS

Café Culebra
103 San Sebastián
No phone

Casa Borinquen
109 San Sebastián
(787) 722–7070

CRISTO STREET

Ambrosia
Cristo
(787) 722–5206

PLAZA DE ARMAS AND SURROUNDING STREETS

Caribbean Deli
205 Tanca
(787) 725–6695

Don Pancho's Café
253 Tanca
(787) 977 6401

El Buen Samaritano
255 Luna
(787) 721–6184

Il Grottino
369 Tetuán
(787) 723–8653

La Bella Piazza
355 San Francisco
(787) 721–0396

Metropolitan San Juan

*H*eading east from Old San Juan, as you transition from ancient to modern, you pass through the area known as Puerta de Tierra. This is the edge of the original settlement that was enclosed by a wall. Continuing east, the other districts of San Juan along the coast include Condado, Ocean Park, and Isla Verde. To their south are Hato Rey, Miramar, Santurce, and Río Piedras.

Many tourists spend their vacations at hotels in these areas, enjoying the ocean view, beaches, fine-dining choices, and nightlife that includes shows, dancing to live music, and gambling in casinos. From Puerta de Tierra to Isla Verde, the waterfront is a highly developed strip these days. You can easily forgo a car, relying on taxis, buses, or walking.

Getting off the beaten path in the metro area may mean a road trip farther east to Piñones or Luquillo. It could be time spent at the new Art Museum of Puerto Rico, or the University of Puerto Rico's botanical gardens in Río Piedras, or the marketplace in Santurce. You can hang with the locals enjoying the Isla Verde *balneario,* watching cockfights, eating at neighborhood restaurants, catching a *beísbol* game, jogging in a city park, or shopping in stores ranging from upscale to bargain.

It's no secret that San Juan is a gay-friendly city. Many establishments in the metro area advertise themselves as gay-owned and -operated. Condado and Ocean Park have a high concentration of these accommodations and nightclubs. Río Piedras, home of the flagship campus of the University of Puerto Rico, offers the ambience of a college town, including book and music stores, cheap restaurants, and great street life. Hato Rey has the combination of ultramodern office buildings and cutting-edge art galleries.

There's something for everybody in the diversity of metro San Juan!

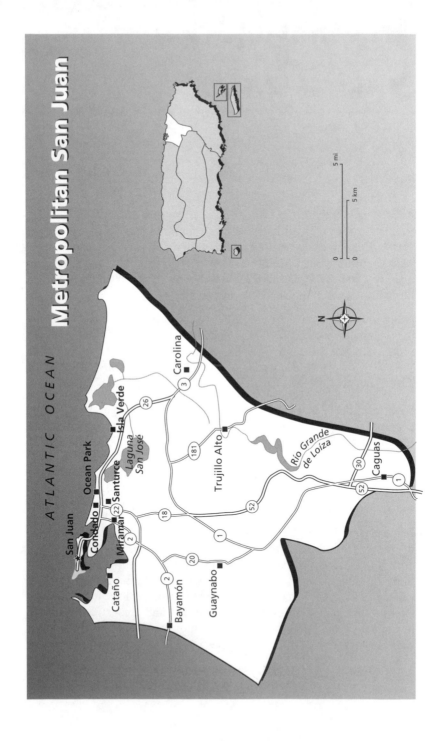

Metropolitan San Juan

ATLANTIC OCEAN

San Juan
Condado
Ocean Park
Miramar
Santurce
Isla Verde
Laguna San José
Cataño
Bayamón
Guaynabo
Trujillo Alto
Carolina
Caguas
Río Grande de Loíza

5 mi
5 km

Puerta de Tierra

Puerta de Tierra is the area located just beyond the wall of Old San Juan. It is named for the gate located there that opened to land *(tierra)* rather than sea. A somewhat shabby neighborhood, it is defined by a working waterfront, public housing, bars, and some government buildings. Gentrification, however, may be making inroads. Perhaps upscale restaurants in former warehouses will someday transform the low-chic setting.

There are two well-known hotels in this area. **Park Plaza Normandie Hotel** (787–729–2929; www.parkplaza.com), on Muñoz Rivera at the corner of Los Rosales, is an Art Deco building built to resemble the classic French ocean liner of the same name. The **Caribe Hilton** (San Gerónimo Grounds, Los Rosales Street; 787–721–0303 or 800–724–7500; www.caribehilton.com) was Puerto Rico's first successful hotel. Founded by Conrad Hilton in 1949, the Caribe Hilton was the first hotel in Puerto Rico designed to appeal to both business travelers and tourists. The hotel features a private beach, a huge exhibition center, Japanese gardens with roaming peacocks, an enviable location, and first-rate bars and restaurants. The circular bar overlooking the pool area is a contender for serving the best piña colada on the island, and some locals credit a bartender here with inventing the famous drink in 1957. The restored ruins of Fort San Gerónimo, which faced a British attack in 1797, are also located here, on a beautiful mount overlooking the Atlantic. The fort's entrance, behind the Caribe Hilton and owned by the Institute of Puerto Rican culture, is currently not open to the public.

Beyond the hotel, the first traffic light you come to marks a good point of entry for both the Balneario Escambrón and the Muñoz Rivera Park. The park is often the scene of special events and is filled with activity on weekday mornings. Skaters and skateboarders, as well as joggers and cyclists, find a welcome environment here. The park's **Peace Pavilion** was inaugurated in 1991 by Nobel Peace prize–winner Oscar Arias, the former Costa Rican president who brokered regional peace accords.

Visitors to Escambrón and related facilities use this entrance by going right at the light to get to the public parking. Pedestrians can also enter the public beach area on foot through the car exit beside the Normandie Hotel.

After turning at the light, you'll see the **Dumas Restaurant** (Reserve Officer's Beach Club; 787–721–3550), which serves up large portions of hearty seafood dishes with *criollo* flourishes. The back porch is the place to sit, overlooking the crashing surf.

Immediately in front of the Dumas Restaurant is a small plaza that overlooks a favored spot for local surfers. The area also attracts local anglers, both on shore and in boats.

The entire Escambrón beach area and adjacent sports complex (built to host the Pan-American Games in the 1960s) is undergoing a much needed face-lift with government plans for the Park of the New Millennium. The Sixto Escobar Stadium, named after the first Puerto-Rican National Boxing Association champion, hosts track-and-field and other sporting events. The Heineken JazzFest is held here every May and June at the outdoor Tito Puente Amphitheater. The palm-lined public beach is very much an urban experience; expect crowds on summer or holiday weekends. Outdoor showers and rest rooms are available, as well as places to barbecue. The more mobile might want to try the **Escambrón Beach Club & Restaurant** (Balneario Escambrón; 787–722–4785). Outside there's an open-air beach cafe serving fried food, cold beer, soft drinks, sandwiches, and hamburgers, while formal dining is available inside an air-conditioned restaurant specializing in Puerto Rican and seafood dishes. The place draws crowds all weekend, beginning Friday afternoon. The indoor restaurant features live music and dancing.

Great Live Music

*T*wo annual events present live Latin music in spectacular festivals in San Juan. A five-day **World Salsa Congress** meets each summer in late July and early August at the Caribe Hilton. For about twenty hours each day, there are dance demonstrations, workshops, and master performances with salsa dancers from around the world (787–274–1601; www.salsa congress.com)

From late May through early June, the

Puerto Rico Heineken JazzFest takes place at the outdoor Tito Puente Amphitheater. From its beginning in 1991, the festival has highlighted Latin jazz while presenting a wide range of jazz music. During the day, faculty from Boston's Berklee College of Music offer workshops. Each night's varied program includes well-known names and international stars who share the stage with local talent (787–277–9200; www.prheinekenjazz.com).

Past the Escambrón entrance, Muñoz Rivera Avenue winds beyond the nondescript condos before coming to great views of grassy, palm-lined bluffs overlooking the surf on the Atlantic side. Across the street you'll see a white wooden shack surrounded by scores of cars. This is *El Hamburger* (402 Muñoz Rivera; 787–721–4269), which serves up the best burgers in town, along with the best hot dogs, onion rings, and fries. A late-night favorite of *sanjuaneros,* El Hamburger also attracts the powerful and politically connected from the nearby capitol and the Popular Democratic Party Headquarters during the day.

El Capitolio (Ponce de León; 787–724–2030, ext. 2638), Puerto Rico's capitol building, is beyond the National Guard Museum and the nearby Armory. The white, domed, classically structured building built in 1925 is the seat of the commonwealth's Senate and House of Representatives and boasts a beautiful rotunda where the Puerto Rican constitution is exhibited. A variety of mosaics, statues, and other touches makes it a worthwhile visit. Open 9:00 A.M. to 4:00 P.M. Monday through Friday, with free guided tours available on the hour.

In front of the capitol is a plaza where you'll see a contemporary stone statue of Saint John the Baptist, the patron saint of San Juan. Descend the stairs to get to a surprisingly well-kept beach, good for lying in the sun, and good for swimming too. The beach is called *Peña Pará* by residents of Old San Juan and Puerta de Tierra. The walkway then

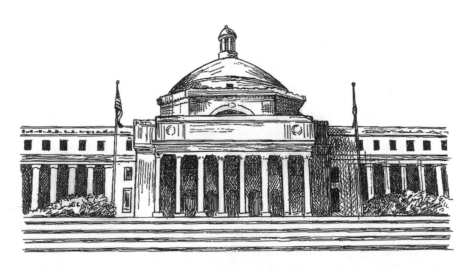

El Capitolio

begins winding around the beginning slopes of Fort San Cristóbal and on into Old San Juan.

Heading east along Ponce de León Avenue takes you past several interesting structures clustered beyond El Casino, in what is generally considered the last vestige of Old San Juan. The *Carnegie Library* (7 Ponce de León; 787–722–4739), which had been shut down for years because of hurricane damage, is now back and better than ever. Built in 1916 with a donation from Andrew Carnegie, it's a nice spot to read newspapers, check your e-mail, or use the Internet. Open 9:00 A.M. to 9:00 P.M. Monday and Wednesday, 9:00 A.M. to 5:30 P.M. Tuesday and Thursday, 9:00 A.M. to 5:00 P.M. Friday and Saturday. Also here is the *Casa de España* (787–724–1041), a blue-tiled structure with towers, built in 1935 by the Spanish expatriate community and now used for a variety of cultural and social occasions. The building can be seen in the movie *The Disappearance of García Lorca,* a thriller about the death of the Spanish poet.

Beyond the capitol is a small retail district. Here you'll find the *Archives and General Library of Puerto Rico* (500 Ponce de León; 787–722–2113), run by the Institute of Puerto Rican Culture. Books, video footage, vintage prints, and photographs are all stored here. Visitors can read up on Puerto Rican culture and even view videotapes of local films, including footage taken during the Spanish-American War. The archives are located in a building constructed in 1877. Built as a hospital, it was the last construction by Spanish colonizing the island. Call ahead for hours.

The Beach District:
Condado, Ocean Park, and Isla Verde

The *San Gerónimo Bridge* into the Condado is a favorite spot, drawing fishermen and swimmers during the day and couples taking romantic walks in the evening. It's easy to see why. The Condado Lagoon pours out to the Atlantic Ocean here, with the ruins of San Gerónimo on one side and the modern skyline of Condado on the other, and the air is always filled with the salty spray of the sea.

A trip across the bridge brings you into a bustling, prosperous modernity. The *Condado* is the closest that San Juan gets to Miami Beach—a world of luxury hotels and casinos, fancy retail shops, restaurants, and towering beachfront condominiums.

METROPOLITAN SAN JUAN

Changes are coming to Condado. The old convention center has been demolished and a new beachfront public park is planned for the area. The project has been dubbed "Window to the Sea." A new convention center will rise at the former naval base nearby. The opening is projected for 2005.

Ashford Avenue, which begins at the bridge into the Condado, is the sector's main strip, running between the ocean and the Condado Lagoon, with modern towers on both sides. Immediately beyond the bridge is the **Condado Plaza Hotel and Casino** (999 Ashford; 787-721-1000 or 800-624-0420; www.condadoplaza.com), a modern structure sprawling over both sides of Ashford Avenue, connected by a pedestrian walkway above the Condado strip. Like most of San Juan's top notch hotels, the Condado Plaza offers casinos, restaurants, and nightclubs. These city hotels are as attractive to San Juan residents as to the tourists staying in them. Even if you're renting more modest accommodations, think about checking out the international scene at one of the big hotels located in the Condado and Isla Verde districts. Whether you want great food in an elegant restaurant, a quiet drink at a bar with a live piano player, or a *cuba libre* (rum and Coke with lime) and a monster salsa band blasting Puerto Rican classics, chances are you can find it at a city hotel. The atmosphere is especially lively on weekends.

The Condado Plaza's casino is one of the biggest and busiest in San Juan, and its restaurants offer quality food. The Fiesta Lounge usually features live bands Thursday through Sunday nights.

Next door to the Condado Plaza is the more moderately priced and modest **Regency Hotel** (1005 Ashford; 787-721-0505 or 800-468-2823), which is so close it almost feels like a part of its larger neighbor. The hotel also houses the well-respected **St. Moritz** restaurant (787-721-0999), known for its pastries and meats.

The tangle of streets on the other side of Ashford Avenue, and extending out to the lagoon, is full of interesting lodging and dining options.

TOP ANNUAL EVENTS

Casals Festival, late January, Luis A. Ferré Performing Arts Center, Santurce

World's Best 10K Race, third week of February

Heineken JazzFest, late May and early June

San Juan Bautista Day, June 23 at bars and beaches

World Salsa Congress, late July and early August

Puerto Rican Symphony Orchestra, September through May, Luis A. Ferré Performing Arts Center, Santurce

San Juan Cinemafest, second week of November, Guaynabo

Feria Bacardi, second week of December, Cataño

On the corner of Ashford is *Ajili-Mójili* (1052 Ashford; 787–725–9195), where Chef Mariano Ortiz serves up Puerto Rican cuisine in a gourmet style with revved-up versions of local favorites like *arroz con pollo, fricasé de cabrito,* and even *mofongo.* The **Comfort Inn Tanama Princess** (1 Mariano Ramiréz Bages; 787–724–4160 or 888–826–2621; www.comfortinn.com) is a low-key alternative to the district's big oceanfront hotels.

Visitors can follow the coast of the Condado Lagoon as it winds around to Baldorioty de Castro Expressway. A nice jogging park surrounds it. Kayak rentals are available at the small parking lot at the lagoon's eastern end.

For every hotel on Condado's bustling oceanside drive, there's a guest house just off Ashford Avenue on a quiet, residential street only steps away. Many of these places are still within a block of the beach and the major hotels, yet they cost significantly less. Many have pools, friendly service, and comfortable rooms. More importantly, they often offer a more intimate experience of Puerto Rico that brings visitors in contact with everyday Puerto Ricans.

A small, quiet hotel, the new **Coral Princess Inn** (787–977–7700; www.coralpr.com) can be found at 1159 Magdalena. This twenty-five-room hotel offers restful tranquility in an otherwise bustling area. Only a short walk from great restaurants, casinos, and the beach, once inside you can relax in the garden courtyard, the comfortable sitting room, the rooftop hot tub or the pool. Rooms are nicely decorated. Continental breakfast is included.

Caruso Restaurant (1104 Ashford; 787–723–6876) is an elegant Italian restaurant serving gourmet dinners; reservations are required. Magdalena, a street that turns away from Ashford through much of the rest of the Condado before merging back into it, has some nice restaurants, too. *Urdin* (1105 Magdalena; 787–724–0420) is an upscale Spanish-influenced restaurant. Reservations are required. *Ramiro's* (1106 Magdalena; 787–721–9049) is considered one of the finest restaurants on the island, with the personal cuisine of owner/chef Jesús Ramiro, described as one of the island's most creative chefs. Reservations are recommended.

The **Atlantic Beach Hotel** (1 Vendig; 787–721–6900), which caters to the gay community, is a well-kept property with a deck bar overlooking the ocean and a restaurant that serves deli and American dishes. The nearby *Alelí by the Sea* (1125 Seaview; 787–725–5313) is a family-run guest house that has a sundeck overlooking the beach. There are nine renovated rooms with shared use of parking, living room, and kitchen.

The *San Juan Marriott Hotel & Stellaris Casino* (1309 Ashford; 787–722–7000 or 800–288–9290; www.marriotthotels.com) has a casino, live entertainment in its main lounge, and good restaurants. Its simple construction has an openness that seems to allow the sea and beach into the hotel. Across the street, on the rooftop of the *Diamond Palace Hotel & Casino* (55 Condado; 787–721–0810 or 800–468–2014), is *Martino's* (787–722–5256), serving good Northern Italian cuisine in a glass-topped penthouse with a wonderful view.

El Canario operates four quality lodgings in the Condado that strive to give their customers a laid-back, Caribbean guest-house experience (all can be reached at 800–533–2649; www.canariohotels.com). Besides *El Canario by the Lagoon* (4 Clemenceau; 787–722–5058), there's *El Canario Inn* (1317 Ashford; 787–722–3861), a cozy bed-and-breakfast. Around the corner on the ocean is *El Canario by the Sea* (4 Condado; 787–722–8640), within steps of the beach. In front of the Marriott, a half block off Ashford, is *Casa del Caribe: A Tropical Bed and Breakfast* (57 Caribe; 787–722–7139), a sleepy guest house with a nice pool, patio, and plenty of shady trees.

The Condado district is one of the finer places to eat in San Juan, and this section of Ashford is one reason why. *Via Appia* (1350 Ashford; 787–725–8711) is a sidewalk cafe serving great Italian food at good prices. The quality rivals that of much more expensive establishments. From the pizza to the veal scaloppini to the sausage and pepper sandwiches, this place delivers. Pitchers of sangria or cold beer entice diners to linger and enjoy the people-watching.

Right next door is *Salud* (1350 Ashford; 787–722–0911), a health-food store with a small cafe serving vegetarian fare. *Il Grottino* (1372 Ashford; 787–723–0499) has one of the island's largest international wine selections and serves fresh pasta and appetizers in an elegant dining

The Le Lo Lai Festival

Sponsored by the Puerto Rico Tourism Company, the *Le Lo Lai Festival* sponsors music and dance performances for visitors. The events are held around San Juan and elsewhere. A purchased card entitles you to admission to various shows featuring cultural traditions in song and dance from the Taíno, African, and Spanish roots of the island. For information, call *(800) 866–7827* or *(787) 723–3135.*

room or on an open-air patio. *Zabó Cocina Creativa* (14 Candina; 787–725–9494) combines a dining room in a restored century-old country house and a bar in its renovated carriage house. It's a beautiful spot, and the food is as inventive as its name suggests: a fusion of Caribbean, Italian, and Asian flavors. The thing to do here is to "graze" on assorted appetizers that you share with your companions. Try the conch fritters. *The Big Apple Deli* (1407 Ashford; 787–725–6345) is a New York–style deli and bakery with corned beef and pastrami sandwiches, bagels, and knishes.

Ashford Avenue turns into McLeary Street as Condado turns into *Ocean Park* and the high-rise condos give way to elegant split-level beach homes interspersed with Art Deco stone beauties from the 1930s. The beach scene here is decidedly more low-key than neighboring Condado and Isla Verde. The sandy, palm-lined beach at Ocean Park, fronted by large homes and an occasional guest house, is a favorite spot for locals. Here you can see all the way from the high-rise-ringed beach of Condado on one side to the palm-fringed beach at the start of Piñones.

Staying in this section could offer the most complete guest-house experience, and the beach might actually be the nicest in San Juan. The young and beautiful come here to play paddleball, windsurf, or just look good. Ocean Park also draws gays and lesbians, who provide a core market for the area's guest houses. Two favorites are *L'Habitation* (1957 Italia; 787–727–2499) and *Ocean Park Beach Inn* (3 Elena; 787–728–7418).

Two restaurants on McLeary are neighborhood staples. *Dunbar's Pub* (1954 McLeary; 787–728–2920) serves a surprisingly wide range of tasty food, with nightly specials around a theme like sushi or Mexican. The bar, which draws a lively crowd, is the other attraction here. Also try the famous *Kasalta's Bakery* (1966 McLeary; 787–727–7340), a fine Cuban-style bakery and deli, open 6:00 A.M. to 10:00 P.M., daily.

The Ocean Walk Guesthouse (1 Atlantic Place; 787–728–0855) has comfortable rooms, suites, and apartments for rent. There's a pool and a nice cafe/bar in an open patio fronting the beach. The establishment caters to a largely gay crowd, but the cafe draws a wide mix of locals and tourists, including the expatriate community. It's about the best place to get a beer at the beach in San Juan. Friendly service by Pablo, Sally, and the others, as well as the reasonably priced food, is also a draw. The beach in front of the guest house is a favorite of San Juan's youth, and the cafe's diverse crowd is frequently quite entertaining. The place really comes alive on sunny holiday weekend afternoons.

The atmosphere is a bit more laid-back in front of the *Numero Uno Guest House* (1 Santa Ana; 787–726–5010). This is a wonderful spot with a variety of comfortable rooms and a fine restaurant/bar, *Pamela's Caribbean Cuisine* (787–726–5010). The restaurant has a Pan-Caribbean focus and serves up some of the best food in San Juan, from jerk chicken sandwiches to the fresh catch of the day with a Caribbean chutney. *Hostería del Mar* (1 Tapia; 787–727–3302) is another beachfront guest house with a restaurant that serves health food.

The *Ultimate Trolley Beach* is a big white crescent at the border of Ocean Park and Punta Las Marías. *Barbosa Park,* which is across a narrow street from the beach here, is filled with soccer players as island aficionados gather to do their thing on weekends. The track here is one of the city's top sites for in-line skating and jogging.

The beach itself looks pretty good today, but it still hasn't bounced back fully from 1989's Hurricane Hugo. The street that winds along the beachfront contains the last guest houses until the district of Isla Verde.

Beyond the Ultimate Trolley Beach lies *Punta las Marías,* a neighborhood of private homes and beach retreats. The beach here is almost nonexistent, and the area is best known for its stretch of restaurants on the way from Ocean Park to Isla Verde. Loíza Street is the main artery into Isla Verde. For the young crowd there's *St. Mick's Irish Pub and Restaurant* (2473 Loíza; 787–727–6620), a typical Irish pub offering a variety of beer, food, classic rock, and televised sports. *Mango's Café* (2421 Laurel; 787–727–9328) maintains a Caribbean focus, from its

Street Festivities

*C*atholicism in Puerto Rico tends to extremes: worrying and celebrating. The celebrating part is manifested in public occasions around the island when communities honor their patron saints. Towns host parades, church services, concerts, and other weeklong fiestas patronales (street festivities) and it's a special way to see a place and its people. Check what's happening during your visit. A schedule of events is posted online at www.gotopuertorico.com.

The patron saint of San Juan, *San Juan Bautista,* is honored June 24. Parties take place all over the city, but many end up on the beach at Isla Verde at midnight, when everyone walks backward into the sea (or pool or fountain if need be) three times for good luck and as a blessing for the coming year. It's a night about baptism, and the tribute of liquid saturation is taken very seriously.

37

jerk chicken to its vegetarian Rasta burgers, serving a wide selection of sandwiches, very few entrees. *Che's Restaurante Argentino* (35 Caoba; 787–726–7202) serves Argentine and Italian specialties but is known for its excellent *churrasco* steaks.

Isla Verde, or green island, bears little vestige of its namesake condition, having grown into a concrete jungle two decades ago. Technically part of the municipality of Carolina, Isla Verde lies between San Juan proper and the Luis Muñoz Marín International Airport. Today it is a main boulevard lined with high-rise luxury condos and hotels, fast-food joints and restaurants, and rental car agencies in small strip-malls.

Isla Verde has the widest beach in metro San Juan, and water sports from kayaks to Jet Skis to parasails are available. The view from the beach is decidedly better than from the main drag, Isla Verde Avenue. The asphalt parking lots that front the hotels and condos on Isla Verde Avenue give way to grassy plazas and gardens and well-landscaped pool areas. As elsewhere in metro San Juan, tourists and locals interact on the beach.

The journey through Isla Verde is marked by fine restaurants. *Casa Dante* (39 Isla Verde; 787–726–7310) is the place to try *mofongo,* a mashed plantain dish that is one of Puerto Rican cuisine's real triumphs. It's served here with whatever you want, from a delicious *churrasco* to shrimp in a tomato sauce to a chicken consommé. A family favorite, the restaurant also offers up a tasty sangria.

Off the beaten path there are still some finds. The *Casa de Playa Beach Hotel* (4851 Isla Verde; 787–728–9779 or 800–916–2272) is one beachfront guest house that is on a quiet stretch of beach. The hotel also runs a friendly, open-air beachfront bar.

Creating a splash in the neighborhood is a glitzy, upscale beach boutique hotel, *The Water Club* (2 Tartak; 787–728–3666; www.waterclub sanjuan.com). Described as sensual, there are waterfalls on every floor. All eighty-four rooms have a water view. The rooftop has a sundeck and plunge pool. The bar, *Liquid,* and the restaurant, *tangerine,* have an Asian accent.

Tartak Street, farther along the strip, is a good place to enter the beach, as access is difficult through the stretch of hotels and private condos that follow. On the beachfront here is the *Hungry Sailor* (Tartak; 787–791–3017), a reasonably priced pub with friendly service, cable television, a jukebox, and a nice open-air porch.

The old Sands Hotel, now known as the *Inter-Continental San Juan*

METROPOLITAN SAN JUAN

Trivia

In 1978 Karl Wallenda, of the Flying Wallendas, fell ten stories to his death while attempting a high-wire cross between two hotels in San Juan.

Resort and Casino (5961 Isla Verde; 787–791–6100 or 800–443–2009; www.intercontinental.com), is known for its live shows at **Martini's**, including *Legends*, with its impersonations of Hollywood and musical stars. It's also home to **Ruth's Chris Steak House** (787–791–6100), serving up the same delicious steaks as it does everywhere else it's located.

Wyndham El San Juan Hotel & Casino (6063 Isla Verde; 787–791–1000 or 800–468–2818; www.wyndham.com) was refurbished in 1999. From its high-energy Las Vegas–style casino to its dark, mahogany lobby to the circular bar and huge chandelier, El San Juan is a class act. The live entertainment in the hotel's disco, **Babylon** (787–791–1000), helps draw an exciting crowd; this is one of the best spots to take in San Juan's intoxicating nightlife. Babylon is open Thursday through Saturday 10:00 P.M. to 3:00 A.M.

Cheaper digs can be found at the **Green Isle Inn** (36 Uno; 787–726–4330 or 800–677–8860), a block away from the beach. The rooms are equipped with kitchenettes, and the property has two pools, a bar, and a restaurant. Another affordable option at the end of Isla Verde Beach is **Hotel La Playa** (6 Amapola; 787–791–1115 or 800–791–9626; www.hotellaplaya.com), which has a big round bar, La Playa Lounge, overlooking the ocean.

Isla Verde is also home to the **Club Gallístico de Puerto Rico** (787–791–1557), at the intersection of Gobernadores and Isla Verde Avenues. The stadium is Puerto Rico's premier spot to watch the sport of cockfighting (Saturdays, 2:00 to 9:00 P.M.; mid-November through August). The sport may offend some, as the cocks are allowed to battle each other brutally (sometimes until the death), but it is a popular and long-standing island sport and tradition. Several similar *galleras* are located throughout the island. The most *auténtico* (authentic) are in Salinas. Bets are also made on the fights, of course, and an honor system ensures payment. All the shouting over bets and money lends the *gallera* something of the hysteria of a Wall Street trading floor.

Next door, at the Club Gallístico Annex, the good service and fine Cuban food of the **Metropol Restaurant** (787–791–4046) draw a steady clientele. It's one of Metropol's several full-service restaurants throughout the metro area.

The Ritz-Carlton San Juan Hotel and Casino (6961 Route 187; 787–253–1700 or 800–241–3333; www.ritzcarlton.com) is an elegant white

Caparra Ruins

The 1508 Caparra Ruins of Puerto Rico's first Spanish settlement include Juan Ponce de León's house.

marble structure located around the bend from the Isla Verde strip on the way to Piñones and Loíza. A casino and a variety of restaurants are among the reasons to come here.

Miramar

Beyond the bridge to Condado lies Miramar, a still-fashionable neighborhood whose shabbier sectors are looking worse. There are, in effect, two Miramars: the one of luxury condominiums squeezed between Ponce de León Avenue and Baldorioty del Castro passing by the Condado Lagoon, and the other between Ponce de León and the harborside Muñoz Rivera Expressway.

Right at the bridge are San Juan's two major marinas: ***Club Náutico of San Juan*** (482 Fernández Juncos; 787–722–0177) and ***San Juan Bay Marina*** (Fernández Juncos; 787–721–8086). Private boat charters and group fishing trips are available.

You'll find some of the area's best deep-sea fishing right off San Juan's coast. The ocean floor here drops off dramatically, meaning big game fish are in the immediate vicinity.

It's easy to find local anglers complaining about the decline in big-game fish, but the fish are still abundant, and the area continues to live up to its nickname, Blue Marlin Alley. Blue marlin are most prevalent in late summer, when Club Náutico runs a world-famous marlin competition. The area also has white marlin, yellowfin and blackfin tuna, sailfish, wahoo, and dorado, or dolphinfish.

It's a quick twenty-minute ride through San Juan Bay and out into the Atlantic to prime marlin grounds. It's literally possible to bag a big game fish in the morning and be back at dock by early afternoon. Two miles off the coast, the sea floor plunges to depths of 600 feet, and 45 miles out is the awesome ***Puerto Rican Trench,*** with a depth of 28,000 feet, the deepest spot in the Atlantic Ocean.

By the way, a fishing trip is worth taking just for the view of Old San Juan and El Morro from this vantage point. ***Benítez Fishing Charters*** depart from Club Náutica (787–723–2292).

Heading out of Old San Juan down what is now Fernández Juncos Avenue, you'll pass through one of Miramar's seedier districts. Immediately after curving past some of the more notorious establishments, the road winds through well-heeled neighborhoods with massive trees and stately century-old houses intermingled with Art Deco walk-ups and modern condos. *Murphy's Camera & Video Repair* (951 Fernández Juncos; 787–725–1565) is a good place to know—it's one of the few camera repair shops in Puerto Rico.

Backtracking through Miramar toward Old San Juan along Ponce de León Avenue is worth your while. The area on the right side, overlooking the Condado Lagoon, is one of the prettiest parts of metro San Juan. There are also several fine restaurants here. *Augusto's Cuisine* (801 Ponce de León in the Hotel Excelsior; 787–725–7700) whips up mostly French-inspired, European gourmet. Formal and expensive, but worth the price. Down the street at *Godfather's* (1426 Ponce de León; 787–721–1556), high-quality Dominican and Puerto Rican favorites such as *mofongo relleno* and *mangú* are sold at dirt-cheap prices. Also in Miramar is the *Fine Arts Cinema* (654 Ponce de León; 787–721–4288), which shows U.S. independent and European releases. The *panadería*, or bakery (which also serves deli food and even full-course Puerto Rican, Cuban, and Spanish meals), at the corner is a good bet, as is the open-air cafe across the street. *Chayote* (603 Miramar in the Olimpo Court Hotel; 787–722–9385) is a favorite of San Juan's elite, with chef Alfredo Ayala serving up Caribbean gourmet. Ayala combines *criollo* cooking with French, Indian, African, Spanish, and Central American cuisines. This restaurant is a "can't miss." Closed Sunday and Monday. Reservations are required.

Santurce

eyond Miramar lies Santurce, with its traditional downtown shopping area. To many Puerto Ricans it is still the heart and soul of San Juan. To the uninitiated this whole stretch through Santurce may be frustrating, because directions are given by the stops to a trolley that stopped running decades ago. Stop 18, for example, is at the intersection of Route 2, or Kennedy Avenue, with Ponce de León and Fernández Juncos. Also, while lack of street signs is an islandwide problem, it reaches ridiculous heights in Santurce. Even attractions such as the Museum of Contemporary Puerto Rican Art are unmarked.

Many locals come here to shop, others come here to work, and nearly everybody comes to eat. The area is loaded with *fondas* serving tasty *criollo* food. *Fondas* are restaurants frequented by the locals; family-run, they serve meals in a homey atmosphere. For island visitors, they offer the opportunity for tasty food, great prices, and wonderful ambience. There are open-air cafeterias featuring cold beer and loud jukeboxes.

Benicio Del Torres

Benicio Del Torres was born in 1967 in Santurce, Puerto Rico, the son of two lawyers. While studying business at the University of California in San Diego, a drama class convinced him to pursue acting. His big break in a major film came in 1995 in The Usual Suspects. *For his role in* Traffic *in 2001, he won a Golden Globe and an Academy Award.*

The area off Fernández Juncos, immediately preceding the towering sky-blue pro-statehood New Progressive Party Headquarters, is on the rise. Many of the homes are Art Deco gems that are being restored by new owners.

Continue down Fernández Juncos to get to **Sacred Heart University** (Colegio Universitario Sagrada Corazón), two blocks over on the other side of Ponce de León Avenue. If you're driving, take the left turn before the bridge into Hato Rey and then turn right at the Patio Shop. Pedestrians should get off at the bus stop before or after the curb and walk toward the university. Do not expect street signs in this neighborhood. The Patio Shop, a half block away on Fernández Juncos, is your best signpost, unless you're a local who knows it as Stop 25.

The university's pretty campus is best known for its small but well-done **Museum of Contemporary Puerto Rican Art** (Barat Building, Sacred Heart University; 787–268–0049). Here you'll find a fine permanent collection and excellent changing exhibits. Open 9:00 A.M. to 5:00 P.M. Monday through Friday, Saturday 10:00 A.M. to 4:00 P.M. Free admission.

Beyond the university the residential neighborhood spreads out over a hill toward the tough Barrio Obrero neighborhood. **La Casita Blanca** (351 Tapia; 787–726–5501) makes the area worth a trip. This is the most renowned *fonda* in San Juan. It serves reasonably priced local cuisine in a funky, Puerto Rican country-house setting, complete with an outdoor patio. This place packs them in and has received notices in *Gourmet* magazine and the *New York Times*. Look for stewed goat and other delicacies.

Once San Juan's premier commercial east–west corridor, Ponce de León Avenue is still the place for a number of the city's most popular nightclubs. Santurce's club scene runs the gamut, including straight and gay, "techno" and Top 40. **Warehouse** (1851 Ponce de León; 787–726–3337) and **El Teatro de Puerto Rico** (1420 Ponce de León; 787–722–1130; www.elteatropuertorico.com) are both popular with the young and hip and feature a lot of Latin pop. El Teatro's gay night is Sunday. Admission varies. The club formerly known as Stargate is now called **Pleasure** (1 Roberto Todd; 787–725–4664). It remains just as popular for dancing with its mix of Latin and gringo music.

José Ferrer

Actor, director, and producer José Ferrer was born in Santurce on January 8, 1912. He is best remembered for his Academy Award–winning performance in 1950's Cyrano de Bergerac. He also starred on stage in Othello, played artist Toulouse-Lautrec in the film Moulin Rouge (1952), and directed the stage version of Stalag 17 (1951). Ferrer died in 1992.

The patch of clubs dotting de Diego Avenue just east of the performing arts center is heavily Dominican. *Music People* (316 de Diego; 787– 724–2123) is a slightly upscale nightclub catering to a crowd that is mature but far from mundane. Merengue, *bachata*, and salsa are rhythms of choice. At 314 de Diego is *Galeria Raices* (787–723–8909) with works by emerging Puerto Rican artists.

Within a half block of Music People are several smaller, quirkier alternatives. The *Tía María Liquor Store* (326 de Diego; 787–724–4011), a few storefronts down, can be best described as an alternative bar for Puerto Rican men who prefer to keep their lifestyle choices under wraps. Local professionals and civil servants unwind after work and check their machismo at the front door. Across the street from Music People is *Margie's Little Professional Cocktail Lounge*—but don't let the name and the red lights mislead you. The women behind the bar will let you *dance* with them only for the price of a drink. Mellow but not melancholy, Margie's is typical of many Dominican pubs that cater to expatriate men who far outnumber their countrywomen in Puerto Rico. Next door to Margie's is *El Pollito #2*, a Puerto Rican–style hole-in-the-wall with cold beer and *criollo* food that manages to draw a lively crowd most Thursday and Friday afternoons and evenings. Occasional live music can be found there, usually *plena*, the spirited music born in the southern coast city of Ponce.

A new spot, *The Unplugged Café* (365 de Diego; 787–723–1423), has become popular for its food, bar, and great live music. You'll hear salsa, rock, jazz, and blues here. Closed Monday. Opens at 11:00 A.M. Tuesday through Friday, Saturday 4:00 to 2:00 P.M., Sunday 3:00 P.M. to midnight.

Farther along Ponce de León Avenue is the *Centro de Bellas Artes* and the *Luis A. Ferré Performing Arts Center* (corner of Ponce de León and De Diego; 787–725–7334). The center was built in 1981 to host theatrical, musical, and other cultural events. A winner of architectural awards, the complex houses three theaters. If you're going to be in town, it's a good idea to check out what's happening here during your stay; the center hosts everything from theater to opera to concerts by top Latin and U.S. performers. It's also the home of the *San Juan Symphony Orchestra* (787–721–7727; www.sinfonicapr.gobierno.pr). The Pablo Casals Festival takes place here, attracting talented classical musicians from around the world. This annual event includes guest orchestras and the Puerto Rico Symphony (787–728–5744).

The area between Ponce de León Avenue and Baldoriority de Castro, running from Canals Street to the Metro movie house, is the neighborhood in which the *Santurce Marketplace* (Mercado Central) is found. The 1912 plaza here has been restored and becomes the scene of a block party on Thursday and Friday nights with music, dancing, eating, and drinking. The market itself is a great place to dine on local food or stock up on fresh fruits and vegetables. Vendors also serve up fresh fruit frappes and other tropical drinks. There are also all sorts of other things for sale, from Santería (a Caribbean mix of Roman Catholicism and African religions) religious artifacts to classic musical recordings.

The neighborhood also features several restaurants that showcase live bands on weekend nights. The area has become a favorite happy-hour spot for *sanjuaneros,* especially on Thursday and Friday evenings. Crowds thread the narrow streets, drinking cold beer and eating *empanadillas* or barbecued *pínchos,* and moving to the music, which seems to come from everywhere. Popular beers include Medalla, a light Puerto Rican brew, and Presidente, a heartier brew from the Dominican Republic.

Directly behind the marketplace, *El Popular* (205 Popular) is a no-frills restaurant that serves good, cheap food during the day. Next door, *Compay Cheo* (103 Capital) has live music on Wednesday through Saturday nights. *Carnicería Restaurant Díaz* (319 Orbeta, corner of Dos Hermanos; 787–723–1903) has the feel of a neighborhood market and sells all sorts of drinks (try the fresh coconut juice) and Puerto Rican food, from *morcilla* sausage to fried codfish. It's a good place to base yourself while enjoying the weekend streetfest.

Across the street, *Restaurant Don Telfo* (180 Dos Hermanos; 787–724–5752) is a sit-down restaurant with reasonably priced Puerto Rican food. The ambience is enhanced by high ceilings, a mahogany bar, and a wall filled with photos of both famous and obscure satisfied customers. Next door, *El Pescador* (178 Dos Hermanos) may be one of the finest seafood restaurants in San Juan. The small restaurant is open Tuesday through Sunday from 11:00 A.M. to 6:00 P.M. Because of the restaurant's popularity, it's difficult to get a table between noon and 2:00 P.M.; try in the late afternoon.

American Vegetable Gourmet Shop (176 Dos Hermanos, 787–723–3299) is the retail outlet of this produce wholesaler. The store has a wonderful selection of Italian, Mexican, and Spanish produce, from fresh *nogales* (an edible cactus) and handmade tortillas to basil and plum tomatoes. If you're cooking in San Juan, this is the place to stock up on ingredients.

A nice vegetarian restaurant one block east of the marketplace is *Sabores Al Natural* (209 Canals; 787–722–4631). Open Monday through Thursday 11:00 A.M. to 5:00 P.M., Friday 11:00 A.M. to 8:30 P.M., and Saturday noon to 7:30 P.M.

Teatro Metro (1255 Ponce de León; 787–722–0465) is a topflight movie house showing current-run hits. It also hosts the annual *Puerto Rico International Film Festival* and *San Juan Cinemafest,* held in October. The movie house lobby has photos of how the place (and Santurce) looked in its 1930s heyday. Next door is *Eros,* a popular nightclub that draws gays, lesbians, and straights with its DJ'ed salsa and house music (1257 Ponce de León; 787–722–1131).

Farther down Ponce de León Avenue, in an area known as Stop 15, is another row of Dominican-run pool halls and dance spots, including *El Merendero Sport Center,* which stands out thanks to the green, hand-painted coconuts adorning the facade. The front half of the Merendero is an open-air sports bar with pool tables and big-screen televisions, while the back serves as a restaurant and, on weekends, a discotheque that features quality bands from the Dominican Republic. Attire is come-as-you-are, and drinks are modestly priced.

Now open at 299 de Diego is the acclaimed new *Museo de Arte de Puerto Rico* (787–977–6277; www.mapr.org). Outside, the building is 1920s neoclassic, but inside the galleries have cutting-edge technology. The MAPR has completed a modern addition to what once was a wing of the San Juan Municipal Hospital. This five-story complex houses important works by *puertorriqueño* artists from colonial times to the present, a gallery designed for children, workshops for classes, and a 400-seat theater named in honor of actor Raúl Juliá. A lush garden covers five acres and includes fourteen sculptures commissioned from Puerto Rican artists. The famous *Pikayo* restaurant (787–721– 6194) is here too, with Chef Wilo Benet blending French, Caribbean, and California cuisines. The museum is open Tuesday through Saturday 10:00 A.M. to 5:00 P.M., Wednesday til 8:00 P.M. Sunday hours are 11:00 A.M. to 6:00 P.M. Adults $5.00, children and seniors $3.00.

Hato Rey

eyond Santurce, Fernández Juncos meets Muñoz Rivera Avenue as it turns into San Juan's "Golden Mile" banking district, a line of high-rise office towers, home to some of the island's biggest names in finance and law.

Puerto Rico's two premier stadiums are named for pioneers in American professional baseball: Hiram Bithorn, the first Puerto Rican to play on an American major-league team, who pitched for the Chicago Cubs in 1942 and 1943; and Roberto Clemente, who joined the Pittsburgh Pirates in 1955, was MVP of the World Series in 1971, National League batting champ four times, Gold Glove winner twelve times, and the eleventh major-league player to record 3,000 hits.

More than 200 Puerto Ricans have now played major-league baseball.

Hato Rey's financial district keeps the sector lively throughout the day and well into the night. Fine restaurants are found on Ponce de León Avenue and on Franklin Delano Roosevelt Avenue into Puerto Nuevo. O'Neill Street, right off Muñoz Rivera, one block before FDR Avenue, is also full of great restaurants. Domenech Avenue is another mecca.

Restaurants specializing in just about every major cuisine in the world operate in this sector, and many are among the best in their class on the island. Four of the best Middle Eastern restaurants in the city are located here: *Jerusalem Restaurant* (1-G O'Neill; 787–764–3265), *Tierra Santa* (284 Roosevelt; 787–754–6865), *El Cairo* (352 Ensenada; 787–273–7140), and *Al Salám* (239 Roosevelt; 787–751–6296). All serve fine Middle Eastern food in comfortable settings and feature belly dancing on weekend evenings.

Hato Rey also boasts some of the finest Mexican food. *Frida's* (128 Domenech; 787–763–4827) is especially recommended, both for its food and for its rustic colonial atmosphere. An unusual ethnic mix is found in the food served at *El Zipperle* (352 Roosevelt; 787–751–4335); German and Spanish flavors combine here. This well-recommended restaurant is popular and expensive. Two Chinese restaurants, *Yuan* (255 Ponce de León; 787–766–0666) and *The Yum Yum Tree* (131 Roosevelt; 787–753–7743), draw Hato Rey execs for power lunches.

La Cueva del Chicken Inn (507 Ponce de León; 787–753–1306) has been a Hato Rey favorite for decades, renowned for its pizza, fried chicken, and barbecued skirt steak (*churrasco*). The domed, white stucco interior hasn't been fashionable in decades, but it's as cool and dark as its name implies, and the food is wonderful.

A hot spot for gay nightlife is *Concepts* (9 Chardon; 787–763–7432), with live music, dancing, and drag shows.

There's much more than food and money in Hato Rey. As you enter the district along Muñoz Rivera Avenue, you can see the *Martí Coll Linear Park* (787–763–0568), a boardwalk along a mangrove canal that runs from the financial district to San Juan's *Central Park* (787–722–1646).

Walkways and bicycle paths here are used by walkers and joggers. Central Park has facilities for tennis, jogging, baseball, and other activities.

Galería Botello (314 Roosevelt; 787–754–7430; www.botello.com) was founded by sculptor Angel Botella in Old San Juan, but the relocated gallery has thrived in Hato Rey as a showcase for contemporary Puerto Rican art.

The district is also home to *Plaza las Américas* (Roosevelt; 787–767–1525), the Caribbean's largest mall, drawing shoppers from across the islands. The mall is also on many tourists' itineraries, not only for shopping but for its restaurants, movies, and art exhibits.

Right across the street is the *Hiram Bithorn Stadium* (787–765–5000), an outdoor baseball park, and the *Roberto Clemente Coliseum*

Play Ball!

*O*ne of the pleasures of a winter visit to Puerto Rico is the opportunity to see baseball. No matter where you go on the island, you can find a municipal ballpark with a grandstand, lighting for night games, and an appreciative corps of fans. But for the most serious action, find a game played among the six teams forming the elite of winter professional-league baseball on the island: the **Bayamon** *Vaqueros,* the **Santurce** *Cangrejeros,* the **Ponce** *Leones,* the **Mayaguez** *Indios,* the **Carolina** *Gigantes,* and the **Caguas** *Criollos. Their season starts at the beginning of November and lasts until play-offs at the end of January. The winning team represents the island in the Caribbean League play-offs in early February. For more information, call the* **Professional Baseball League of Puerto Rico** *at (787) 765–6285.*

When it's Puerto Rico's turn to host the Caribbean series, the games are played in the **Roberto Clemente Walker Stadium** *(787–781–2256) on Highway 3. Tickets for the series are about $20 for general admission. Attending regular season games costs $5.00 to $10.00. Beer and piña coladas sell for $2.00. Printed programs don't exist, but Web sites for some of the teams carry rosters. And autographs can be obtained!*

Another important ballpark, the **Hiram Bithorn Stadium** *(787–765–6285), is located in Hato Rey, across from the Plaza las Américas shopping mall on Route 23. This is becoming the part-time home of the Montreal Expos, who committed to playing twenty-two games—almost a third of their regular season—on the island in 2003. If they decide to completely relocate from Montreal, Puerto Rico has been named as a potential site. During the winter season, the Santurce Cangrejeros (the "Crabbers") play here.*

(787–781–2258), an indoor sports complex. Puerto Rico has its own professional baseball and basketball teams that use these facilities, which are also used for track and field and volleyball tournaments. The stadiums also host concerts, festivals, traveling amusement parks, and fairs.

Behind the stadium and coliseum is the *Muñoz Marín Park* (787–763–0568), with picnic areas, bicycle and jogging paths, miniature lakes, and beautiful gardens. The park's main entrance is on Piñero Avenue. An auditorium gives regular presentations on the island's flora and fauna, and an open-air amphitheater hosts reggae, pop, and jazz concerts at night.

Down Roosevelt and Piñero Avenues lies the Puerto Nuevo district, which has its own fair share of fine restaurants. *Fishes and Crabs* (301 Matadero; 787–781–6570) and *Casa del Mar* (435 Andalucia; 787–782–3594) are two long-standing seafood restaurants that are favorites among locals. Casa del Mar serves until very late in the evening and often has live Latin jazz, especially on weekends.

Río Piedras

R ío Piedras is home to the University of Puerto Rico, as well as the Río Piedras Marketplace, two worthwhile reasons to come here.

The campus of the *University of Puerto Rico* (787–764–0000; www. upr.edu) is a sprawling, green oasis of trees, sculpted gardens, and stately buildings. A thriving bird population, including the rare Puerto Rican parrot, can be seen and heard here. The university has more than 25,000 students and faculty from throughout the world. Art openings and music and theatrical performances take place here at a handful of auditoriums. The university's *Museum of Anthropology, History and Art* (Ponce de León; 787–764–0000, ext. 2452) has an informative Taíno Indian exhibit as well as Francisco Oller's masterwork, *El Velorio,* or *The Wake.* Open Monday through Friday 9:00 A.M. to 4:30 P.M., Thursday until 9:00 P.M., and weekends 9:00 A.M. to 3:00 P.M. Free admission. The library has a Puerto Rico periodicals room that contains local publications—a good spot to catch up on current events or history. The campus is a wonderful attraction in itself, mixing its tropical garden feeling with a traditional collegiate ambience.

A few blocks from the pastoral campus is the *Mercado de Río Piedras* and adjacent shopping district. There's a lot of food for sale within the marketplace and in little stands lining the bustling streets that surround it. The market here is even bigger than at Santurce and offers fresh tropical fruits, vegetables, and herbs from around the island. Try the food stalls within the marketplace that serve fresh fruit drinks and fried *empanadas* or *pastelillos*.

There's a lively air inside the shops lining the **Paseo de Diego** pedestrian mall and other streets surrounding the marketplace, as customers and merchants haggle over prices. This area rivals Plaza las Américas, the mall in Hato Rey, as a draw for shoppers from across the Caribbean. It's not as fancy, but the prices can't be beat.

Behind the marketplace is the recently restored *Juan A. Palerm Transportation Center*, a bus, taxi, and *público* station. The best place to eat in the Río Piedras area is at **La Bodega del Hipopótamo** (880 Muñoz Rivera; 787 767–2660), located at University Avenue, the turnoff for the university and marketplace districts. Reasonable prices, an extensive menu that ranges from simple breakfast sandwiches to Spanish gourmet, and a long wine list are among its attributes. The restaurant has been a favorite of *sanjuaneros* for years. **Shannon's** (Centro Comercio Caribe; 787–281–8466) is an Irish pub popular with university students.

Most visitors will want to go to the **Botanical Garden of the University of Puerto Rico** (Jardín Botánico) at the traffic-congested intersection of Highway 1 and Route 847 (787–767–1710), located about ten minutes away from the main campus. Once inside, you'll be treated to another pastoral respite from the big city. Here on seventy-five acres are more than 200 plant species, an orchid garden with 30,000 specimens, a lotus lagoon, a palm garden, and extensive bamboo-lined paths. Many of the tropical and subtropical plants are from Australia and Africa. Open daily from 9:00 A.M. to 4:30 P.M., with guided tours and trail maps available. Free admission.

PLACES TO STAY IN
METROPOLITAN SAN JUAN

THE BEACH DISTRICT
(CONDADO, OCEAN PARK,
AND ISLA VERDE)
Arcade Inn
8 Taft, Condado
(787) 725–0668

At Wind Chimes Inn
1750 McLeary at Taft,
Condado
(787) 727–4153 or
(800) 946–3244
www.atwindchimesinn.com

Beach Buoy Inn
1853 McLeary, Ocean Park
(787) 728–8119 or
(800) 221–8119

Best Western Hotel Pierre
105 de Diego, Condado
(787) 721–1200 or
(800) 468–4549
www.hotelpierre
sanjuan.com

Borinquen Beach Inn
58 Isla Verde, Isla Verde
(787) 728–8400
www.borinquenbeachinn.
com

Days Inn Condado Lagoon
Hotel
6 Clemenceau, Condado
(787) 721–0170 or
(800) DAYS–INN
www.daysinn.com

El Consulado
1110 Ashford, Condado
(787) 289–9191 or
(888) 300-8002
www.ihppr.com

El Prado Inn
1350 Luchetti, Conado
(787) 728–5925 or
(800) 468–4521

Embassy Guest House
1126 Sea View, Condado
(787) 725–8284 or
(800) 468–0615
www.embassyguesthouse.
com

Embassy Suites Hotel and
Casino–San Juan
8000 Tartak, Isla Verde
(787) 791–0505 or
(800) EMBASSY
www.embassysuites.com

Empress Oceanfront Hotel
2 Amapola, Isla Verde
(787) 791–3083 or
(800) 678–0757
www.empresshotelpr.com

ESJ Towers
6165 Isla Verde, Isla Verde
(787) 791–5151 or
(800) 468–2026
www.esjtowers.com

Hampton Inn Resort–San
Juan
6530 Isla Verde, Isla Verde
(787) 791–8777 or
(800) 426–7866
www.hamptoninn.com

Hotel Casa Mathiesen
14 Uno, Isla Verde
(787) 726–8662 or
(800) 677–8860
www.casamathiesen.com

Hotel El Portal
76 Condado, Condado
(787) 721–9010

Hotel Iberia
1464 Wilson, Condado
(787) 723–0200

Hotel Villa del Sol
4 Rosa, Isla Verde
(787) 791–2600
www.villadelsolpr.com

La Condesa Inn
2071 Cacique, Ocean Park
(787) 727–3698

Mango Inn
20 Uno, Villamar
(787) 726–4230 or
(800) 777–1946

Mario's Hotel and
Restaurant
2 Rosa, Isla Verde
(787) 791–6868

Radisson Ambassador
Plaza Hotel and Casino
1369 Ashford, Condado
(787) 721–7300 or
(800) 333–3333
www.radisson.com

San Juan Beach Hotel
1045 Ashford, Condado
(787) 723–8000 or
(800) 468–2040
www.sanjuanbeach.com

Tres Palmas Inn
2212 Park, Ocean Park
(787) 727–4617 or
(888) 290–2076
www.trespalmasinn.com

Tu Casa Guest House
2017 Cacique, Ocean Park
(787) 727–5100
www.tucasaguest.com

MIRAMAR
Hotel Excelsior
801 Ponce de León
(787) 721–7400 or
(800) 289–4274

Hotel Miramar
606 Ponce de León
(787) 977–1000 or
877–MIRAMAR
www.miramarhotelpr.com

Hotel Toro
605 Miramar
(787) 725–5150

Olimpo Court Hotel
603 Miramar
(787) 724–0600

PLACES TO EAT IN
METROPOLITAN SAN JUAN

THE BEACH DISTRICT
(CONDADO, OCEAN PARK,
AND ISLA VERDE)
Antonio's
1406 Magdalena, Condado
(787) 723–7567

Back Street Hong Kong
Wyndham El San Juan
Hotel
6063 Isla Verde, Isla Verde
(787) 791–1224

Café de Angel
1106 Ashford, Condado
(787) 643–7594

Casa Dante
39 Loíza, Ocean Park
(787) 726-7310

Cielito Lindo
1108 Magdalena, Condado
(787) 723-5597

Cobia Tapas Bar and
Seafood Grill
999 Ashford, Condado
(787) 721-1000

Greenhouse Restaurant
Diamond Palace Hotel
55 Condado, Condado
(787) 725-4036

Hacienda Don José
1025 Ashford, Condado
(787) 722-5880

Hermés Creative Cuisine
1108 Ashford, Condado
(787) 723-5151

Hostería del Mar
1 Tapia, Ocean Park
(787) 727-3302

José José
1110 Magdalena, Condado
(787) 725-8496

La Belle Epoque Creperie
Bistro de Vin
1400 Magdalena, Condado
(787) 977-1765

La Patisserie de France
1504 Ashford, Condado
(787) 728-5508

La Scala
1369 Ashford, Condado
(787) 725-7470

Los Faisanes
1108 Magdalena, Condado
(787) 725-2801

Marisquería Atlántica
2475 Loíza, Ocean Park
(787) 726-6654

Marisquería Dorada
1105 Magdalena, Condado
(787) 722-9583

Marisquería Miro
Hotel El Portal
74 Condado, Condado
(787) 723-9593

Napa
1018 Ashford, Condado
(787) 724-3686

Pepin's
2479 Isla Verde, Ocean Park
(787) 728-6280

Pinky's
51 Maria Moczo,
Ocean Park
(787) 727-3347

Repostería Kasalta
1966 McLeary, Ocean Park
(787) 727-7340

Stone Crab Alley
1214 Ashford, Condado
(787) 722-8438

Van Gogh
60 Condado, Condado
(787) 723-8193

Yerba Buena Café
1350 Ashford, Condado
(787) 721-5700

MIRAMAR
Pizzaiolo
47 Isla Verde
(787) 268-0622

SANTURCE
Compostela
106 Condado
(787) 724-6088

Havana's Café
409 del Parque
(787) 725-0888

La Casona
609 San Jorge
(787) 727-2717

Mangere
311 de Diego
(787) 792-6748

HATO REY
Allegro Ristorante
1350 Roosevelt,
Puerto Nuevo
(787) 273-9055

Aurorita's
303 de Diego, Puerto Nuevo
(787) 783-2899

Deli Restaurant Argentino
235 Roosevelt
(787) 753-1853

El Belén
312-A Piñero
(787) 282-6332

El Muelle
191 O'Neill
(787) 767-7825

Los Chavales
253 Roosevelt
(787) 767-5017

Margarita's Restaurante
Mexicano
1013 Roosevelt, Puerto
Nuevo
(787) 781-8452

Metropol II
124 Roosevelt
(787) 751-4022

Spice Restaurant and
Tapas Bar
1646 Pinero
(787) 782-0503

RÍO PIEDRAS
Café Valencia
1000 Muñoz Rivera
(787) 764–4786

El Buen Gusto
1117 William Jones
no phone

El Isleno
Plaza Olmedo
1790 Lomas Verdes
(787) 250–8046

La Bodega del Hipopstamo
880 Muñoz Rivera
(787) 767–2660

Middle East Restaurant
207 Padre Colón
(787) 751–7304

East of San Juan

To the east of the city, beyond Isla Verde and the airport, is a bit of untamed coastline. Leaving San Juan on Highway 26 or Route 37, get on Route 187 east and cross the bridge over Boca de Cangrejos and into Piñones.

Piñones

Although it could geographically be described as a San Juan suburb, the term doesn't fit here. Despite its proximity to the city, Piñones is remarkable for preserving a unique identity in the face of urban sprawl. What you'll notice by the road are battered shacks with food cooking outdoors, tall pines leading to the water's edge, and thick mangrove forest. Besides the wild scenery, the draw for visiting Piñones is eating, drinking, and music.

Depending on the day, places get progressively busier as the locals come to relax, teens play pool and the jukebox, and tourists get in on a good thing. If you're there while the sun is high, you can bike or walk the new government-built trail, the Paseo de Piñones, which takes you through coastal and forest areas. Beaches for swimming and surfing await you farther east.

Many of the open-air discos, restaurants, and bars are reached by turning left on a dirt road just past the bridge. Even if you're not going to stop to partake in the action, the view is worth a quick detour. Looking to the west you see the sweep of city coastline. Sunsets can be impressive here, and after dark, the metropolis is a veritable Milky Way of sparkling lights.

The first sizable establishment here, the **Reef Bar and Grill** (787–791–1374), has a nice veranda for this view. With a jukebox, pool tables, and a bar dominating the room, this place has a honky-tonk

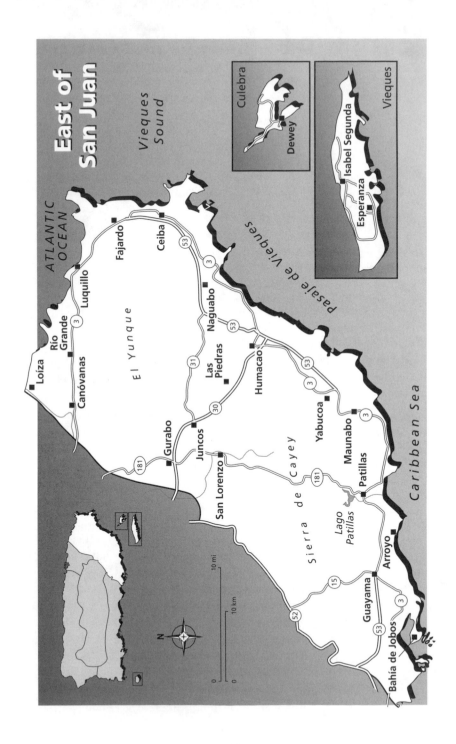

East of San Juan

Vieques Sound

Culebra

Dewey

Isabel Segunda

Esperanza

Vieques

pasaje de Vieques

ATLANTIC OCEAN

Fajardo

Ceiba

Luquillo

Río Grande

Loíza

Canóvanas

El Yunque

Naguabo

Las Piedras

Humacao

Gurabo

Juncos

San Lorenzo

Yabucoa

Maunabo

Patillas

Sierra de Cayey

Lago Patillas

Arroyo

Guayama

Bahía de Jobos

Caribbean Sea

10 mi

10 km

N

EAST OF SAN JUAN

feel. Open Sunday through Thursday 8:00 A.M. to 11:00 P.M., Friday and Saturday 9:00 A.M. to 2:00 A.M. Along the dirt road following the shore are more places to check out, little shacks and "clubs" on a spit of sand parallel to the road, each with its own personality. *Pulpo Loco* (787–791– 8382) is close by. A booth outside rents bicycles at $10 for the first hour or $20 for the day. On Sundays from 2:00 to 7:00 P.M., there's live salsa and *merengue*. The menu offers a wide choice of seafood, including the locally famous land crabs.

Check out *La Terraza,* which is owned by Dominicans. *Mangú* is served here, their version of *mofongo* (mashed plantains). There's live music on Saturday nights. *La Vereda* is a colorful place, decorated with strings of lights and holiday swags, where families come to enjoy meals of *comida criolla.* Thursday through Sunday evenings feature live music. *Bebo's* (787–253– 3143) is a nightclub catering to a gay and lesbian crowd.

La Soleil Beach Club (787–253–1033; www.soleilbeachclub.com) is a solid-looking establishment with a wide range of food on the menu. You can feast on *camarones* (shrimp), *pulpo* (octopus), *carrucho* (conch), and *cangrejo* (crab). Open Sunday through Wednesday from 11:00 A.M. to 11:00 P.M., Thursday to 1:00 A.M., and Friday and Saturday to 2:00 A.M. Live music on Sunday from 2:00 to 5:00 P.M. features *bomba* and *plena.* There's live jazz on Wednesday from 7:00 to 10:00 P.M., live '70s and '80s funk on Thursday from 10:00 P.M. to 1:00 A.M. live salsa on Friday from 10:00 P.M. to 1:00 A.M., and live blues on Saturday from 10:00 P.M. to 1:00 A.M. Farther along is *Playa 79,* a disco club. On the main road, Route 187, are more beach bars, including *La Pocita #2* and *Hemingway's Place* (787–791–4212).

One drink to stop for while passing through this area is *coco frío,* sold at stands along the road. *Coco frío,* the quintessential drink of Puerto Rico, is the cool water of a green coconut sipped from an opening cut across the top with a heavy machete, done with a flourish. Similar to a visit to the famous line of food kiosks at Playa Luquillo, this is a place where you might sample your way through the neighborhood, trying different specialties. With quite an array of fried finger foods, mainly fritters, you could try *bacalaítos* (salted cod), *alcapurrías* (mashed platain and yautia filled with beef, pork, or seafood), *piononos* (cup-shaped plantains

Surf's Up!

*T*he best surfing on the northeastern coast is at **Aviones, Chatarra,** and **Tacones** in Pinoñes; **Sheraton, Sunset, La Punta** and **La Parada Ocho** (Bus Stop 8) in the Condado section of San Juan; and **La Pared** and **Costa Azul** in Luquillo. The best waves are during the winter, November through March.

Farther down the east coast, surfing is good at **El Convento, El Faro,** and **Racetrack** in Fajardo; **Pedregales, El Cocal,** and **Sharkey's**

in Yabucoa; **Palmas del Mar** in Humacao; **Los Bohíos** in Maunabo; and **La Escuelita, Las Lajas,** and **Inches** in Patillas. Waves are best in the summer, July through September.

The best time to surf is as the sun is rising, around 5:30 A.M. The island's water temperature is always between 74 and 80 degrees Fahrenheit. Visiting surfers should ask about reefs and riptides in the area. There have been no reports of shark attacks.

holding beef, chicken, or seafood), and *arañitas* (patties of grated plantain and garlic that look like little spiders).

Paseo de Piñones, which has become popular with cyclists, joggers, walkers, and skaters, is also wheelchair accessible. Open daily from 6:00 A.M. to 6:00 P.M., the maintained path covers more than 6 miles. Bike rentals are available through *Piñones Ecotours* (787–253–0005), which also offers kayak tours of the lagoons. The best swimming beaches are about a mile east of the food stands. Pick a place where other cars and bathers have located; experience shows this is not where you want to leave your vehicle or your belongings unsupervised. Depending on the weather, the surf may be up. A good beach for surfing is *Aviones* (Airplanes); it's the last land aircraft fly over when taking off from Isla Verde. Six miles of beach lead to *Punta Vacía Talega,* a scenic bluff of sea-carved rock.

Shortly past that point, you cross the *Río Grande de Loíza* and pass into the municipality of *Loíza Aldea.* (Piñones is actually one of its districts.) Seeing Loíza will bring into focus how much this area retains of its African roots. Slaves brought to Puerto Rico came here first, beginning in the sixteenth century, after the Spanish decimated the Indian population. Still hoping great reserves of gold would be found in the rivers, the Spanish put Africans to the task. But with little to find, the slaves soon went to work in the sugarcane fields. They dispersed to plantations around the island, but Loíza remained the center of their new homeland. Freed slaves returned here to live and farm in a setting that seems evocative of the West African coast they left behind. Outdoor cooking, drumming and *bomba* music, Santería, and dark-skinned complexions relate directly to this heritage.

When residents of Loíza celebrate their patron, Saint James, culminating on July 25 with the Fiesta de Santiago festival and parade, their ceremonial costumes are strikingly similar to dress of the Yoruba tribe, their West African descendants. The *vejigantes* march in handmade masks of coconut husks or gourds painted with garish colors and bold decoration. The primitive faces are meant to scare nonbelievers into the faith and bring back those who have strayed. Picture a combination of Mardi Gras, Rio's Carnaval, and Halloween. This occasion, including traditional *plena* and *bomba* music and dance, attracts a huge turnout of spectators. Despite the logistical headache of traffic, it is one of the most vivid celebrations in Puerto Rico and well worth seeing.

Appreciated for their artistic value, the *vejigante* masks attract shoppers to Loíza. The master artisan was Castor Ayala, who died in 1980. His family carries on the tradition at the **Artesanías Ayala** family business (Route 187, km 6.6; 787–876–1130), 1 mile east of Loíza's center. Open most days from 10:00 A.M. to 5:00 P.M.; call for exact times and directions. Prices range from $50 to $350. There are twenty other mask-makers in the area. Call the **Loíza Tourism Office** for a listing (787–886–6071), or visit the office on the Plaza de Recreo, Monday through Friday, 8:00 A.M. to noon and 1:00 to 4:30 P.M.

Son of Loíza: William Cepeda

*W*illiam Cepeda was born into a family of musicians with proud roots in the African and Taíno traditions of Loíza Aldea. He grew up immersed in the island's traditional music of bomba and plena, also appreciating jíbaro, gospel, blues, flamenco, and jazz. Studying music and composition, Cepeda earned two bachelor's degrees from Berklee College of Music in Boston and the Conservatory of Music in Puerto Rico, and a master's in jazz performance from the Aaron Copeland School of Music at Queens College in New York.

Cepeda is considered a pioneer of contemporary Puerto Rican music, building on its roots and transcending into what he calls AfroRican jazz. He performs with the United Nations Orchestra and his Grupo Afro Boricua, playing trombone, conch, and percussion, as well as vocals. Cepeda plays in San Juan venues such as the Nuyorican Café and La Rumba, and at the Heineken Jazzfest. With as many as twenty-five accomplished musicians and dancers on stage, his show is electrifying and inspired.

Loíza 's *Iglesia del Espíritu Santo y San Patricio* (10 Espíritu Santo; 787–876–2229) is one of the oldest churches on the island, dating from 1646. The building is usually open only on Sunday for its 10:00 A.M. service. Honoring Saint Patrick was a tribute to the Irish who came to Puerto Rico to help defend the island (and who designed the fort San Cristóbal in San Juan).

A cave, *La Cueva de Maria la Cruz,* located near the intersection of Routes 187 and 188, is where Puerto Rico's oldest Indian skeletons were unearthed. The art studio of *Samuel Lind* (Route 187, km 6.6; 787–876–1494) shows Lind's paintings focusing on nature and Puerto Rican culture. Open daily, 10:00 A.M. to 5:00 P.M.

If you leave San Juan via Highway 3, which parallels Route 187 farther below the coast, you come to *Canóvanas.* This town is home to the *El Comandante Hipódromo* (Highway 3, km 15.3; 787–876–2450; www.comandantepr.com), the largest horse track in the Caribbean. Eight thoroughbred races are run each Sunday, Monday, Wednesday, Friday, and Saturday beginning around 2:45 P.M.

The *Belz Factory Outlet World* (Highway 3, km 18.4; 787–256–7040; www.belz.com) gives you more than eighty brand-name outlets to browse. Open Monday through Saturday 9:00 A.M. to 9:00 P.M. and Sunday 11:00 A.M. to 5:00 P.M. You can find accommodations off the beaten

Paying Homage

*L*oíza has paid homage to the virtues of warriors in its own way. The selection of Saint James, or Santiago, as the town's patron was a connection the African slaves saw between Santiago (who, in a fleshly manifestation long after his death, appeared in Spain to help drive out the Moorish invaders) and their own Yoruba god of war, Changó. Not permitted by the Catholic Spaniards to practice Yoruba religion and worship Changó, they substituted Santiago, who seemed to appreciate the desire to live free of conquerors. Loíza 's tradition of honoring

warriors may have roots in its Taíno era. When the settlement was first visited by Juan Ponce de León and his Spanish troops, the chief was a powerful woman warrior and ruler, a caciqua they referred to as Luisa (hence their name for the village). Under her strong leadership, women were considered equal to men, an empowering situation for both sexes. Additionally, the area was known to be home to the most powerful spirits existing in nature. This combination brought the Taíno community strength and respect.

The Goatsucker of Canóvanas

N ot too long ago Canóvanas was best known for its racetrack. That is until the appearance of **El Chupacabra,** or The Goatsucker.

El Chupacabra is most often described as a skinny, hairy, 4-foot-tall creature with a large head, lipless mouth, lidless eyes, and fangs. It has spiky protrusions along its backbone and webbed arms. Since first sighted in 1994, it is alleged to have killed farm animals across the Puerto Rican countryside in a particularly hideous manner that always includes completely draining the animals of their blood. Explanations as to the beast's origin range from the offspring of wild rhesus monkeys to an alien being.

El Chupacabra is just the latest flavor in a long line of creatures that have surfaced in Puerto Rico over the last thirty years. Others have included the Moca Vampire, a batlike being that "terrorized" the mountain town of Moca in 1975; the Comecogollo, a monkeylike creature that gorges on plátano plants; and the Creature from Fajardo's Black Lagoon, also known as garadiablo, or sea demon, which caused hysteria in the early 1970s.

Although the jury's still out on the existence of El Chupacabra, the legend lives on in song and drink, and on T-shirts and Web sites.

track by heading south on Route 857 off Highway 3. In rolling countryside that eventually becomes the Caribbean National Forest is **Caribe Mountain Villas** (787–769–0860; www.caribevillas.com), with three landscaped acres, seven villas, a pool, and a tennis court. New owners Jeff and Mitchell are emphasizing personalized service and catering to special events, no matter how small. Off of Highway 3 past the racetrack, **Lechonera Carmelo** (Route 185, km 4.5; 787–256–6452) offers the range of food served at *lechoneras,* including roasted pork, chicken, sausage, and rice and vegetable side dishes. Open every day until 10:00 P.M. with live music on Sunday.

Río Grande

The next town on Highway 3 is Río Grande, which shares its name with the river that runs through it. The area boasts a stunning landscape, with a backdrop to the south of the majestic mountain range of El Yunque, greenery that stretches north to the ocean's edge, and beautiful white sandy beaches. There are four golf courses here. Two are reached by driving slightly north off Highway 3 on Route 187. The **Bahía Beach Plantation** (Route 187, km 4.2; 787–256–5600; www.golfbahia. com) is the closest eighteen-hole course to San Juan. The *Berwind Country Club* (Route 187, km 4.7; 787–876–3056) is open to the public Monday through Friday. The other two courses are part of the *Westin Río Mar Beach Resort and Country Club* (Route 968, km 1.4; 787–888–6000 or 800–WESTIN–1; www.westinriomar.com). If you're not staying at the resort, call twenty-four hours ahead to reserve a tee time. The Westin Río Mar is set on almost 500 acres with a mile of beachfront. Built in 1996, the complex features 600 units, nine restaurants, four bars, a casino, a children's program, two pools, a spa and fitness center, and twelve tennis courts. The hotel, in an isolated setting, enjoys a fantastic location, with views to El Yunque and a beautiful beach. As with other luxurious but remote resorts, it is most conducive to a stay-put-and-unwind vacation (or attending a convention, which is common at the Westin). Despite its proximity to Luquillo and Piñones, the Westin Río Mar feels a world apart. Villas rented by Westin that share the hotel facilities are available at *Ocean Villas* (787–888–6000 or 800–WESTIN–1; www.theoceanvillas. com). Other lodging can be found at *Río Grande Plantation Resort* (Route 956, km 4.2; 787–887–2779; www.riograndeplantation.com), a complex of fifteen two-story villas with a pool and a conference center, combining comfort with a rustic setting on the mountainside of El Yunque. It's the perfect location for hiking and horseback riding.

On the peninsula of Miquillo de Rio Grande at Coco Beach, several new resorts are shaping up, including the *Paradisus Puerto Rico* (787–809–1770; www.solmelia.com), a new, all-inclusive resort built by the Spanish hotel chain Sol Meliá. Accommodations include villas, bungalows, and 490 suites. In addition there are five restaurants, four bars, a lagoon-style pool, a children's pool and program, lighted tennis courts, two golf courses, a spa, a fitness center, a casino, and a disco. All-inclusive bookings include room, all meals and beverages, live entertainment, non-motorized water sports, and kids camp. Ground has been broken nearby for construction on a five-star *Fairmont Coco Beach Resort and Spa.* Two golf courses are planned, as well as a 400-room hotel, a spa, and conference space.

Artist Monica Linville Laird has a gallery in Río Grande for her paintings. Call for directions to her *Tree House Studio* (787–888–8062; www.treehousestudio.com) and a listing of workshops she offers. *Eco Xcursion Aquatica* (Route 191, km 1.7; 787–888–2887) will help you with tours and equipment for kayaking, mountain biking, or hiking.

El Yunque

E l Yunque—both the name and the place—had positive associa-tions for the Taíno. *Yukiyú* was a protective spiritual being, a good force, ruling from his mountaintop home. Even today the place feels majestic and blessed. Covering 28,000 acres in the Sierra Luquillo range, this tropical forest is managed and protected by the USDA Forest Service as the **Caribbean National Forest** (www.southernregion. fs.fed.us/caribbean). About a million people a year visit El Yunque, sixty percent of whom are Puerto Rican. Over the course of a day, you can learn about the forest at the visitor center, hike one of the trails of vary-ing lengths, picnic, and take a refreshing dip.

The trip directly to El Yunque on Highway 3 from San Juan will take about an hour by car. The entrance is in the village of Palmer, also

Hike with Care

A s you hike in the Caribbean National Forest, observe some impor-tant precautions.

• Stay on the marked paths.

• Walk with a buddy, never alone.

• Carry water, a light snack, insect repellent, sunscreen, a small first-aid kit, a map, and a compass.

• Wear shoes—ideally boots—that protect your feet, with grip for rough and wet terrain.

• Pack a waterproof windbreaker and hat; rain showers are inevitable.

• During the hurricane season between June and November, always check a weather forecast first. Heavy rains will cause flash floods.

• Climbing rocks along streams and waterfalls can be risky because mossy surfaces will be slippery.

• Don't drink the water: River snails produce schisto, a bacteria that can cause liver damage.

• Long pants will shield legs from razor grass (which lives up to its name) and a poison oak growing along some trails.

• Pack bathing suits for dips in waterfall and pool areas. Swimming is a popular family activity, so don't assume you'll have the privacy to skinny-dip.

• No fishing is allowed in the park.

• If you plan to camp, obtain a permit first at the Catalina office near the park entrance. There are no facilities for camping; everything must be car-ried in and out.

• Only one road is open to mountain bikers, a closed section of Route 191.

• At all times, it is important to respect the life of the forest. Going off-trail, littering, and damaging vegetation are destructive intrusions into a delicate ecosystem.

Puerto Rican parrot

known as Mameyes, on Route 191, with a well-marked right turn off Highway 3. Take Route 191 south for about five minutes until you see the Caribbean National Forest sign. *El Portal Tropical Forest Center* (787–888–1880), near the main entrance, is open daily 9:00 A.M. to 5:00 P.M. Admission is $3.00 for adults, $1.50 for children and seniors; children under four get in free. (Admission to the park itself is free.) In an attractive, modern building with a walkway that puts you at tree canopy height, you can see a short film (shown every half hour, alternating English and Spanish versions) and view interactive exhibits that prepare you for the terrain you'll tour. The gift shop here is worth a look too. Around the park are several other information stations and rest room facilities.

El Yunque is home to 240 types of trees including twenty-six indigenous species in four distinct forest zones, as well as 150 types of ferns, and fifty different kinds of orchids. The elusive and endangered bright-green Puerto Rican parrot is one of the sixty-eight bird species that can be found here, along with the Puerto Rican boa (at 7 feet long, it's the island's largest snake) and the ubiquitous *coqui,* the small tree frog whose song sounds like its name. Protection of this special place began in 1876 with Spanish laws. Some of the trees are more than 1,000 years old! Another impressive number is the amount of water arriving as precipitation here. The area receives about 240 inches of rain per year, equaling 100 billion gallons.

UFOs over Puerto Rico

A round the island, stories abound describing close encounters with unidentified flying objects. On the south coast, at La Parguera, part of Lajas, reports described low-flying spacecraft. In 1997, what was believed to be the site of a crashed UFO there was closed off to the public by the military, with no official explanation.

El Yunque was often the focus of rumored sightings. In the early 1980s it was widely believed Martians had landed there, and the rain forest drew crowds looking for aliens. Residents of Adjuntas, in the mountains above Ponce, reported the presence over five years of mysterious lights, as if from UFOs, traveling a path from Adjuntas to Laguna Cartagena in Lajas. Observers described tremors, strange noises, and other inexplicable phenomena at the lagoon in Lajas.

It is tempting to attribute all of this to an overactive imagination, a kind of hysteria, or a paranoid state of mind. Paranoia would be understandable for an island with a legacy of invasions, a military presence, and a history of colonization. Why shouldn't little green creatures from somewhere else find Puerto Rico an inviting place to sightsee or make a home for themselves?

There are ten different hiking trails covering more than 23 miles. The Forest Service Web site provides good descriptions and maps. This information is also available at all the visitor stations at the park. The shortest and least strenuous trails are Big Tree and La Mina, each less than a mile long. Big Tree begins on Route 191, km 10.4, and ends at La Mina Falls. La Mina begins at the Palo Colorado visitor center and joins Big Tree at the falls. The Mt. Britton trail, which brings you to the Mt. Britton tower, is also less than a mile long, but it is a more vigorous climb in higher terrain. Staying at this altitude, in the cloud forest, you can hike the Mt. Britton spur almost a mile to the 2.5-mile El Yunque trail, which climaxes at the peak of El Yunque at 3,496 feet. This hike could take almost two hours. From here, the Los Picachos trail is a short hike to the Los Picachos lookout tower. The 4-mile Tradewinds trail, wilder than other trails, is popular with serious hikers and campers. Passing through all four ecosystems of the park, a four-hour hike leads you to El Toro, the forest's highest peak, at 3,522 feet. The El Toro trail, about 2 miles long, heads west through cloud forest.

If you prefer to drive, you can still enjoy great vistas and picnic facilities. On Route 191 are La Coca Falls, the Yokahú Tower with views to the northeastern coast, and the information centers at Sierra Palm and Palo Colorado. Recreational areas are open daily from 7:30 A.M. to 6:00 P.M. If you're unable to put in the time or energy getting out on trails, a visit here

La Coca Falls at El Yunque

is still immensely rewarding and provides an important experience in an endangered environment that deserves our attention and support.

Luquillo

ack out on Highway 3, slightly farther east, are **Playa Luquillo,** with its *balneario* and kiosks, and the town of Luquillo. Describing the beach provokes much debate. Some claim it is one of the nicest and cleanest on the island; others lament that as a popular destination, it is growing shabby. The fact is that the setting, with *balneario* facilities and nearby refreshment kiosks, distinguishes it from other beaches. The combination of El Yunque and Luquillo captures much of the essence of Puerto Rico. With a curved beach protected by offshore coral reefs, the water is great for swimming and snorkeling. Coconut palms provide

TOP ANNUAL EVENTS

Luquillo Patron Saint Festival, late April

Maunabo Patron Saint Festival, last week of June

Arroyo Patron Saint Festival, second week of July

Loíza Patron Saint Festival, last ten days of July

Fajardo Patron Saint Festival, last week of July

Vieques Patron Saint Festival, last week of July

Festival Jueyero, last weekend of August, Maunabo

Yabucoa Patron Saint Festival, late September and early October

Naguabo Patron Saint Festival, second week of October

Festival de los Platos Típicos, third week of November, Luquillo

shade along the shore. A ramp and special water-proof equipment provide access to the water for those using wheelchairs. There are also camp-sites, but call ahead to check availability. For more information, call the *balneario* at (787) 889-5871.

There's something relaxing about basking in the sun on Luquillo's beach while watching heavy, rain-laden clouds hover over El Yunque. When you've worked up an appetite or thirst, head over to the line of kiosks at the large parking area just west of the beach. These establishments vary in size and style. Some offer counter service for *pastelillos*—finger food you eat as a snack—while others offer full-service with tables and meals. There are lots of places to sit and enjoy *comida criolla* and a cold drink. Evenings and weekends the place gets crowded, and live music dominates the scene.

A popular nightspot is the **Brass Cactus** (Route 193, km 1.3; 787-889-5735) with live music Thursday through Saturday from 11:00 P.M. to 3:00 A.M. Some accommodations in the nearby area include the **Luquillo Beach Inn** (701 Ocean Drive; 787-889-3333), **Le Petit Chalet** (Route 186, km 22.1; 787-887-5802), and **Trinidad Guest House** (6A Ocean Drive; 787-889-2710).

The town of Luquillo has succumbed to the siren song of development, and condos are rampant. Some beaches, such as La Pared and La Selva, offer good swimming and surfing, but the area looks built up these days. La Pared is the site of local surfing competitions throughout the year. Surfboards and other equipment can be rented at **La Selva Surf Shop** (250 Fernández García; 787-899-6205). For diving trips and scuba equipment rentals, try **Divers Outlet** (787-889-5721) or **Alpha Scuba** (787-327-5108), both on Fernández García.

Horseback riding is also popular on some beaches. Just off Highway 3, **Hacienda Caribaldi** (Route 992, km 3; 787-889-5820) is a ranch that arranges excursions with horses on trails of El Yunque's foothills, beside the Mameyes River, and along an empty stretch of Luquillo beach.

Heading along the coast about 5 miles to the east is another attractive beach, *Playa Seven Seas* (Route 987, km 4.6; 787–863–8180), in the village of Las Croabas. Many islanders say this is one of the best *balnearios*. Tent sites are available as well as a picnic area, refreshment stand, showers, and changing rooms.

Fajardo

Once frequented by pirates and smugglers, Fajardo is still a busy port today, with marinas for pleasure craft and government-operated ferries that run to Culebra and Vieques, Puerto Rican islands 6 miles off the coast. Fajardo isn't as scenic as it is functional, offering accommodations, food, an airport that provides quick hops to the islands or San Juan, and a variety of stores.

Many visitors to Fajardo come for the day to get out on the water aboard a sailboat. Usually a catamaran large enough to carry between ten and twenty passengers and provisions with an experienced captain, the boats cruise for about six hours, with stops for swimming and snorkeling and lunch on one of the small cays. A number of these offer sunset cruises as well.

At the *Puerto del Rey Marina* (Highway 3, km 51.4; 787–860–1000; www.marinapuertodelray.com) are *Erin Go Bragh Charters* (787–860–4401; www.egbc.com), *East Wind II Catamaran* (787–860–3434 or 877–WE–R–4–FUN; www.eastwindcats.com), *Chamonix Catamaran* (787–885–1880; www.snorkelparty.com), and *Ventajero Sailing Charters* (787–863–1871; www.sailpuertorico.com). The East Wind offers both sailing and power catamarans, with all-day excursions to Culebra's Flamenco Beach and Culebrita or to Bioluminescent Bay in Vieques. Future trips are planned to St. Thomas.

Two restaurants at the marina offer Italian food, *Portofino* (787–860–0414) and *A La Banda* (787–860–9162). For scuba and snorkeling trips, contact *Sea Ventures Pro Dive Center* (787–863–3483; www.divepuertorico.com).

The *Autoridad de Transportacíon Maritima ferry terminal* (787–863–0705 or 800–981–2005) is at Playa de Fajardo, 1½ miles from the center of town on Route 195. There are a few places to eat here, as well as parking lots for vehicles left by those traveling to the outlying islands, including St. Thomas of the U.S. Virgin Islands. *Caribe Cay* (787–863–0582; www.caribecay.com) is a high-speed passenger boat that crosses to Charlotte Amalie, a two-hour trip it makes Saturday and

Sunday leaving Fajardo at 8:00 A.M. and departing St.Thomas at 4:30 P.M. For ferries to Culebra and Vieques, arrive one hour before departure time. Each trip takes approximately one hour. Schedule information is described in the sections that follow about the two islands. The *Aéropuerto Diego Jimenez Torres* (Route 976, km 1.1; 787–860–3110) is west of Fajardo near the intersection of Highway 3. Two companies offer air service to Culebra and Vieques from Fajardo: *Isla Nena* (787–741–6362) and *Vieques Air Link* (787–741–8331).

Next to the ferry dock is a small hotel, *Hotel Delicias* (787–863–1818), probably best for overnight accommodations before boarding a ferry. *Fajardo Inn* (787–860–6000; www.fajardoinn.com) and the adjacent *Scenic Inn* (787–863–5195) on Route 195 have a pool, a restaurant, two bars, and a view encompassing the Atlantic, Caribbean, and El Yunque. *Rosa's Sea Food Restaurant* (536 Tablazo Street; 787–863–0213), off Route 195, is touted as one of the best around by some; others claim it is overpriced and has stiff competition.

North of Fajardo on Route 987 is the fishing village of Sardinera. Day cruises are available at the *Villa Marina Yacht Harbor* (Route 987, km 1.3; 787–863–5131; www.villamarinapr.com). Choices include *Fajardo Tours* (787–863–2821), *Catamaran Getaway with Captain Mingo* (787–860–7327; www.getawaypr.com), *Club Náutico International* (787–860–2400), the *Catamaran Fun Cat* (787–728–6606) that will bus passengers from San Juan, the *Traveler* (787–863–2821 or 877–919–2821), and the *Spread Eagle* (888–523–4511; www.snorkelpr.com). Sardinera has two other marinas: *Marina Puerto Chico* (Route 987, km 2.4; 787–863–1915) and *Sea Lovers Marina* (Route 987, km 2.3; 787–863–3762).

Following Route 987, you come to *Anchor Inn* (Route 987, km 2.7; 787–863–7200). Set atop a bluff, this small hotel has a pool, restaurant, and good proximity to the beach. Lobster is the dining room's specialty, and weekends feature live Latin music.

If you're looking for luxury, the road brings you to the *Wyndham El Conquistador Resort and Country Club* (Route 987, km 3.4; 787–863–1000; www.wyndham.com). From 1968 through much of the 1970s, the original El Conquistador was the epitome of Caribbean splendor. Its black and stainless-steel circular casino was featured in the James bond movie *Goldfinger,* and the hotel was a haven for U.S. celebrities and jet-setters. It then fell on hard times following the Middle East oil embargo and the ensuing recession, and closed in 1977. The hotel reopened in 1996 after a $200 million renovation. The resort's design draws its influences from several Mediterranean sources, including Spain's Moorish gardens and the neoclassic elegance found in northern Italian architecture. Nine hundred units perch along a hillside. Guests are ferried to nearby Isla Palomino for beach and water activities. There are twelve restaurants, an eighteen-hole golf course for hotel guests only, a spa and fitness center, six pools, tennis courts, and a casino.

Also at the resort is *Las Casitas Village,* a separate, upscale section of ninety deluxe villas with high-end services. At El Conquistador's marina complex, *Tropical Fishing Charters* (787–266–4524; www.tropicalfish ingcharters.com) at Piers 15 and 16 will take you out angling for marlin and tuna. *Palomino Island Divers* (787–863–1000) rents scuba gear.

With more modest quarters, *La Familia* is a twenty-seven-room hotel and restaurant down the road (Route 987, km 4.1; 787–863–1193; www. hotellafamilia.com). It's a mile inland from the coast with a peaceful view of the El Conquistador greens.

The small fishing village of *Bahía Las Croabas* is reached off Route 987 at the end of the spur, Route 9987. There is some scenic quality to it, with a scattering of seafood restaurants and the old-style fishing boats called *nativos.* To arrange a ride on one, call *Captain Freddie Rodriguez* (787–863–2471 or 642–3116). For dining, try *El Picazo, Restaurant Croabas,* or *Rocar Seafood.* For some fun in the water, contact *Yokahu Kayak Trips* (Route 987, km 6.2; 787–863–5374). The *balneario Playa Seven Seas* (Route 987, km 4.6; 787–863–8180) includes campsites on the beach. Walking along the shore about a half mile east brings you to a quieter spot, *Playa Escondido.* With offshore reefs here, it's a good place for snorkeling and swimming. Tranquillity at any of these beaches, however, is never guaranteed. Jet bikes can take over an area and not only create noise but a hazard to swimmers, and aircraft sometimes fly in low patterns from the nearby U.S. Naval Station, *Roosevelt Roads.*

Las Cabezas de San Juan

At the northeast tip of the island is a special spot that preserves pristine coast, mangrove swamps, a dry forest, coral reefs, a bioluminescent lagoon, a coconut plantation, and a restored lighthouse. Every ecosystem of the island except rain forest is represented in this unique location. Under the auspices of the Conservation Trust of Puerto Rico (www.fideicomiso.org), whose headquarters you may have visited in Old San Juan, 316 acres are being protected here. Las Cabezas de San Juan (the headlands, Route 987, km 5.9) is open to the public and has a

Sixto Escobar

Born in Puerto Rico in 1913, Sixto Escobar began boxing profession- ally in 1930. By 1936, he was declared World Bantamweight Champion. Over his nine-year career of sixty-four fights, he had forty-two wins with twenty-one knockouts. He died in 1979. An outdoor stadium in San Juan, home to the Heineken Jazzfest, is named for him.

nature center in the lighthouse, *El Faro,* to educate visitors about the different ecosystems. Two miles of trails are traversed by trolley on the guided tour. Reservations are required in order to control the impact of visitors in the fragile environments. Call the San Juan office weekdays at (787) 722–5882 or Las Cabezas weekends at (787) 860–2560. The reserve is open Wednesday through Sunday 8:00 A.M. to 4:00 P.M. A two-hour tour in English is available at 2:00 P.M. Three tours daily are in Spanish: 9:30 A.M., 10:00 A.M., and 2:00 P.M. Admission for adults is $7.00, $4.00 for children and seniors. In order to best appreciate the bioluminescent *Laguna Grande,* check for kayak tours; moonless nights are preferable. Call *Eco Xcursion Aquatica* (787–888–2887) or *Caribe Kayak* at (787–889–7734).

Vieques and Culebra

So you're already on a tropical island. Why leave to go to a different one right next door? When it's to visit Vieques or Culebra off Puerto Rico's eastern coast, the answer is clear: These islands are different. They're sometimes referred to as the Spanish Virgin Islands because they are geologically related to the chain of American and British Virgins that follow. As a result of dry conditions and no river runoff bringing silt into the ocean, they enjoy clear water. For snorkeling and scuba diving, Culebra is especially notable for spectacular visibility underwater.

Still relatively undeveloped, the beaches are also considered some of the most beautiful in the Caribbean. What the islands lack in choices for nightlife they make up for in the daytime with activities like sailing, fishing, hiking, swimming, exploring underwater, biking, kayaking, bird-watching, beachcombing, and just plain relaxing. This being Puerto Rico, however, you can find some good food, music, and dancing to mix in. And if quiet is what you want, you can certainly find it here.

Getting to Culebra and Vieques isn't hard. Ferries run from Playa de Fajardo and planes leave from San Juan's international and Isla Grande Airports and Fajardo's Diego Jimenez Airport. The trip by boat to either island is about an hour; from San Juan it's a half-hour flight, from Fajardo it's fifteen minutes. There is finally, as of February 2003, a ferry running passengers between Culebra and Vieques.

Culebra, a small, one-town island, is just acquiring its first big hotel, the Casa Bonita Sea Resort, but not without controversy. Vieques is larger, with two towns, and for more than fifty years has had the distinction of serving as home to war games, bombing practice, and military maneuvers offshore and on the two-thirds of the island the U.S. Navy controlled. The Navy departed in May 2003 after citizens grew increasingly dissatisfied with intrusions into normal life. Residents are already enjoying the repatriation of some beaches they had been prevented from using, including Red Beach, known as Caracas, and the Blue Beach, known as Manuel Key. Development will likely accelerate; an unfinished high-end resort that passed like a hot potato among hoteliers over the last four years opened in February 2003 as Wyndham Martineau Bay Resort. The airport is gearing up for more and bigger planes.

The 4-by-21-mile island of *Vieques* may be the most Caribbean part of Puerto Rico, combining dry rolling hills and pastures with coastal roads. Here egrets fly overhead as cattle lazily chew in pastures. The interior of Vieques is more hilly than its coast, with forested, winding country roads. There are fields of exotic flowers, wild horses, and mongoose. Ruins of sugar and pineapple plantations are scattered throughout the island, as are historic artifacts and archaeological digs.

It's possible to go horseback riding through trails in the island's central hills and along the mangrove lagoons that attract more than one hundred bird species. The island's forty-plus beaches are among the Caribbean's finest. Many are isolated, accessible only by powerful jeep along dirt roads or by hiking down narrow trails. Probably the prettiest *balneario* in all of Puerto Rico is *Sun Bay,* or Sombé as locals call it, on the south coast. Note that nude sunbathing in Vieques is illegal.

In the center of the north coast, *Isabel Segunda,* the island's main town, will likely be your first point of reference. The ferry docks are located here, and the airport is just outside of town. As beautiful an island as Vieques is, its main town is only ordinary, reminiscent of nearly every other small Puerto Rican town. But if you stick around long enough, you will witness a certain laid-back pace. Eating, exploring the water's depths, discovering quiet beaches, and relaxing are the highlights here.

Vehicles can be ferried over, but you'll do better renting one, preferably with four-wheel drive. *Publicos* will take you around the island at reasonable rates; bicycles and motorized scooters are also available.

Travel to Vieques and Culebra

*H*ow you go to Vieques or
Culebra depends on your schedule
and your budget.

FLIGHTS

Vieques Air Link flies from Isla
Grande in San Juan and Fajardo to
Vieques and Culebra. Call (877)
622–5566 for information on flights
from San Juan, (787) 863–3020 for
flights from Fajardo, (787) 741–8331
for flights from Vieques, and (787)
742–0254 for flights from Culebra.

Isla Nena flies from Luis Munoz
Marín International Airport, San
Juan, and Fajardo. Call (888)
263–6213 for information on San
Juan and Fajardo departures, (787)
741–1577 for Vieques, and (787)
742–0972 for Culebra.

Air Flamenco flies charters only;
(787) 742–1040 (Culebra).

Air Culebra flies chartered flights with
up to five passengers from San Juan
international airport to Vieques or
Culebra. Call San Juan, (787)
268–6951; Culebra, (787) 379–4466;
or log on to www.airculebra.com.

PASSENGER FERRIES

Fajardo–Vieques
Weekdays 9:30 A.M., 1:00 P.M., 4:30 P.M.
Weekends 9:00 A.M., 3:00 P.M., 6:00 P.M.

Vieques–Fajardo
Weekdays 7:00 A.M., 11:00 A.M., 3:00 P.M.
Weekends 7:00 A.M., 1:00 P.M., 4:30 P.M.

Fajardo–Culebra
Weekdays 9:30 A.M., 3:00 P.M.
Weekends 9:00 A.M., 2:30 P.M., 6:30 P.M.

Culebra–Fajardo
Weekdays 6:30 A.M., 11:30 A.M.
Weekends 6:30 A.M., 11:00 A.M., 4:30 P.M.

CARGO FERRIES

Fajardo–Vieques
Daily 4:00 A.M., 9:30 A.M., 4:30 P.M.

Vieques–Fajardo
Daily 6:00 A.M., 1:30 P.M., 6:00 P.M.

Fajardo–Culebra
Daily 3:30 A.M., 4:00 P.M.

Culebra–Fajardo
Daily 7:00 A.M., 6:00 P.M.

On Wednesday and Friday, a cargo
boat also departs Fajardo for Culebra
at 10:00 A.M. and Culebra for Fajardo
at 1:00 P.M.

No pets are allowed on passenger ferries. All cars must have reservations
and have lower priority than commercial vehicles. Bicycles are now allowed
on passenger ferries. Call the ferry office
ahead to secure reservations. The offices
are open weekdays from 8:00 to 11:00
A.M. and 1:00 to 3:00 P.M.

Always call ahead to confirm the current ferry schedule.

Fajardo terminal: (787) 863–0705
or (800) 981–2005

Vieques: (787) 741–4761

Culebra: (787) 742–3161

As of March 2003, a ferry runs between
Vieques, leaving at 6:30 A.M., to Culebra, leaving Culebra at 4:30 P.M. Primarily to assist workers commuting,
availability is first come, first served.

Públicos travel from San Juan, departing Río Piedras, to Fajardo for about
$10. Taxis will also transport you from
the international airport to Fajardo for
about $60. Cars can be parked at the
Fajardo ferry for about $3.00 a day.
Passenger fares are $2.00 each way.

It was around Isabela Segunda in 1843 that the Spanish began building what would have been their last fort in the Americas. It was never completed. Today the building houses the *Fort Conde de Mirasol Museum* (787–741–1717), named after the Spanish governor who convinced his countrymen to begin building the fortress. The museum features a permanent exhibit on the island's history, from its Taíno past to its Spanish heritage to a chronicle of the U.S. Navy's presence. The museum, under curator Robert Rabin, also hosts changing shows featuring local and visiting artists, as well as frequent lectures and talks. It is open Wednesday through Sunday 10:00 A.M. to 4:00 P.M. The island's sleepy main square is where you'll find a statue of Latin America's "Great Liberator," *Simón Bolívar*, who also visited here. The statue was given to the people of Vieques in 1972 by the government of Venezuela (Bolívar's birthplace) in recognition of the fact that Vieques was the only Puerto Rican town visited by Bolívar.

Bravos of Boston, east of Isabel Segunda, is a beachfront area of modern Malibu Beach–style homes. The water here is clear blue and protected by a coral reef, which makes for some good snorkeling. A convenient alternative to staying on the south coast, many of the homes are available on a weekly or even weekend basis.

Most visitors head to *Esperanza,* a charming fishing village on the south coast that was once an important sugar production center. Today it is marked by its oceanfront road lined with guest houses and restaurants facing the water. The country road leading to Esperanza crosses the entire island, giving you a glimpse of the beautiful interior of the island.

Before reaching Esperanza, the road passes by *Casa del Francés* (Esperanza; 787–741–3735), a real Caribbean classic some call the "world's most laid-back hotel." It's certainly one of the most colorful. The hotel is a 1910 plantation home built by a French general for his bride. Today palms, mango trees, banana plants, bamboo, and riotous wildflowers and orchids are scattered throughout the plantation's twelve acres. Two sweeping verandas surround the place, and the rooms are huge, high-ceilinged, and comfortable. Fine meals, which attract locals, are served on mahogany tables on a protected back porch or beside the pool beneath a towering tree that also shelters the outdoor bar.

There are a few interesting shops and galleries along the strip and, if you're in the mood for nightlife, you'll find a couple of rickety dance clubs and open-air bars by the beach.

The town is a center for water-sports operators, whether you want to scuba or windsurf. Sun Bay is just a fifteen-minute walk away. Beyond

Sun Bay are two more secluded beaches, Media Luna and Navío. Media Luna is an ideal beach for children, where the water stays shallow for 40 feet into the bay—great for snorkeling! Navío has a small beach and a strong surf. The *balneario* Sun Bay also offers campsites. Note that theft has been a persistent problem here and gear should not be left untended.

If none of the restaurants or guest houses grabs your attention on your first stroll down Esperanza's main boulevard, retrace your steps—this is as cosmopolitan as Vieques gets. Rates at most inns in town start at $65. The *Amapola Inn & Tavern* (144 Flamboyán; 787-741-1382), *Bananas* (142 Flamboyán; 787-741-8700), and *Trade Winds* (107C Flamboyán; 787-741-8666) have clean, affordable, and comfortable rooms for rent. Bananas has a bar, loud music, and it's open late. Trade Winds is better for a quiet sit-down meal. The Amapola, right next door to Bananas, has Caribbean cuisine. *Hacienda Tamarindo* (Route 996, km 4.5; 787-741-8525) is one of the nicest small hotels in the region, with a beautiful pool and a hilltop location overlooking the Caribbean. A huge tamarind tree grows in the middle of the hotel. The place was decorated by its owner as a swan song to a fifteen-year career as a commercial interior designer and is filled with art, antiques, and collectibles.

Overnight options include the gorgeous *Inn on the Blue Horizon* (Route 996, km 4.2; 787-741-3318). The name says it all. Located on a grassy bluff overlooking Esperanza and the Caribbean, the inn has a great restaurant, *The Blue Macaw,* and a large outdoor bar where sculpted walkways and gardens compete with the sea for the view. The bluff has a

Simón Bolívar

Simón Bolívar *(1783–1830) was a South American hero whose life was dedicated to uniting South America. Although he managed to create the independent republic of New Granada (where present-day Colombia is located), Bolívar's attempt to liberate Venezuela in 1815 failed, prompting him to sail to Jamaica in voluntary exile. It was there that he penned his celebrated Jamaica Letter, one of the documents in which he set*

forth his vision for a united republic of the Americas.

Bolívar next went on to Haiti and stopped off in Vieques in August 1816, on his way back to South America and more battles. During his weeklong stay in Vieques, the Liberator and his men stocked up on supplies. Historians believe Bolívar was brought to the island by one of his generals, Antonio Valero de Bernabé, a native of Fajardo.

natural walkway down to a miles-long beach. The place was opened by two stylish ex–New Yorkers who have created a chic hotel popular with a trendy crowd of models, actors, and jet-setters.

There are several other lodging and dining options outside of Esperanza. The twelve-room *Crow's Nest* (Route 201, km 1.6; 787–741–0033) is set on five acres of rolling hillside in barrio *Florida,* the quiet middle of the island. It's just a six-minute ride from the center of town or from the beaches in Esperanza. The pool and adjoining deck have a spectacular bird's-eye view of the island's countryside. Nice grounds, and the friendly staff will help arrange all sorts of activities.

Even better is to go up to *Pilón,* in the island's hilly central region. *La Finca el Caribe* (Route 995; 787–741–0495) rightly bills itself as a "rustic getaway." There's a central guest house plus small cabins for rent, providing comfortable, laid-back lodging in the heart of the country. *Casa Cielo* (Route 995, km 1.1; 787–741–2403) is an architecturally interesting inn described as "a James Bond set with a bossa nova beat." *Hix Island House* (Route 995 near Route 201; 787–741–2302) has zen-inspired architecture and offers yoga classes.

Pilón is also home to *Chez Shack* (Route 995; 787–741–2175), started by Duffy, a legendary figure who has been operating various guest houses and restaurants in Puerto Rico for the last four decades. Monday is "Reggae Grill Night," which always draws a crowd.

The Fiery Waters of Mosquito Bay

M osquito Bay, on Vieques, is one of the best examples in the world of a bioluminescent bay. The shimmering waters are especially breathtaking on moonless nights. The bay's magic glow comes from the billions of tiny protozoan organisms called Pyrodinium bahamense. *At night these organisms glow, a phenomenon that increases when the water is disturbed, giving the currents a fiery look. The organisms are kept in the bay by its narrow channel. Be sure to take a swim in the glowing waters, so you can see their dazzling spray erupt around you.*

If someone offers you a ride on a boat that is gas-powered, decline. Pollution from boat engines can kill the organisms that give the bay its glow. Most tour operators give electric boat or kayak tours, which cause no harm. Call Island Adventures (787–741–0720) or Blue Caribe Dive Center (787–741–2522). To learn more about the phosphorescent bay, see the Web site www.biobay.com.

On the north coast by the airport is *Mount Pirata,* which has a cave at its summit where the ancient Taíno chief Bieque supposedly hid his people's treasures from the Spanish conquistadors. The higest point on the island, it is reachable with a four-wheel-drive vehicle and lots of care negotiating a rough road.

The newest resort on Vieques, **Wyndham Martineau Bay Resort and Spa** (Route 200, km 3.4; 787–741–4100; www.wyndham.com) includes three beaches, tennis courts, use of sailboats and kayaks, a fitness center, 156 units, and several restaurants. A casino and golf course may be added in the future.

Just 7 miles long and 4 miles wide, *Culebra* is smaller than Vieques and it's so laid-back that Vieques's Esperanza seems downright cosmopolitan in comparison. Although its name means "snake," it was named for its shape, not the presence of the reptiles.

Culebra has dozens of small cays and islets, which boaters find perfect for gunkholing. Magnificent reefs and hard and soft coral ridges surround the Culebra coast. Lumbering nurse sharks, tropical fish, and other sea life thrive in Culebra's shallow waters, which rarely exceed a depth of 100 feet. Visibility underwater is 70 feet or more.

Throughout the 1500s Culebra served as a home for the Taínos, who fled the Spanish colonization of Puerto Rico. It then became a refuge for pirates, whose buried treasure is still said to be hidden on the island. In the late 1800s, farmers growing tamarind, mango, and other tropical crops began to settle here. The U.S. Navy first established itself on Culebra shortly after the end of the Spanish-American War and left in 1975. Today Culebra is home to about 3,000 residents, with many wealthy Puerto Ricans and North Americans maintaining vacation or retirement homes on the island.

In 1909 a *National Wildlife Refuge* was established in Culebra. Today more than 1,000 acres of Culebra, as well as much of its coastline and twenty-four offshore islands, are managed by the U.S. Department of Fish and Wildlife. The island teems with bird species, such as brown boobies, laughing gulls, Bahama ducks, and brown pelicans. Between May and July the island's pristine beaches such as Playa Brava serve as a nesting ground for rare leatherback turtles. You can even go on turtle-watching expeditions, on which you quietly and patiently stand guard through the night, waiting to glimpse the large creatures lumbering across the beach to bury their eggs and protect them. The *Culebra Leatherback Project* (P.O. Box 190, Culebra, PR 00775; 787–742–0015) has more information.

Several guest houses are located in the island's main town of **Dewey**, which also hosts the ferry dock, post office, town hall, and several eateries. Most of the lodgings offer transportation to the beautiful Flamenco Beach, so staying here makes a lot of sense. It's also the site for scuba and fishing expedition departures. The *Culebra Calendar* (787-742-0816) is a bilingual newspaper published about six times a year, that also puts out a handy tourist guide.

In the middle of Dewey's Bay is **Pirate's Cay**, a favorite spot for holiday beach picnics. At the corner of Pedro Márquez Street you'll find the town hall, which has a tourist information office (787-742-3291).

Mamacíta's (66 Castallen; 787-742-0090) and **Posada La Hamaca** (68 Castallen; 787-742-3516) are two of the best places to stay in town, and they're located right next to each other on the lagoon. For breakfast and dinner, Mamacíta's has a good restaurant on the dock overlooking the water. There are three rooms for rent here. Evenings, a DJ spins salsa and merengue mixed with American pop, attracting a crowd of locals and tourists. At La Hamaca there's a barbecue on the back deck for guests' use, and coolers are supplied. Both places provide transportation to Flamenco Beach.

Around the corner from these two establishments is a drawbridge over the lagoon. **The Dinghy Dock** (787-742-0581) is a restaurant on an open dock on the lagoon beside the drawbridge. The menu ranges from grilled T-bones and vegetarian specials at dinner to eggs over easy for breakfast. Around the bend, directly across the lagoon from Mamacíta's and La Hamaca, is a municipal entertainment complex with pool tables and video games. It's the scene of rowdy dance parties on weekend evenings.

Following the main road from the drawbridge will take you to **Ensenada Honda** (Deep Bay), a favorite resting spot for Caribbean boaters. **Club Seabourne** (787-742-3169 or 800-613-1511) is a charming wooden clubhouse with high ceilings, a wooden lobby, and a screened-in dining room with an adjacent open-air bar. The dining room serves the best food on the island. The hotel also has the only freshwater public swimming pool on the island.

Taking the road from the drawbridge out of town the other way leads to the airport and **El Batey** (787-742-3828), a brew and burger place. Bearing left at the airport takes you on the road to Flamenco Beach. **Tamarindo Estates** (787-742-3343) is an isolated hotel and restaurant down a long gravel road overlooking a beautiful coastline. The bar

CULEBRA'S PRETTIEST BEACHES

Flamenco

Carlos Rosario

Cayo Luís Peña

Resaca

Brava

Cayo Norte

Zoni

Casa La Pelá

Culebrita

and restaurant here are worth visiting even if you don't stay. It has that edge-of-the-world feeling to it, with a seemingly endless empty beach fronting the property.

The crescent-shaped and palm-lined *Playa Flamenco* has a campground (787–742–0700), rest rooms, freshwater showers, and some lodging. Most guest houses in Dewey will bring you here in the morning and take you back in the afternoon, so many guests prefer staying in town. Flamenco's white sandy beach is great for swimming. The tanks at the far end of the beach are a grim reminder of the military exercises that used to take place on these peaceful shores. Uphill a half mile from the beach is the island's highest point, *Mount Resaca,* covered by forest and giving a panoramic view of the countless cays and the Virgin Islands.

A right turn at the airport leads to secluded *Playa Zoni,* a mile-long strip of white beach that has the feeling of being your very own. Zoni is well worth the trip, even though the roads are bad and a four-wheel-drive vehicle is required.

Culebrita, a mile-long islet off Culebra's coast, has an old lighthouse and gorgeous beaches. It's a great spot to snorkel. Businesses on the island rent snorkeling and scuba gear, as well as bikes, wind surfers, sailboats, kayaks, and outboards.

Ceiba, Naguabo, and Humacao

South of Fajardo is the U.S. Navy's Roosevelt Roads, the biggest American naval base in the world. With 8,000 acres, it occupies one-quarter of Puerto Rico's east coast. Responsible for servicing and fueling American and allied military ships in the region, it also traditionally supported the war games and practice maneuvers carried out at sea and across the water on the nearby island of Vieques. Now that Vieques is no longer used by the Navy, the role of Roosevelt Roads may be redefined as well. The base is located in the town of *Ceiba,* which has not been a hot tourist destination. The City Hall will help you visit one of the four historic sugarcane plantations in the area; call (787) 885–2180.

There are several laid-back places to stay here and enjoy the proximity to El Yunque's quiet south side. Cars cannot enter the park from the south because this section of Route 191 was destroyed by hurricane. Outside of Naguabo, *Casa Cubuy* (Route 191, km 22; 787–874–6221; www.casacubuy.com) offers hiking trails, streams to soak in, and a comfortable tropical decor. Also reached from Naguabo off Route 191 is *Cabañas de Yunque* (787–874–2138), formerly known as Phillips Family Budget Cabins. Owner Robin Phillips gets rave reviews from visitors for his rustic cabins with great views, his extensive orchard, and the services he offers, such as guided hikes and camping sites.

Several houses near the Cubuy River are available at *Casa Flamboyant* (787–874–6074; www.casaflamboyant.com). *Casa Marshall* (14 Las Quinta; 787–885–4474) rents as a four-bedroom house in the hills. The *Ceiba Country Inn* (Route 977; 787–885–0471) is a bed-and-breakfast in an old family manor home. Set in the rolling countryside, this nine-room inn also provides peace and quiet in a natural setting.

Inter-Continental has plans to build a megaresort in Ceiba on 2,000 acres with beachfront that would include more than 300 units, golf, spa, restaurants, heliport, and marina. No date has been set for its opening.

South of Ceiba, Route 3 brings you to *Playa de Naguabo,* a fishing town with a picturesque harbor and seafood restaurants along its *malecón* (waterfront promenade). For a stroll and meal, this is a great

Monkey Business

*L*ess than 1 mile offshore is *Cayo Santiago,* a thirty-nine-acre island that is home to about 700 rhesus monkeys. The monkey colony was started under a Columbia University grant in 1938, when the first group of monkeys was brought over from India. Even though the monkeys were hit by a tuberculosis epidemic and then nearly starved to death when research money ran out during World War II, the colony is still thriving under the administration of the University of Puerto Rico's Caribbean Primate Research Center.

Because the monkeys live in a natural environment but are contained on the island, scientists can study their behavior and development throughout their entire life span. More than 300 scientific articles have been written based on research conducted here, which is also credited with several breakthroughs in human medicine. To avoid disturbing the research, visitors are forbidden. But boats can be hired that anchor offshore close enough to see the monkeys, who can be seen having a good time on the beach or swinging from the trees.

stop. *Castillo Villa del Mar,* a Victorian home on the waterfront, is listed on the National Register of Historic Places. The beach itself is south of town, a thin strip of sand several miles long. *Playa Húcares* has a new boardwalk and places to eat.

Continuing on will bring you to *Playa Humacao* and the *balneario* and *centro vacacional Punta Santiago* (Route 3, km 77; 787–852–1660) with rental accommodations for cabins and campsites. In the neighborhood are several popular restaurants offering the local catch, including *Daniel's Seafood* (7 Marina; 787–852–1784) and *Tulio's Seafood* (5 Isidro Andreu; 787–850–1840). Offshore here is *Cayo Santiago,* a small island that's off-limits to the public and home to a laboratory run by the Caribbean Primate Research Center of University of Puerto Rico. A population of hundreds of rhesus monkeys are studied here for behavioral and medical research. Being the amusing critters they are, boat trips to watch from offshore are available. Call Captain Frank Lopez at (787) 850–7881.

Another natural scene worth observing is the *Humacao Wildlife Refuge* (Refugio de Vida Silvestre de Humacao, Route 3, km 74.3; 787–852–6088), protecting 28,000 acres with a series of lagoons. Great for bird-watching, it also is home to sea turtles that nest their eggs here. The entrance is just past the *balneario.* The park office is open weekdays from 7:30 A.M. to 3:30 P.M. Kayaks can be rented from *Proyecto Peces* (787–285–0696).

Another megaresort is located off Routes 3 and 906 in Humacao, the *Candelero Resort at Palmas del Mar* (170 Candelero Drive; 787–852–6000; www.palmasresort.com), with hotels and time-share villas. Palmas is also packaged as a second home for many residents who winter here, and it is increasingly becoming an upscale gated community for year-rounders who commute to jobs only forty-five minutes north in the San Juan area. It feels like a town, with its own school, fire and police departments, shopping center, bank, and medical facilities. Its 2,700 acres once were plantations of coconuts and sugarcane. There is still some rolling countryside, including two eighteen-hole golf courses (open to the public; 787–285–2256), but the center of the complex is an intensely developed area of residences and accommodations. There are also a casino, a myriad of restaurants and bars, a sandy 3 miles of beach, marina, twenty tennis courts, and an equestrian center. Gourmet French dishes are served at *Chez Daniel* (787–850–3838), open for dinner daily except Tuesday, lunch Friday through Sunday. What some might find most interesting about a place like this is a drive through to note the architecture. For others, this could be paradise.

You can still see sugarcane fields in this area, but the mills have closed. Two once thriving mills dating from the nineteenth century can be viewed, **Hacienda Lucía** off Route 901 and **Central Roig** on Route 3 at km 96. In the town of Humacao, **Casa Roig** (66 Lopez; 787–852–8380), is a 1920s home whose design by Puerto Rican architect Antonin Nechodoma shows Frank Lloyd Wright's influence. It's open as a free museum, Wednesday through Friday and Sunday, 10:00 A.M. to 4:00 P.M. This is the former home of the Roig family, who made their fortune raising cane.

Yabacoa and Maunabo

South of Humacao in the town of **Yabucoa** is **Hotel Parador Palmas de Lucía** (Route 901 at Route 9911; 787–893–4423; www.palmasde lucia.com). A fairly new, friendly hotel with comfortable rooms, a pool, and a restaurant, it is just off **Playa Lucía.** Known for a strong undertow, Playa Lucía is not always conducive to swimming, but the beach is great for walking. As at many beaches on the island, homeless dogs living here take an interest in you in a curious but timid way. Palmas de Lucía also operates **Costa del Mar Guest House** nearby (Route 901, km 5.6; 787–893–4423). Nine rooms are available here, as well as a pool and a restaurant specializing in Mexican food.

El Cocal and **Sharkey's Beach** are the local places for surfing. A good place to eat breakfast or lunch is at the outdoor counter at **El Tivoli** (Route 901, km 3.7; 787–893–2727). For dinners with an emphasis on seafood, **El Nuevo Horizonte** (Route 901, km 9.8; 787–839–5492) serves memorable *mofongo*. The view from here is impressive, looking off a hilltop to the expanse of the Caribbean Sea.

Yabucoa is the eastern starting point of the **Ruta Panorámica,** the scenic route that runs across the island's mountains to the west coast. More on this route is described in the Central Mountains chapter. Below Yabucoa, continuing south on Route 3, is the town of **Maunabo.** At **Punta Tuna,** a late nineteenth-century lighthouse is still in use and maintained by the U.S. Coast Guard. It is reached by taking Route 760 east off Route 901. There is a nice beach here, **Playa Larga,** reached by a path from the lighthouse.

A beach at **Puerto Maunabo,** on Road 7760 off Route 901, is also worth visiting. Pack a picnic with provisions from one of the supermarkets found in local shopping centers and you'll be set for the day. Go native by combining fresh-baked Puerto Rican bread with sandwich makings.

Be sure to include whatever fruits of the island are in season. A ripe papaya cut lengthwise then seeded and sprinkled with lime juice, or pineapple, coconut, bananas, mango, or oranges (*chinas*) will be emblematic and delicious. Of course, one could also argue the same thing about rum combined with fruit juice.

Providing accommodations here is *Playa de Emajaguas* (Route 901, km 2.5; 787–861–6023), a family-run guest house set on a bluff overlooking a pretty, mostly deserted beach. There are comfortable, well-worn rooms, some with an ocean view, and an outdoor deck. A pool and tennis courts enhance the inn. Guests enjoy the setting atop a bluff in the middle of fields. It seems the advantages of Maunabo being an overlooked corner of the island are about to change, when a resort complex similar to Las Palmas is built. *Villas del Faro* (Route 760; 787–861–1464; www.tier ranueva. com) is described as a combination of residences and tourist accommodations. First to be built will be 212 apartment units, followed by a resort called Point Tuna Nature and Beach Resort and Condohotel, comprising an "ecological park," restaurants, pools, tennis courts, and beach facilities, all with an Art Deco motif.

Patillas, Arroyo, Guayama, and Aguirre

After passing through Maunabo, Route 3 flattens in the coastal area of sugarcane fields and heads toward *Patillas*. Entering the semiarid southern coast, the sun and heat are so intense here that the town looks deserted at midday, when everyone takes refuge in shaded and air-conditioned spaces. One thing enjoying the climate is the grape crop that local vineyards sell to the United States for wine production. If you spend time here, there are some lodging choices, but the beachfront has eroded, leaving only a token strip. *Caribe Playa* (Route 3, km 112; 787–839–6339; www.caribeplaya.com), *Villa de Carmen* (Route 3, km 113; 787–839–7576), *Sunset Beach Village* (Route 3, km 113.7; 787–724–3434; www.sunsetpr.com), and *Caribbean Paradise Hotel* (Route 3, km 114; 787–839–5885) offer various amenities; all have pools. Also nearby is *Inches Beach,* known for good surfing. *Restaurante El Mar de la Tranquilidad* (The Sea of Tranquility) specializes in seafood (Route 3, km 118.9; 787–839–6469).

South of Patillas is *Punta Guilarte* (Route 3, km 126; 787–839–3565), with a *balneario* and *centro vacacional* renting cabins and campsites. There is a nice stretch of beach here. Shortly after this you enter *Arroyo*.

Step into the past by getting off the highway and driving into town on Morse Street. If that name sounds familiar, you may have guessed correctly that Samuel Morse, the American inventor of the telegraph, is associated with the town. In 1848, Morse came here to visit his married daughter and installed the first telegraph lines in all of Latin America. In the main plaza, a monument honors him.

When sugarcane plantations dominated this area during the nineteenth century, Arroyo was the shipping port for the crop brought by train from neighboring Guayama. Warehouses line the harbor and *malecón*, now reclaimed by bars and restaurants. Another relic of the period, the *Tren del Sur de Arroyo* (Route 3, km 130.9; 787–271–1574), combines a trolley ride around town and a 3.5-mile train trip to Guayama through fields still growing cane, although it's no longer harvested. The fare for adults is $3.00, $2.00 for children, and $1.50 for seniors. Call ahead to confirm times. Winter hours are Monday through Friday 8:00 A.M. to 4:30 P.M., Saturday and Sunday, 9:00 A.M. to 5:00 P.M. Summer hours 9:00 A.M. to 4:00 P.M. daily.

The Old Customs House, *Antigua Casa de Aduana* (65 Morse; 787–839–8096), is a museum open Wednesday through Friday from 9:00 A.M. to noon and 1:00 to 4:30 P.M. and Saturday and Sunday 9:00 A.M. to 4:30 P.M. This combination is a popular family outing and a chance to learn about the chapter of Puerto Rico's history when sugar was king. Earlier in Arroyo's history, the port had a long association with smuggling during Spanish rule, when little attention was paid to the island's south coast. The waterfront may seem sleepy now, but it is nearing a major overhaul. Plans are afoot to revive it in the near future as the government looks at the development of both Ponce and Arroyo as regional ports handling more shipping traffic. The dredging of Ponce's harbor to deepen it is beginning in 2004.

Past Arroyo, rejoin Route 3 west for *Guayama.* Set back from the coast where there are breezes and shade in the foothills, Guayama was a more desirable address than hot and dusty Arroyo. Wealthy merchants built their impressive homes here. The central plaza retains a dignity and the city prides itself as being Puerto Rico's "cleanest." One of the stately homes, on Ashford Street, is the birthplace of Luis Pales Matos, a poet who celebrated Puerto Rico's African legacy. A plaque identifies the house, now a private residence.

Museo Casa Cautiño (Palmer Street; 787–864–9083) is on the plaza's north side. It was a residence built in 1887 by Don Genaro Cautiño Vazquez, a plantation owner also described as a robber baron. He invoked worldly sophistication, using Victorian furniture, Persian carpets, a Murano glass chandelier, a bathroom bidet, bronze sculpture, and French architecture. In 1974, the house was taken by the government for unpaid taxes, and was opened as a museum in 1987 by the Institute of Puerto Rican Culture. What history lessons can be learned here? Decide for yourself. Open Tuesday through Saturday 10:00 A.M. to 4:30 P.M., Sunday until 5:00. A trolley departs from here on Sundays, providing a loop tour around town from 10:00 A.M. to 3:30 P.M.

Down Route 3 is the *Centro de Bellas Artes* (787–864–7765), open Tuesday through Saturday 9:00 A.M. to 4:30 P.M. and Sunday 10:00 A.M. to 4:30 P.M. In this beautifully restored courthouse, eleven rooms display historical exhibits and artwork.

As you leave Guayama on Bypass Route 54, some of the structures you'll see are the ruins of chimneys and windmills from the former sugar mills. There's also a large shopping center and a hotel, *El Molino* (Bypass Route 54, km 2.1; 787–866–1515). Set on a former plantation, El Molino (The Windmill) has a large pool, a restaurant, and comfortable accommodations.

You have a choice for the route you travel heading west. Highway 53 west to 52 south is faster, but Route 3 is closer to the coast and provides local color as you drive through cane fields and small communities. The highlight of this area is *Aguirre Forest and Jobos Bay,* a national estuarine research reserve, open daily 7:30 A.M. to 4:00 P.M. You can enter the mangrove forest off Route 3 on Route 7710, and visit the 2,883-acre estuary, which includes salt flats, fifteen cays offshore in the brackish bay, freshwater wetlands, and pristine coast. Manatees can be sighted here early in the day. The reserve's visitor center in Aguirre (Route 705, km 2.3; 787–853–4617) explains how the estuary works. Sign up for a guided hike or kayak tour, or learn which trails and boardwalks offer bird- and manatee-watching. The center is free and open weekdays 7:30 A.M. to noon and 1:00 to 4:00 P.M., weekends 9:00 A.M. to noon and 1:00 to 3:00 P.M. You can apply for a camping permit to stay in either Aguirre Forest or Jobos Bay. Information on the campgrounds is available at the reserve office located at the park entrance (787–724–3724). Kayaks can be rented nearby from *Marina de Salinas* (8G Chapin; 787–824–3185) .

The town of *Aguirre* owed its very existence to sugar, with one corporation's dominance making it a company town. The Central Aguirre Sugar Company created the town, named it Central Aguirre (still shown as that on many maps), and outfitted it with the facilities employees needed. When the sugar business went sour, everything was shut down practically overnight. The company's collapse turned it into a ghost town in 1990, but some facilities have gone on to new lives. The nine-hole golf course (Route 705, km 2.5; 787–853–4052), once used exclusively by company executives, is now open to the public daily 7:30 A.M. to 6:00 P.M. The train used to transport cane has been relocated to Arroyo, now operated as the *"Tren del Sur."* The bowling alley is an environmental center. Empty buildings continue to deteriorate, however. A coal-fired power plant is due to open here in 2003.

Beyond Guayama, Route 3 connects with Highway 52, which is the quickest route north over the Cordillera Central to San Juan.

**PLACES TO STAY
EAST OF SAN JUAN**

LUQUILLO
Villa Falcon Resort
8 First Street
(787) 889–7185

VIEQUES AND CULEBRA
Acacia Apartments
236 Acacia, Esperanza, Vieques
(787) 741–1856

Adventures Inn
Isabel Segunda, Vieques
(787) 741–1564
www.adventuresinn.com

Bay View Villas
Culebra
(787) 742–2961

Casa de Amistad
27 Benitez Castaño, Isabel Segunda, Vieques
(787) 741–3758
www.casadeamistad.com

Casa Ensenada Waterfront Guest House
142 Escudero, Culebra
(787) 742–3559

Costa Bonita Sea Resort
Carenero Point, Culebra
(787) 791–2332

Casa La Lanchita
Bravos de Boston, Vieques
(800) 774–4717
www.viequeslalanchita.com

Culebra Island Villas
Punta del Soldado Road, Culebra
(787) 742–0333

Culebra Ocean View
201 Jesús María Ortíz, Culebra
(787) 742–2601

Green Villas
4 Punta Aloe, Culebra
(787) 742–3112

Harbour View Villas
Playa Melones, Culebra
(787) 742–3855
www.culebrahotel.com

Hostal Bahía Marina
Fulladoza, km 2.7, Culebra
(787) 742–0366

Hotel Kokomo
Next to the ferry terminal, Culebra
(787) 742–0719

Hotel Puerto Rico
56 Salisberi, Culebra
(787) 742–3372

Isla Bonita
Playa Flamenco, Culebra
(787) 742–3575

La Piña
222 Acacia, Vieques
(787) 741–2953

Ocean View
751 Plinio Peterson, Isabel Segunda, Vieques
(787) 741–0622

Posada Vistamar
Almendro, Esperanza, Vieques
(787) 741–8716

Sea Gate Guest House
Isabel Segunda, Vieques
(787) 741–4661

Villa Arynar
South of Dewey, Culebra
(787) 742–3145

Villa Boheme
Punta del Soldado Road, Culebra
(787) 742–3508
www.villaboheme.com

Villa Flamenco Beach
Playa Flamenco, Culebra
(787) 742–0023

Villa Fulladoza
Punta del Soldado Road,
Culebra
(787) 742–3576

Villa Naniqui
Barriada Clark, Culebra
(787) 742–3271

Villa Nueva
Barriada Clark, Culebra
(787) 742–0257

Waters Edge Guest House
Isabel Segunda, Vieques
(787) 741–1128
www.watersedgeguest
house.com

CEIBA, NAGUABO, AND
HUMACAO
Intercontinental Cayo
Largo Resort
(787) 801–5000
www.intercontinental.com

YABACOA AND MAUNABO
Hotel Campo Viejo
Route 901, km 5.6, Yabacoa
(787) 266–1294

PATILLAS, ARROYO, GUAYAMA,
AND AGUIRRE
Hotel and Restaurant
Brandemar
61 Coral, Guayama
(787) 864–5124

PLACES TO EAT
EAST OF SAN JUAN

RÍO GRANDE
Antojítos Puertorriqueños
Route 968, km 0.4
(787) 888–7378

El Dajao
Route 191, km 0.4
(787) 888–6716

Las Vegas
Route 191, km 1.3, Palmer
(787) 887–2526

LUQUILLO
Chef Wayne
Off Route 992
(787) 889–1962

Las Vegas
Route 191, km 1.3
(787) 887–2526

Lolita's
Highway 3, km 4.8
(787) 889–5770

Sandy's Seafood Restaurant
and Steak House
276 Fernandez Garcia
(787) 889–5765

Victor's Place Seafood
2 Jesús T. Piñeiro
(787) 889–5705

Villa Pesquera
Route 877, km 6.6
(787) 887–0140

FAJARDO
La Fontanella
Las Croabas Roads
767–860–2480

Sardinera
Calle Croabas
(787) 863–0320

Star Fish Restaurant
Fajardo Inn
Route 52
(787) 860–6000

VIEQUES AND CULEBRA
Bayaond
Playa Monte Santo, Vieques
(787) 741–0312

Café Media Luna
Antonio Mellado, Isabel
Segunda, Vieques
(787) 741–2594

Coconuts Beach Grill
Flamenco Beach Villas
Playa Flamenco, Culebra
No phone

Culebra Deli
Dewey, Culebra
(787) 742–3277

El Caobo/Tina's
Barriada Clark, Culebra
(787) 742–3235

El Oasis
Dewey, Culebra
(787) 742–3175

Happy Landings
Culebra Airport
(787) 742–0135

Juanita Bananas
Harbour View Villas
Playa Melones, Culebra
(787) 742–3855
www.juanitabananas.com

Island Steak House at the
Crow's Nest
Route 201, km 1.6, Vieques
(787) 741–0011
www.crowsnestvieques.com

La Casa del Frances
Route 996, Esperanza,
Vieques
(787) 741–3751

La Sirena
Flamboyán, Esperanza,
Vieques
(787) 741–4462

Mar Azul
Isabel Segunda, Vieques
(787) 741–3400

Marta's Al Fresco
Dewey, Culebra
(787) 742–3575

Mucho Gusto
121 Muños Rivera, Isabel
Segunda, Vieques
(787) 741–3300

Naniqui Café
Villa Naniqui, Culebra
no phone

Panadería El Patio
Culebra Airport
(787) 742–0374

Paso Fino
Wyndham Martinequ
Bay Resort
Route 200, km 3.4, Vieques
(787) 741–4100
www.wyndham.com

Posada Vista Mar
Almendro, Esperanza,
Vieques
(787) 741–2900

Restaurante El Pesquerito
Fish Co-op, Culebra
(787) 742–3506

Richard's Café
Antonio Mellado, Isabel
Segunda, Vieques
(787) 741–5242

Taverna Española
Carlos Lebrún at Benitez
Castaño, Isabel Segunda,
Vieques
(787) 741–1175

Tiki Hut
Malecón, Esperanza,
Vieques
(787) 741–4992

Tropical Baby
Esperanza, Vieques
No phone

Tropico
Isabel Segunda, Vieques
(787) 741–4000

Vieques Country Club
Playa Monte Santo, Vieques
(787) 741–1863

Wai Nam Chinese
Restaurant
Dewey, Culebra
no phone

White Sands
Club Seabourne,
Punta del Soldado Road,
Culebra
(787) 742–3169

CEIBA, NAGUABO, AND
HUMACAO
A Lo Natural
Calle Tejas, Humacao
(787) 852–0945

El Jíbaro
Route 3, Playa Húcares,
Naguabo
(787) 874–0690

El Navegante Restaurant
Route 3, Playa Húcares,
Naguabo
(787) 874–1652

Punta Lima Restaurant
Route 3, Playa Húcares,
Naguabo
(787) 874–1448

Tacomiqueo
Route 3, Playa Húcares,
Naguabo
(787) 643–7168

YABACOA AND MAUNABO
Bella Vista Restaurant and
Sea Terrace
Route 901, km 4.6,
Maunabo
(787) 861–1501

Los Bohíos
Route 760, km 2.5,
Maunabo
(787) 861–2545

PATILLAS, ARROYO, GUAYAMA,
AND AGUIRRE
El Balco Café
47 Hostos, Guayama
(787) 864–7272

El Molinito
Molino Inn Hotel, Bar, and
Restaurant
Route 54, km 2.1, Guayama
(787) 866–1515

El Puerto
Route 3, at Route 7710,
Guayama
(787) 866–2664

Frenesi
Parador Caribbean
Paradise
Route 3, km 114.3, Patillas
(787) 839–7388

King's Pizza
2 Vinente Pales, East,
Guayama
(787) 866–4331

La Familia
53 Morse, Arroyo
no phone

La Llave del Mar
Paseo de Las Américas,
Arroyo
(787) 839-6395

Hotel Restaurant
Brandemar
Barrio Branderi, Arroyo
(787) 864-5124

Restaurante y Bar Vino y
Candela
La Fuente Town Center
Route 54, km 0.9, Guayama
(787) 864-2256

Seaview Terrace
Hotel Caribe Playa
Route 3, km 112.1, Patillas
(787) 839-6339

Ponce and the South

Gone are the days when Puerto Rico's southern coast was separated from the capital by grueling one-lane roadways through steep mountain terrain. The completion of a freeway in 1975 put the south coast within easy reach of San Juan, and a recent extension that skirts downtown Ponce has cut trips to the southwest by about forty-five minutes. Now Ponce is a quick ninety-minute drive, and almost anywhere in the southwest can be reached within another hour or so from there.

Despite increased contact with San Juan, the south still retains its own ways. This is the Caribbean side of Puerto Rico, and the south coast sizzles throughout the year. The sun is almost always strong and high. This has a big effect on the pace of the days and nights here. Puerto Rico's southerners are distinct from their northern neighbors; they're used to a slower-paced, more relaxed way of life. History seems closer at hand here, where an agricultural way of life lives on in sugarcane plantations and cattle fields that punctuate the drive along the southern coast. The region's capital, Ponce, is a provincial city of turn-of-the-century grandeur and immaculate plazas. From Guánica to Lajas to Cabo Rojo, southwestern Puerto Rico has some of the island's best beaches. Along with large hotels and casinos, the region also has pristine natural reserves, from coastal mangroves to cliffs to dry forests.

There are many reasons to visit this region, and no one should forego the trip—even if it's just a Ponce day-tour from San Juan. But those who come to this region to stay for a few days will definitely be rewarded. Puerto Ricans love this part of the country, and they flock here in droves during holiday weekends.

South of San Juan

Heading south from San Juan means taking the Luis A. Ferré Expressway (Highway 52), which cuts through San Juan's southern suburbs and then straight over the top of the *Cordillera Central* mountains to the steaming southern coast.

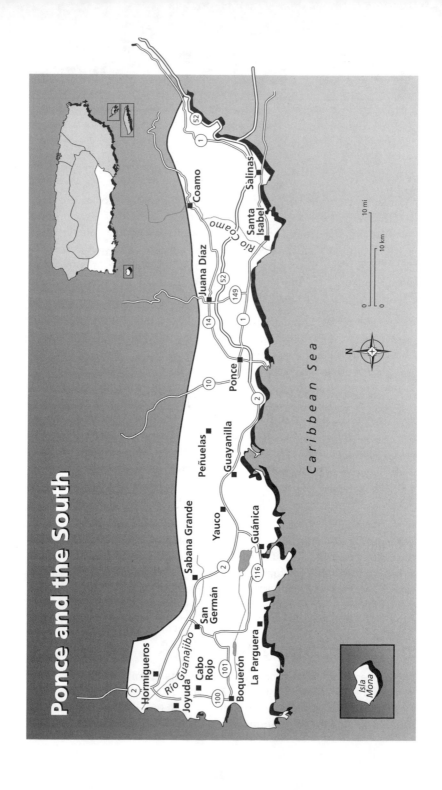

Ponce and the South

Coamo

Salinas

Santa Isabel

Juana Díaz

Río Coamo

Ponce

Peñuelas

Guayanilla

Sabana Grande

Yauco

Guánica

San Germán

Hormigueros

Río Guanajibo

Joyuda

Cabo Rojo

Boquerón

La Parguera

Caribbean Sea

Isla Mona

N

10 mi

10 km

PONCE AND THE SOUTH

Although it's only about a forty-minute drive from San Juan to the top of the central mountain range, the climatic changes are dramatic. The area is often draped in dark clouds, and it's generally much cooler here than on the coasts. As the highway soars upward, it passes lushly covered hillsides.

The descent to the Caribbean coast along the mountain range's southern side is always impressive. The roadway descends into the foothills that, depending on the season, are either a lunarlike terra-cotta or a lush tropical green. The hot sun above the turquoise sea sends shimmering waves of haze across the southern coastal plains.

After passing over the Cordillera Central, the expressway turns into a coastal road through cattle farms and foothills.

Whether your travel sees you heading down from the north or continuing west along the coast, the Salinas area you enter around the junction of Highways 52 and 53 and Route 3 has some points of interest. Off Highway 53 is the **Albergue Olímpico** (Route 712, km 3.4; 787–824–2607 or 800–981–2210; www.albergueolimpico-pr.org), where athletes train for participation on the Puerto Rican Olympics team. On Sundays there are tours at noon, 1:00, 2:00, and 3:00 P.M. (Visitors are advised to confirm times in advance.) The grounds include a small water park, playground, botanical garden, and the Puerto Rican Museum of Sports. Open daily, 10:00 A.M. to 5:00 P.M.; there is an admission fee.

The **Puerto Rico International Speedway** (Route 3, km 155.2; 787–824–0020; www.salinasspeedway.com) holds races on Wednesday from 5:00 P.M. to midnight, Saturday 4:00 P.M. to midnight. For Sunday hours, which vary, call ahead. The recent residency of athletes and race car drivers carries on the tradition of brawn and bravery in Salinas, traditionally home to cane workers. A life working in fields certainly required such attributes.

Because there is a protected harbor here, Playa Salinas does have a waterfront offering yachting services. There are two places to stay in town: **Puerta La Bahía Hotel and Restaurant** (Calle Principal; 787–824–7117) and, at the harbor, **Marina de Salinas and Posada El Náutico** (Route 701; 787–824–8484; www.prhtasmallhotels.com) with its restaurant, **Costa Marina.** Playa Salinas is famous for its numerous seafood eateries ranging in price and style. To kayak the bay, Marina de Salinas has hourly and daily rentals (787–752–8484).

(Note: Playa Salinas is located on Bahía de Rincón, not to be confused with Bahía Salinas at the southwest corner of the island, where the Cabo Rojo lighthouse is located).

Continuing west on Route 1 brings you to the town of Santa Isabel, and out Route 538 is **Playa Santa Isabel.** There's a *malecón* here with places to eat. The best restaurant around may be **La Fonda de Angelo** (6 Betances; 787–845–2886), which attracts day-trippers from San Juan for a meal with original recipes. One specialty of the town is the number of artisans making *bomba* drums. A new hotel, **Hacienda Santa Isabel** (Route 153, km 3.3; 787–845–7777), is scheduled to open in 2003.

This area of cane fields is home to horses, ranches, stables, and shows. You can find the island's *paso fino* breed in both Salinas and Santa Isabel. Santa Isabel also boasts a natural reserve at Punta Petrona. The beach at **Playa Jauca** is touted as excellent for windsurfing, with winds at 18 to 25 knots and 2 to 4 foot waves. As an insider explained, it has some "great bump and jumps conditions."

While in this area, you may want to see **Baños de Coamo,** the hot springs famous in Puerto Rico's history. From Route 52 headed west, turn north on Route 546. After 3 miles, turn left at the **Coamo Springs**

Mojo Isleno

*T*he traditional salsa from Salinas, mojo isleno *accompanies grilled, baked, or fried fish. This version uses fresh tomatoes instead of canned tomato sauce. The recipe is enough for two pounds of fish.*

¼ cup olive oil
2 tablespoons chopped garlic
1 large onion, chopped
2 peppers, seeded and chopped
        (Italian frying or green bell)
3 large ripe tomatoes, chopped
½ cup chopped alcaparrado
        (manzanilla olives, capers,
        and pimientos)

Salt and ground black pepper to taste
2 whole bay leaves
1 tablespoon wine vinegar

In a heavy saucepan, heat olive oil. Add garlic, onion, and peppers and sauté. Add tomatoes and remaining ingredients. Cover; simmer slowly on stovetop, stirring frequently. If more liquid is needed, add small amount of water, tomato sauce, or more tomatoes. When thickened, remove and discard bay leaves. Serve sauce over cooked fish. If desired, garnish with strips of roasted red peppers. Rice is a good side dish to accompany this.

PONCE AND THE SOUTH

Top Annual Events

San Blas Marathon, early February, Coamo

***National Coffee Harvest Festival,** late February and early March, Yauco*

***Carnaval de Salinas,** first week of April*

***Semana de la Danza,** second week of May, Ponce*

***Festival de San Pedro,** late June, La Parguera*

***Fiesta del Pueblo de Guánica,** July, Guánica*

***Lola Rodríguez de Tió Festival,** second week of September, San Germán*

***Yauco Patron Saint Festival,** October*

***Las Mañanitas,** December 12, Ponce*

***Ponce Patron Saint Festival,** third week of December*

Golf and Tennis Club, a new eighteen-hole course that welcomes visitors daily from 7:00 A.M. to 6:00 P.M. (787–825–1370; www.coamosprings. com). Wind along the road through here to a parking lot and *parador* on the left. Dating from when the *Taínos* lived here, the hot springs have been valued for their healing powers. Legend has it that this was the fountain of youth Juan Ponce de León was searching for. The fashionable resort that thrived here in the early decades of the twentieth century drew the likes of Franklin D. Roosevelt, Alexander Graham Bell, Frank Lloyd Wright, and Thomas Edison. There are two places to take the waters.

Staying at *Parador Baños de Coamo* (Route 546; 787-825-2186; www.banosdecoamo.com) gives you access to the thermal pools maintained by the hotel, including a larger, standard pool. Day passes can be purchased for the use of these pools and locker room facilities ($5.00 for adults, $3.00 for children; 10:00 A.M. to 5:30 P.M. daily). The *parador* has a certain charm to it once you're inside the compound, which includes low-key buildings with stone, stucco, and balconies, an outdoor bar at the pool area, and the restaurant, *Café Puertorriqueño.* (The rooms, nothing fancy, get mixed reviews.) In the courtyard, the landscaping is shady, green, and lush, an oasis in the heat of the day.

To get to the *public thermal pools,* free and open daily 8:00 A.M. to 6:00 P.M., walk outside the *parador* (opposite the parking area) along a dirt road. Right beyond the *parador*'s walls, you walk up a short path on your left to two adjacent pools in the rock. The hottest water—about 110 degrees Fahrenheit—is in the first pool; the water then spills into the second, cooling off slightly, and finally cascades over the edge, creating a stream people stand under on ground level. Although the public baths are not well maintained, it is a popular spot with locals who believe in the water's curative powers. In years past, a visit to this spa was rejuvenating for many reasons, and the peaceful countryside encouraged complete relaxation. Now you arrive at the hot springs after driving through burgeoning suburbia, including the luxury condos built right in front of the *parador.* Sadly, it isn't the same respite anymore.

Already populated by *Taínos,* Spaniards established a town at Coamo in 1579, one of their first settlements on the island along with San Juan, Aguada, and San Germán. The plaza boasts an eighteenth-century church with artwork by two important Puerto Rican artists, José Campeche and Francisco Oller. In a former residence from the nineteenth century, the **Museo Historico de Coamo** (29 José Quinton; 787–825–1150) has several rooms decorated to the period. Open weekdays 9:00 A.M. to 4:00 P.M.; call for weekend hours.

Ponce

once, known as the "Pearl of the South," is a pretty, provincial city that still maintains its late-nineteenth-century feeling, when Ponce was not only the most important city in Puerto Rico, but in much of the Caribbean as well. The city was named in 1692 in honor of Ponce de León's great-grandson.

The sun-bleached, pastel-painted historic zone is laced with a whimsical Creole-Caribbean architecture built from the 1850s through the 1930s, when Ponce was the rich port city of a region bursting with agricultural activity. It was also a center of intellectual life, and many poets, painters, and politicians hailed from this area.

Ponce residents initially favored a simple, colonial architectural style, but as the city grew richer so did local tastes. In the nineteenth century, homes began displaying ornate neoclassic and Art Nouveau flourishes. Interiors were also elaborately decorated so that the sunlight coming through intricate stained-glass panels would fall in splashes of color over patterned, mosaic tile floors. Punched-tin ceilings and fixed jalousies in back corridors were also prevalent.

Until 1995 the Luis A. Ferré Expressway ended at Ponce, meaning that drivers heading for the southwest went through the city center in order to catch Highway 2. Now the road has been lengthened so that the expressway spills onto Highway 2 on the western edges of the city. While the extension only added a few miles to the expressway, it has shaved an hour off most trips by circumventing the traffic-clogged city.

Most people who want to visit Ponce, however, will still get off at the old Ponce By-Pass, a built-up roadway that runs through a modern retail district and connects the old Highway 1 and Highway 2. Here you'll find plenty of places to gas up, and roadside fruit vendors selling everything from *queñepas* to pineapples, depending on the season. There are also several shopping centers, with the biggest being Plaza del Caribe on Highway 2.

To get to Ponce's historic district, take Route 133, which runs over the Río Portugues before becoming Calle Comercio, the historic district's main artery. Two bronze lions by sculptor Victor Ochoa tower over the entrance to Ponce's historic zone.

Plaza Las Delicias, also called Plaza Degetau or Plaza Central, is the main square in the historic zone. It captures the city's charm with its clean, shaded walkways and opulent fountains and flower gardens. Big trees hang over stone benches and antique gas lampposts, while pink granite pathways roll through the plaza. Trolleys and horse-drawn carriages ply the narrow historic streets as well dressed *ponceños* stroll slowly in the Caribbean heat.

The plaza is dominated by the *Lion Fountain,* a bronze and marble fountain made for the 1939 World's Fair. It was modeled after the fountain of the same name in Barcelona, Spain. Be sure to view it after dark. The most photographed building on the plaza is undoubtedly

Celebrations in Ponce

*W*ith a combination of influences from Spanish and African traditions, Ponce's Carnaval in February includes masks, a blend of pagan and religious imagery, and street parades with floats, marchers, music, and dance. The weeklong celebration concludes the night before Ash Wednesday with the burial of a sardine. The center of action is Plaza Las Delicias.

The distinctive forms of music with deep roots in Ponce are bomba, plena, *and* danza. Bomba *music of drumming accompanied by dance came from Africa with slaves brought to Puerto Rico, originally in the Loíza area of the northeast coast.* Plena *developed on the southern coast in the nineteenth century. Spanish lyrics, usually about current events, are sung to music blending African, Taíno,* jíbaro, *and* danza *influences. An islandwide event, the Fiesta Nacional*

de Bomba y Plena attracts performers who sing, dance, and drum every year in November. The Fiesta Nacional de Danza takes place each May, with orchestras and formally donned couples performing the danza *in Plaza Las Delicias. The stylized steps from a Spanish dance similar to the waltz are combined with music that blends European classical elements and island vernacular.*

The patron saint of Ponce is the Virgen de Guadelupe, also Mexico's patron saint. She was chosen in honor of the long and close relationship Ponce had with Mexico as partners in trade. Ponce was a major source for horses and cattle. How better to celebrate than with mariachis, margaritas, and fireworks? The week leading up to December 12 has parades and all the usual rituals involving music, food, and drink.

the *Parque de Bombas* (Plaza Las Delicias; 787–284–3338), the city's famous Victorian firehouse, which was built in 1883 as the centerpiece of an annual agricultural fair. It has red and black walls, a myriad of poles and cornices, and many passageways. Admission is free. Open 9:30 A.M. to 6:00 P.M., closed Tuesday.

Also on the plaza, the **Cathedral of Our Lady of Guadalupe** (Catedral Nuestra Señora de Guadelupe, Concordia and Union; 787–842–0134), named after the city's patron saint, has unique silver spiral protrusions that sparkle in the sun of the Ponce afternoon. The church was first built here in 1660, but it was destroyed on several occasions by natural disasters, from fires to earthquakes. The present Gothic-inspired structure was built in 1931.

Helpful tourist information centers are scattered throughout the downtown area. Free trolley rides from the Plaza are offered daily from 8:00 A.M. to 9:00 P.M. There are three different routes. The attractive **Casa Alcaldía,** City Hall (787–284–4141), across from the Plaza, dates from 1840. It's open weekdays 8:00 A.M. to 4:30 P.M. **Hotel Meliá** (2 Cristina; 787–842–0260 or 800–742–4276; http://home.coqui.net/melia/) is the place to stay downtown. Among its features are a rooftop terrace where continental breakfast is served, friendly staff, and **Mark's at the Meliá** (787–284–6275), a fine restaurant with renowned local chef Mark French, which takes traditional *comida criolla* and raises it to new heights. Also on the plaza is **King's Cream** (Plaza Las Delicias; 787–843–8520), a local ice-cream parlor famous for its delicious homemade creations. You'll want to try more than one flavor.

Paseo Arias, also known as the *Callejón del Amor* (Lovers Lane), is a pedestrian passage built in the 1920s between two banks. Today the buildings house air-conditioned mini malls filled with African tulips and open-air cafes. The **Fox Delicias Mall** (78 Isabel), on the north end of Plaza Las Delicias, was built in the 1930s. The red-tile-roofed building, originally a movie theater, combines Hollywood Art Deco flourishes with a Mediterranean style. It now houses a food court and stores.

Teatro La Perla (Calle Mayor; 787–843–4322) remains a center of Ponce's cultural life, with concerts and theatrical and dance performances taking place throughout the year, as well as more low-brow (and popular) affairs such as beauty pageants. A late-afternoon stroll by here often rewards the visitor with a warm-up practice of the evening's performance. The theater was designed along the lines of New York's Carnegie Hall and is famous for its acoustics. Restored in 1941, it was originally built in 1864 by the Italian-born Juan Bertoli Calderoni,

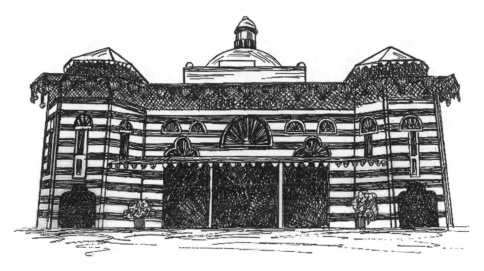

Parque de Bombas

who is considered the father of Puerto Rico's neoclassic architectural style. Bertoli also built the Creole-style residence that now houses the **Museum of Puerto Rican Music** (Museo de la Música Puertoriqueña, Calle Salud between Cristina and Isabel; 787–848–7016), where you can see displays of the Taíno, African, and Spanish instruments that have helped create the island's unique music, including the *bomba, plena,* and *danza.* Open 9:00 A.M. to 4:30 P.M. (closed Monday and Tuesday). Admission is $1.00.

Also worth a visit is the **Casa Salazar,** which houses **The Museum of the History of Ponce** (Museo de la Historia de Ponce, 51-53 Isabel; 787–844–7071). The museum, which opened in 1992, traces Ponce's storied history from the time of the Taínos to the present. The 1911 building mixes Moorish and neoclassic styles and is filled with the decorative displays that typify this southern city: from its stained-glass windows, pressed-tin ceilings, and fixed-window jalousies to its wooden and iron columns and full balconies. Open daily except Tuesday 9:00 A.M. to 5:00 P.M. Admission is $3.00 for adults, $2.00 for seniors, and $1.00 for children.

Paseo Atocha, a pedestrian mall that is also the downtown area's main shopping district, is housed in century-old buildings. The **Plaza del Mercado** (two blocks north of Plaza Central between Estrella and Castillos Streets) is also worth a visit. There you'll find all the browsing, haggling, and liveliness you'd expect at a Caribbean market.

For souvenirs, two stores on the plaza offer typical goods from across the island, including vejigante masks, musical instruments, and santos, as well as refrigerator magnets, decals, T-shirts, and postcards. *Mi Coquí* (9226 Marina; 787–841–0216) and *Utopia* (78 Isabel; 787–848–8742) are open 10:00 A.M. to 6:00 P.M. daily.

Other places to see around the plaza include the *Casa Armstrong-Poventud* on Calle Union on the plaza's west side, a 1900 home now serving as the Institute of Puerto Rican Culture's southern office (787–844–2540), open weekdays 8:00 A.M. to 4:30 P.M. The exterior boasts a gingerbread Victorian style.

Over one block at the corner of Reina and Meléndez Vigo is *Casa Wiechers-Villaronga* (787–843–3363), built in 1911 by Alfredo Wiechers, a Ponce architect. Inside and out this home is full of interesting details. Free admission; open Wednesday through Sunday 8:00 A.M. to 4:30 P.M.

Another must-see is *Castillo Serrallés* (787–259–1770), which over-

The World of Ponce

*P*onceños will be the first to tell you that they're, well, different. There's a saying, "Ponce is Ponce." Residents take enormous pride in their city, with a gentility and dignity that are palpable. Ponceños care about gritty details like having clean streets, restored buildings, and an active city center. The town's mayor, the most powerful politician in the south, works out of plush trappings that rival La Fortaleza, the governor's mansion in San Juan. Ponce is one of Puerto Rico's few "autonomous" municipalities, a status that grants the city a wide range of oversight. It has also been Ponce's advantage to be home to two of the island's twentieth-century governors, Rafael Hernández Colón and Luis A. Ferré.

Ponce's early days were busy as a port popular for smuggling. When plantations in the southern part of the island prospered in the nineteenth century, it was Africans brought to Ponce who worked the fields. This was where ships from all over came for coffee, rum, and sugarcane. Aristocrats in Latin America, fleeing their newly independent countries in order to continue to live in Spanish domain, came to Ponce. The result was a city with a blend of successful merchants, plantation owners, old money and new fortunes, and many different ethnicities.

The city's attractions illustrate this history. The downtown benefited from wide-scale renovations in the 1990s and hosts not only Ponceños enjoying the main plaza, businesses, and cultural offerings, but large numbers of tourists. Whether at the art museum or a souvenir shop, most of the visitors are Puerto Ricans, including many who don't live on the island and are learning more about their roots.

looks the city from El Vigía Hill. The mansion, built in the 1930s Spanish Revival style, was originally home to the Serrallés family, makers of Don Q rum. In 1986 the city of Ponce bought the mansion and painstakingly restored it. Today it houses a museum that attempts to replicate life in the era of the sugar barons. The museum also shows documentary films on the sugar and rum industries. Open Tuesday through Sunday 9:30 A.M. to 5:30 P.M. Admission is $3.00 for adults, $1.50 for children, and $2.00 for seniors. Forty-five-minute tours are available, but no rum-tasting. The mansion sits below the cross-shaped *El Vigía Observation Tower* (admission $1.00, open Tuesday through Sunday 9:00 A.M. to 5:30 P.M.), which affords a magnificent view. A ride in the elevator costs $3.00. You can climb to the El Vigía neighborhood from Ponce's Plaza Las Delicias. This hilly sector overlooks the old mansions of Ponce's elite and the Caribbean Sea.

Starting with breakfast at 7:30 A.M. *El Patio Colonial* (Calle Luna at Calle Marina; 787-848-3178) offers a full day of meals, culminating with live Latin jazz and rock in the evening. Music Tuesday through Saturday; closed Sunday. *Hollywood Café* (Highway 1, km 12.5; 787-843-6703) is the place for live rock and roll, including lots of Latin pop. Open Sunday through Thursday 5:00 P.M. to midnight, Friday and Saturday until 3:00 A.M.

The waterfront district of *Playa de Ponce,* sometimes referred to as El Muelle de Ponce, is a fisherman's village that lies on the opposite side of the Ponce By-Pass from the historic sector. This area, along with the adjacent waterfront area of Paseo Tablado La Guancha, is loaded with casual open-air restaurants, bars, and kiosks. Known as *La Guancha,* this half-mile-long boardwalk comes alive Wednesday through Sunday evenings when bands and DJs blast merengue, salsa, and rock into the salt-scented breezes. It's a multigenerational scene, from infants to great-grandparents. Lots of families go together, although teenagers inevitably find their own crowd. Sometimes everybody is dancing, and sometimes there are couples everyone stops to watch. There are places to sit and eat and drink. Although it's a local scene, visitors—especially those appreciative of the music—are made to feel welcome. The parking area adjacent to La Guancha is large, well-lighted, police-patrolled, and free. This is also the home of the *Ponce Yacht Club,* whose members' boats are docked just offshore.

In the La Guancha area, you can take boats to offshore cays such as *Caja de Muertos* (Coffin Cay), which is the biggest and most popular of the offshore islands. Eight miles off the coast of Ponce, the 2-mile by 1-mile island is one of three cays in the Caja de Muerto Nature Reserve

The Ponce Art Museum

The Ponce Museum of Art (2525 Las Américas Avenue; 787–848–0505; www.museoarteponce.org) is one of the largest and most impressive museums in the Caribbean. Its holdings range from European classics to contemporary Puerto Rican, with good examples of Baroque and pre-Raphaelite painting. Located across from the Catholic University of Ponce, the building itself is a beauty. It was designed by Edward Durell Stone, the architect of the Museum of Modern Art in New York. The museum's core collection was donated by former governor and pro-statehood New Progressive Party founder Luis Ferré.

The museum features a huge, shell-shaped wooden staircase and a series of skylit, angular galleries that give an overview of European painting from the fourteenth to nineteenth centuries. There are also traveling exhibits of contemporary art. Surrounding the staircase are such classics as Leandro Rosanno's sixteenth-century masterpiece The Flood. Other highlights include Sir Edward Burne-Jones's Sleeping Beauty, Sir Frederick Leighton's Flaming June, Peter Paul Rubens's The Greek Magus, José Campeche's Dama a Caballa, and Francisco Ollers's La Ceiba de Ponce. Open 10:00 A.M. to 5:00 P.M. daily. Adults $4.00, children $2.00, students $1.00.

The island has rest rooms, picnic areas, and fine swimming beaches.

Island Ventures (787–842–8546) runs trips here. *Isla de Cordona,* which lies a nautical mile from La Guancha and takes less than one hour to reach, is another option for a day trip. Although there are no public facilities, the island is much less trampled and features a nice beach and an old lighthouse. The shallow waters off both islands and the surrounding reef make for great snorkeling. Two submerged century-old wrecks lie just off of Cordona, and some snorkelers have found antique bottles and pottery in their explorations. San Juan–based *Las Tortugas Adventures* (787–725–5169) runs a kayaking trip to Cordona. A $75 fee provides transportation from San Juan, kayak, snorkeling equipment, and lunch, which includes drinks and beer. The tour operators set up a beachside picnic area on the island, so guests are very comfortable.

The luxury accommodations for Ponce are at the *Ponce Hilton,* next to La Guancha on the waterfront (1150 Caribe; 787–259–7676; www.hilton.com). On eighty acres, the southern coast's biggest resort includes the gourmet restaurant *La Cava,* a casino, spa, children's playground and programs, pool, tennis courts, fitness center, driving range, three bars, shopping, arcade, and 153 rooms.

Just outside Ponce is the *Tibes Indian Ceremonial Center* (Route 503, km 2.2; 787–840–2255), the largest indigenous settlement, and the oldest burial ground and ceremonial center in the Caribbean. Ancient pre-Taíno plazas dating from A.D. 700 were uncovered here in 1975 when a tropical storm flooded the area. There are also ten *bateyes,* or ball courts (where the Taínos played a soccerlike game), and two dance grounds. The center also houses a museum with indigenous ceremonial objects, pottery, jewelry, and a small gift and snack shop. A video presentation and guided tour explain the site's significance. Open Tuesday through Sunday 9:00 A.M. to 4:00 P.M. Admission is $2.00 for adults and $1.00 for children and seniors.

North of Ponce, the **Hacienda Buena Vista** (Route 123, km 16.8; 787–722–5882 or 787–284–7020; www.fideicomiso.org) is a restored corn and coffee plantation that dates from 1833. It has been faithfully restored by the Conservation Trust. It's a fun trip, as you're free to wander around the plantation, which is decorated with nineteenth-century antiques and artifacts. The experience is authentic—the waterwheels and mills function and the manor house retains some of the original furnishings. The place is open Wednesday through Sunday. Spanish-language tours are given at 8:30 and 10:30 A.M. and 1:30 and 3:30 P.M.; English-language tours are given at 1:30 P.M. only. Reservations are necessary for all tours. Please call ahead to secure a space. The guided tour lasts ninety minutes. Admission is $5.00 for adults and $2.00 for children.

About 3 miles west of town lies **El Tuque,** a long stretch of beach fronting the Caribbean. The closest thing Ponce has to its own beach, it now also boasts **Complejo El Tuque,** a recreation complex featuring a water park, the Ponce International Speedway Park, and the **Hotel El**

Communing with Cohoba

*O*ne ceremonial ritual the Taíno shamans (medicine men) and caciques (chieftains) practiced at Tibes, believing it allowed them to reach a higher level of understanding, was imbibing an alcoholic beverage of fermented cassava and inhaling powdered seeds from a variety of the native cohoba tree, sometimes mixed with tobacco. In the ritual, the shaman or cacique sat facing a cemí, an idol in the image of a god, carved of stone or wood. The cemí held the powdered cohoba, symbolically offering a gift of the gods. The cohoba was inhaled into the nose through a hollowed bone or tuberous vegetable. Entering into a higher state—what we might call a drug-induced hallucination—allowed one to speak directly with the deities. These consultations provided important guidance for decision-making.

Hacienda Buena Vista

Tuque (787–290–2000; www.eltuque.com) with seventy-five rooms and the Pub Club, a sports bar and grill.

Highway 2 westbound then passes *Las Cucharas,* a beautiful coastal area where the narrow shoreline and the highway curve in a gentle arc beside the Caribbean. The *balneario* Las Cucharas is located here. On the other side of the highway is a row of famed seafood restaurants that serve fresh fish and Puerto Rican specialties. While all of them are worthy, *Pito's Seafood Café* (787–841–4977) is the most famous, with live music on weekends.

Highway 2 west of Ponce is a beautiful, rolling coastal road, with the glistening Caribbean to the left and dry, gnarled hills to the right. The one blotch on this scene is the petrochemical plant that spreads over the Peñuelas/Guayanilla border. All along the southern coast, petrochemical and power plants have sprawled across land that was once agricultural.

Playa de Guayanilla, less than 15 miles west of Ponce, is a nice place to stop and catch a real slice of Puerto Rican life. The little waterfront can be found just beyond the site of the old chemical production facility. The block-long stretch of weathered restaurants and food stands draws crowds on weekends with delicious seafood and loud music. This area, a protrusion in the staggering 3-mile-wide Guayanilla Bay, is surrounded by Punta Verraco and Punta Guayanilla, making it one of the Caribbean's best natural harbors.

Near the waterfront is *Parador Pichi's* (Route 132, km 204; 787–835–3335; www.pichis.com), with a pool, fifty-eight air-conditioned rooms, and courtyard gardens. Its restaurant, *Pichi's Steakhouse and*

Seafood, is a member of the government's *Mesón Gastronómico* program, known for its fine food. Open Wednesday through Sunday 11:00 A.M. to 11:00 P.M.

Beyond Guayanilla is the town of *Yauco,* an important coffee-growing center for more than a century. Today, the cropped hills above the city are still filled with coffee trees, and many former residences of the coffee barons have been elegantly restored. One of the region's most charming inland cities, Yauco remains a center of agricultural activity.

Coffee: "The Gold In Them Thar Hills"

*E*arly in the nineteenth century, immigrants arrived at Puerto Rico from the island of Corsica in the Mediterranean. Wanting to farm, they looked for undeveloped land, which they found in the southwestern mountains near Yauco. The Corsicans decided to specialize in coffee. The clay-based soil and climate of Yauco, along with persistent dedication, created a coffee soon considered the best in the world. By the late 1800s, Puerto Rican coffee—primarily from Yauco—received a premium price in Europe. The Vatican as well as royalty insisted on it.

In 1899, unfortunately, the area was hit by San Ciriaco, a devastating hurricane. The coffee crop, valued at more than $7 million, was completely destroyed. Establishing new trees and harvesting beans would take several years. In the meantime, the replacement of Spanish with American ownership meant a change of economic priorities. Mainland America didn't need coffee from Puerto Rico (that market was guaranteed to Brazil), but U.S. corporations eager to grow more sugar on the island ushered in the era of monoculture when "sugar was king."

Now that sugar too has been phased out, coffee grown and marketed by small-scale Puerto Rican companies is again asserting some importance and prestige. Yauco's continues to be considered one of the best.

Coffee producers are also successfully growing beans in mountainous areas such as Maricao, Utuado, Adjuntas, and Lares. Any supermarket shelf on the island will attest to the broad variety of brands available. Growers emphasize that their top concerns are not only quality, but paying competitive wages and growing the crop with environmentally sensitive methods. In this way, they hope to develop a niche in the world market to compete with coffee grown in developing countries that is mass-produced and lower priced.

Yauco celebrates its coffee-growing with a **National Coffee Harvest Festival** in late February and early March every year; Maricao also hosts a coffee harvest festival in mid-February. Both feature parades, live jíbaro music, exhibits related to coffee growing, a crafts fair, and coffee—in all its glory—both in drinks and in desserts.

Luchetti Lake

*One good side trip is to **Luchetti Lake**, which is about a half-hour drive up winding country roads from Highway 2. Exit the highway at Yauco Plaza and continue straight on Albizu Campos Boulevard (Route 128). As it climbs north, the road turns from four lanes to two, passing through massive bamboo and towering trees. This change happens almost instantly, and before you know it the road is overlooking dizzying drop-offs that offer vistas of rolling farmland and Yauco's charming center.*

You'll know you're nearing the lake when you begin passing all manner of roadside cantinas with such magical names as El Pozo de los Milagros (The

Well of Miracles) and El Vete y Vuelve (The Leave and Come Back). Lake Luchetti, like all of Puerto Rico's lakes, is an artificial one. The lake's name comes from engineer Antonio Luchetti, who designed and constructed the dam and reservoir in 1952. Today the lake is stocked with bass, and anglers can be seen along its shores or on the roadway bridge that passes over the dam.

Since a number of the restaurants around the lake have fallen into disrepair, a picnic lunch is probably your best bet. Camping around the lake is possible with a permit from the Department of Natural and Environmental Resources (call in San Juan 787–724–3647 or 787–724–3724).

Here you'll find a quaint historic town center and sleepy country roads that begin as soon as you exit the highway.

La Guardarraya (Route 127, km 6; 787– 856–4222) is an impressive, informal restaurant with towering trees and enclosed-porch seating for lunch and dinner. This is strictly local fare, good and filling. The specialty is *chuleta de kan kan* (breaded and deep-fried pork chops). Also try the *arroz Mamposteao,* a fried rice concoction. Closed Mondays.

Campo Alegre (Route 127, km 5.1; 787–856–2609) offers pony rides and horseback tours on its 204 acres. The camp's **Hacienda Restaurant** serves *chuleta de kan kan* and other *criollo* specialties.

Southwest Puerto Rico

Southwest Puerto Rico is arguably the most beautiful part of the island, filled with everything a Caribbean-bound tourist expects. The scores of beaches (many of them hidden down sandy, forested roads), and the coral reefs and cays make this one of the better places for snorkeling and swimming close to shore.

Deep-sea sports fishermen also come to the southwest to go after big game fish, such as marlin and tuna. Scuba divers relish the 100-mile-long underwater cliff that runs from Ponce to the Mona Passage. The waters here are teeming with fish and have good visibility.

The area's natural wonders extend to land as well. Its most famous is the Guánica Forest Reserve, a rare subtropical dry forest that looks like a giant bonsai reserve. The forest is a haven for over one hundred species of tropical birds. It tumbles down rocky cliffs to one of the most beautiful coastlines on the island.

Guánica

The coastal town of Guánica is the first town you'll come to on Route 116. Dubbed *el pueblo de la amistad* (the town of friendship) Guánica lives up to its name. Asking a few questions of locals about the town's great past or its natural wonders will likely prompt long and interesting conversations with proud people wanting to share their knowledge of this special place. In fact, sometimes it seems as if everybody in Guánica is an amateur historian or naturalist. The town's tourism office at City Hall (25 de Julio at Carlos del Rosario; 787–821–2777) might be able to recommend a guide, but asking questions along the *malecón* (waterfront promenade) may get you just as far or, with a bit of luck, even farther.

Language should not be a barrier here. Although it's true that you'll find the greatest level of English proficiency in San Juan, Guánica (like most small Puerto Rican towns) has been greatly affected by the waves of immigrants leaving the island to search for a better life stateside. Just about everyone in town has a brother, cousin, or aunt living in New York or in another stateside location and knows enough English to get by. Guánica, just like other island towns, has more than its fair share of residents who spent their productive years laboring in the United States only to return to the beloved town of their birth to retire. English is a required class in schools, and its influence among the younger generations continues to increase through cable television, Hollywood movies, and American music.

At most times the Guánica harbor is a peaceful, sleepy area, but on weekend nights it can get crowded and a bit rowdy. The *malecón* is lined with open-air bars and seafood restaurants. Try an *empanadilla de carrucho* (conch turnover) or some *escabeche de pescado* (pickled fish) at any of these places. The buildings along the harbor are classic Caribbean colonial structures.

Heading southeast out of Guanica on Route 333 will lead to one of the prettiest roads in Puerto Rico. The road climbs up in gripping curves around the hilly terrain overlooking the bay and then comes down the other side, offering cliffside vistas of the bay at each bend before flattening out to the calm, crystal-blue waters of the shoreline.

Halfway up the hill, the road passes the ruins of an old lighthouse and Spanish fortress, both of which are barely standing. As quickly as it rises, the road drops down again, and the hot black asphalt descends into the mangrove and white-sand beachfront, the beautiful coastline running through Guánica's Caña Gorda, San Jacínto, and Ballena sectors.

One of the island's nicest *balnearios,* **Caña Gorda** (Route 333, km 5.9), is located here. The **Copamarina Hotel & Beach Resort** (Route 333, km 6.5; 787–821–0505 or 800–468–4553; www.copamarina.com), a locally owned and managed resort, is as popular with visitors as it is with Puerto Ricans. Even from a distance, with its red-roofed, open-air Caribbean

The Back Road from Yauco

If you're coming to Guánica from Yauco, avoid the main roadway and instead take quiet country Route 333. To pick it up, go underneath Highway 2 from the Yauco Plaza exit and continue straight. You'll have to pass another shopping center, Cuatro Calles, before the road returns to its country roots.

The road then passes through shaded areas of small wooden homes and farmland with sprawling nurseries selling plants and flowers. At one point the road turns into a one-lane bridge over a trickling stream. Farther along is **El Convento de Fátima** *(Calle de la Fátima, off of Route 333), a beautifully restored, active convent located at the Hacienda Santa Rita sugar plantation. The convent is not open to the public. Beyond the convent, the road meets up with Route 116 before coming to Guánica.*

The McDonald's at the corner of Route 116 and Guánica's main boulevard, 25 de Julio, is where to turn to get to the main town. The street is lined with charming, weather-worn wooden homes. Hardware stores and bakeries operate out of historic brick structures. The road also passes by Guánica's attractive city hall and its adjacent main square. From certain points in the town, it's possible to forget if not which century, then at least which decade it is.

Continue on 25 de Julio to the town's harbor area, which overlooks picturesque **Guánica Bay,** *a wide mouth of protected Caribbean water between two promontories. Immediately to the right on the waterfront is a rock monument to the American invasion, placed there by the local chapter of the Daughters of the American Revolution.*

Where It All Began

A rock—**La Piedra**—stands at the waterfront in Guánica, marking the site where American troops invaded Puerto Rico on July 25, 1898. Some of the defending Spanish soldiers were killed by the Americans as Gen. Nelson Miles took the harbor. There was shelling of the town by the U.S. forces and shooting in the streets. Victorious, the soldiers hoisted the first American flag to fly over the island at Guánica

To this day, almost anything you can say about the event remains impolite conversation in San Juan social circles. For starters, you can't even describe the event without showing your political cards. For independentistas, "the invasion" was the start of U.S. colonialism. Pro-statehood supporters, meanwhile, see it as the long period of great benevolence under Uncle Sam.

architecture, this luxurious, small, low-key resort is a rarity in Puerto Rico, where glitz is a fact of life. The hotel's 106 rooms are lovely and comfortable. The eighteen-acre complex has two pool areas, beautifully landscaped grounds, and a narrow swath of white-sand beach extending from the public beach. The resort offers all sorts of water activities, including charters for deep sea scuba diving. In addition, on-site tour operators will take you on a number of adventures, from a nature and bird-watching tour of the nearby Guánica Forest Reserve to climbing at the famed San Sebastián canyon or a scuba adventure in Culebra. Part of the sense of relaxation here is the friendly atmosphere provided by the staff. Visitors inevitably feel very welcomed and cared for.

The big attraction for divers is likely the *La Parguera* seawall, which extends from Ponce to the Mona Passage between Puerto Rico and the Dominican Republic to the west. The seawall is a major magnet for all sorts of marine life, from nurse sharks to angelfish. There is a variety

Fresh-Picked Pineapples

P ineapples thrive in the southern coastal plains of Puerto Rico. A trip to Guánica when they are in season during the spring and summer months will feature roadside vendors offering the crop. Pineapples available in mainland Amer-

ican markets usually come from Costa Rica or Hawaii, so this is your opportunity to consider the merits of a fresh-picked, ripe Puerto Rican pineapple.

¡Que rico!

of dive sites, from challenging tunnels in the seawall to shallow coves on its shifting top.

Some other excellent places to stay in this area are just around the bend. Passing by Copamarina and heading east on Route 333, you come to the area called **San Jacinto**. There are two special establishments in this neighborhood. First is the **Caribbean Vacation Villa** (15 San Jacinto; 787–821–5364; www.caribbeanvacationvilla.com). Paul Julien, a champion windsurfer, runs this small guest house as an "ecosports center." That means that guests can use kayaks, snorkeling equipment, windsurfers, and mountain bikes gratis when staying here. Visitors can pay a day fee of $50, $35 if staying at another local guest house or hotel. There are four different units here. The site is right on the water, and each unit is comfortable, with a kitchenette and a great view. Paul will give lessons and/or tours; Lynn Gudjonsson, a licensed massage therapist, offers shiatsu, reflexology, aromatherapy, and various massage techniques. They are gracious hosts who want you to share their passion for the place.

Just as welcoming is Mary Lee at her accommodations down the street, **Mary Lee's by the Sea** (25 San Jacinto; 787–821–3600; www.marylees bythesea.com). Ten different units, loosely connected, share a rocky outcropping at the water's edge. Privacy and peace are clear priorities here. The suites are decorated in a sumptuous tropical style, all with kitchenettes and varying sleeping accommodations.

Besides the close access to the dry forest and a nearby white-sand beach, both places offer boat transportation to the nearby offshore cay of Gilligan's Island. You can also catch a ferry to Gilligan's from the dock at **San Jacinto Restaurant** (next to the Copamarina Hotel on Route 333, km 6.8; 787–821–4941). The joint offers fried seafood, beach snacks, and cold beer. Shaded tables out back overlooking the water are quite nice. Whether you enjoy the loud jukebox music will be a matter of taste. The range goes from seventies disco to Latin pop.

Route 333 continues beyond the San Jacinto cutoff. The inland side of the road is undeveloped land, forested flatlands, and climbing hills, all covered by a brown-green scrub forest. About a half mile past the Copamarina, the road rises to give a view of an impressive field of palm trees. This is the heart of Ballena, perhaps one of the most magnificent pieces of natural landscape in the Caribbean.

The **Guánica Forest Reserve** (Department of Natural and Environmental Resources; 787–724–3724 or 787–724–3647) is a United Nations Biosphere Reserve that sprawls over 9,500 acres, with 36 miles of trails and roads running through it. The two main access points are from Route 116 (turn left on Route 334) and via the coastal Route 333. Most visitors take the latter route, and many come simply to enjoy the beaches on the reserve's southern edge.

The unique look of the forest, with twisted trees and cacti spouting from red soil, stems from the area's extreme heat and dryness. Guánica is sheltered from rain clouds by the mighty back of the Cordillera Central mountain chain. Within the forest, temperatures can vary by 10 degrees—the difference between a hillside exposed to the sun and a steep ravine in the forest shade.

Amid the cacti and forest are a variety of coffee plants, the white fragrant flowers of the gumbo limbo tree, and the majestic Guayacán tree, which produces one of the densest woods in the world and blooms blue flowers. Among its many treasures, the forest is home to forty-eight endangered plant species, many found in the moist ravines and caves. Half of Puerto Rico's bird species are also found here, including the endangered Puerto Rican whippoorwill, lizard cuckoos, pearly-eyed thrashers, and Puerto Rican mangos. There are plenty of lizards, mongooses, and endangered sea turtles too.

The reserve is divided into the dry scrub forest on its northern edge and the coastal forest that lines the southern edge. The latter consists of deep-rooted plants whose thick stems and leaves were built to retain every drop of water. There's sea grape and giant milkweed, buttonwood mangrove and sea blight. The grounds of the reserve are formed of limestone riddled with water holes that in some spots have formed caves and sinkholes. Off the coast, massive coral reefs have formed on the seafloor.

If you want to explore the forest, take the drive up Route 334. Most of the hiking trails run off this main route. Your first stop should be at the parking lot at road's end and the small information booth located there. This is where you can pick up the Department of Natural and Environmental Resources' *A Guide to Trails of Guánica State Forest and Biosphere Reserve* by Beth Farnsworth. The booklet has a map and description of the reserve's walking trails, a good description of the reserve's plant and animal life, and a general overview of the weather system and terrain. When hiking, be sure to wear protective clothes, shoes, hat, sunscreen, and insect repellent. Carry a map and water. It will be bright and hot during the day; the island's highest temperatures are recorded here.

There are eleven trails in all. If you park at the dead-end of Route 333, you can walk along the coast on the Meseta trail. This is an easy walk on

---

Household Names

All these successful pop musicians are Puerto Rican: José Feliciano, Ricky Martin, Marc Anthony, Jennifer Lopez, Chayanne, and India.

a flat 2 miles. Some of the stunted cedars look like bonsai and could be one hundred years old.

Take Route 116 to visit Guánica's other half: the old sugar plantation town Ensenada and the Playa Santa beach community. Turn right at Route 325. Immediately past the underpass, the road curves right and squeezes between Ensenada Bay on the left and a green hillside. Towering trees surround the stately 1930s plantation homes that overlook Ensenada Bay from the prettiest perch in town.

Ensenada was built on sugar money, and the ruins of the old Guánica Central sugar mill still dominate the place. The community never really recovered from the closure of the mill in 1980, and today fishing and a few local apparel plants provide most of the jobs here. In many ways Ensenada is a forgotten place; the economic bonanza being enjoyed elsewhere in Puerto Rico has bypassed this beautiful town.

After passing by the bay, the road comes to a split. Bearing right takes you into Ensenada's sleepy downtown full of quaint shops, barbers, and bakeries, small *colmados* (markets), churches, and schools. The charming **Ensenada Public Library** (which keeps irregular hours) was recently named a historic structure. Staying on the road out of town will lead back to Route 116, which will take you farther west along the beach route and back toward Ponce along Highway 2.

Bearing left, the road winds around the grounds of the sugar mill. The old post office, a hospital, and other plantation structures are still standing. The road then passes by a blue gymnasium and an adjacent field that is most often used as a parking lot. If you're lucky, the orange portable kiosk of **Miguelito's Pinchos** will be parked here. By all means take a break and try some of Migeulito's specialties, including fish broth soup, chicken, and pork kabobs, and a cool drink. Across the lot lies the **Parque de Las Flores,** a lovely landscaped park filled with tropical flowers. Next door is the **Club de Artesanos,** a wooden plantation structure now used as a meeting place and party hall.

The road then bears to the right as it passes into the small fishing village of **Barrio Guaypao.** Most visitors driving through this area are headed toward **Playa Santa,** a low-key, slightly scruffy beach town of open-air bars and seafood snack shops. But it's a good idea to take it slowly, since much lies between Guaypao and Playa Santa, which locals also call Salinas.

The main road (Route 325) from Guaypao passes dry fields filled with scrub pine, *flamboyán* trees, wild cotton, and cacti. This is the second half of the Guánica dry forest, an ecosystem related to its other half across Guánica Bay. There are a few dirt road cutoffs on the right side of the road. Although the entrances of some of these roads have been used as clandestine dumps, every dirt road between Guaypao and Playa Santa leads to hidden beaches such as Las Espaldas, Manglillo Grande, Manglillito, and La Jungla. These beaches are mostly used by locals who come here to fish and bathe, and who fill the beaches with great barbecues on summer Sundays and holiday weekends. At most other times, however, the beaches are empty. Although they are safe, there are no services available.

Right before Playa Santa, the road passes *Papi's Pinchos,* a family-run seafood shack specializing in barbecued shark kabobs and marinated conch salad (open Wednesday through Sunday noon to 6:00 P.M.). The big blue monstrosity of a building facing the beach is a vacation center of the Commonwealth Employees Association. It may be an eyesore, but it does have a beautiful white-sand beach with a protected reef. Kayak rentals and other water sports are available. Any of the open-air restaurants is a good place for a snack and a cold drink, and the place is lively on weekends.

The Coastal Highway

uánica is just the start of what is Puerto Rico's most enjoyable coastal area: a series of beach towns that ring the southwest coast from Guánica to Cabo Rojo. Here the sun is at its hottest and the protected waters are among the most welcoming on the island. Route 116 is your ticket to this world.

Beyond Guánica you'll pass long, rolling pastures with the massive Cordillera Central mountain range rising dramatically from the fields in the distance. If Puerto Rico has a big sky country, this is it.

La Parguera, the next beach community along Route 116, is accessible by taking a left on Route 304. Before entering the village proper, a right turn takes you to *Avenida Pedro Albizu Campos,* a road that climbs a big hill overlooking the town. From the top of the road (a popular place to stop) you can see the endless cays—the small islands—that lie off the coast.

Because the town lacks a great beach, the thing to do is rent a boat or take one of the scheduled ferry trips to one of the offshore islands, such as *Isla Mata de Gata.* The town also makes a good base from which to explore the southwest region, with several beaches and other attractions all within a short drive.

There's a kind of honky-tonk feel to La Parguera itself, and it's a favorite of vacationing Puerto Rican families and college students. Most of the businesses are centered along the main street, which is filled with small restaurants, hotels, and shops.

La Parguera is especially crowded on summer and holiday weekends. Particularly hopping are the **Mar & Tierra Restaurant and Bar,** between the main street and the docks as you enter town, with pool tables, food, and a good jukebox; and the **Blues Cafe** (El Muelle Shopping Center on Avenida Los Pescadores; 787–899–4742), which often has live music and draws a younger crowd. Also try **Sangria Coño,** right across the alley to the left of the big lot from Tony's Pizza. The owner has the place decorated with newspaper articles and artwork of Puerto Rican artists, patriots, and other cultural icons from the past and present, as well as posters of local events such as the annual Lajas Kite Festival held each April. Pro-independence folk music, ballads, and salsa are the music of choice. There's also assorted food and very good sangria. On weekends live merengue or salsa bands play behind the bar and in the recreation room adjacent to the town square.

Oh, the Things You Can See

S ome of the creatures living here sound like critters out of a Dr. Seuss book. There are sea cucumbers, queen angelfish, scrawled cowfish, peppermint bass, trumpetfish, black bar soldierfish, elkhorn coral, spiny lobsters, snook, dog snappers, Spanish hogfish, tube sponges, and butterfly fish—just to mention a few! Offshore from La Parguera and Guánica, the diving is remarkable, with depths as great as 600 feet and visibility up to 100 feet. With at least fourteen different sites ranging from novice to expert ability, the wall dives here and the views they offer are spectacular. Scientifically speaking, the coexistence of coral reef,

seagrass, and mangrove communities has created a complex ecosystem with high biodiversity.

All of this special landscape is extremely vulnerable to stresses, such as pollution, in the environment. If mangrove areas are cut down and salt marsh is filled along the coast to make space for housing, there are fewer natural resources supporting ecosystem habitat for foraging and reproducing. The seagrass beds at edges of mangrove islets, a convenient place to anchor small boats, are damaged by motor propellers. Please act responsibly when enjoying this beautiful place.

Various casual eateries in town serve everything from pizza to sand-wiches to seafood to barbecued chicken. A good choice for dinner is *La Casita Restaurant* (301 Calle Principal; 787–899–1681), right beyond the *paradores*, which specializes in seafood. Open daily from 11:00 A.M. to 10:00 P.M.

There are several lodging options in town. Two of the nicest spots are *Parador Villa Parguera* (Route 304; 787–899–7777) and *Parador Posada Porlamar* (Route 304; 787–899–4015 or 800–223–6530). Both are set on the water, with a small shoreline and docks. Villa La Parguera's restaurant, *El Pescador*, is also quite popular, and there are dinner shows on many nights. Although there is no beachfront, the hotel has a nice lawn and pool area that are perfect for children. There are also many smaller guest houses in town. A new hotel, *Torres de la Parguera* (Route 304; 787–808–0808; www.torresdelaparguera.com), is in the center of town. The facilities include a saltwater pool, the restaurant *Majimo*, and a rooftop terrace. It is located one block from the waterfront.

Playita Rosada (at the end of Calle 7) is the public beach and a natural reserve run by the Department of Natural and Environmental Resources. Named after the red mangrove trees that grow along much of the water in the park, this is a very interesting area. It can get crowded, especially on weekends, and you're much better off going offshore by renting a small outboard boat or taking a tour or a scheduled trip to one of the islands, all of which are within about 4 miles of the shore.

Behind the parking lot at the center of town are the docks used by most of the boat operators in town, including *Cancel Boats* (787–899–5891). A good idea may be to go out for a two- or three-hour snorkeling trip in the morning and then arrange for the boat to drop you off at *Isla Mata de Gata*, which has beaches and basic facilities such as picnic areas and rest rooms. *Isla de Magueyes* is one of the bigger islands in the small offshore chain and is home to a group of gigantic iguanas. Stop to admire and photograph them at the University of Puerto Rico's dock (sorry, no admission for uninvited guests at this private facility).

There are also water-sports operators that can take you on fishing and scuba charters. Try *Parguera Fishing Charters* (787–382–4698) or *Paradise Scuba Center* (787–899–7611) at Hostal Casa Blanca. *Aleli* (787–899–6086), located right at the central boat docks, offers kayak rentals.

Even if you don't take a daytime excursion, you'll want to come here on a moonless night to see the sparkling waters of La Parguera's *Phosphores-cent Bay*. Like Esperanza's Mosquito Bay, its greenish glow is produced by the billions of microorganisms known as *pyrodinium bahamense.* Boats ply the bay waters in ninety-minute trips most nights. Passengers usually get into the act by leaning over the side of the boat to wave their hands and arms through the water, which brings movement to the water's glow. Even though the effect is not as dramatic as Vieques's bay due to pollution, the boat trip is pleasant and the phosphorescence is magical.

La Parguera is actually part of the town of **Lajas,** which, besides its valley, is known for frequent UFO sightings, as well as roving rhesus monkeys, loose from research labs on Isla Magueyes. The UFOs, according to local news reports, appear over the Lajas lagoon with great frequency. You are more likely to see one of the monkeys. Depending on what you catch them doing, it could be a sight of shock or awe.

Farther west is **Cabo Rojo,** which sprawls across the island's southwest corner and encompasses several communities that are favorite vacation spots of islanders. This area can also lay claim to some of the nicest beaches and dramatic coastline in Puerto Rico.

Most places of interest are down Route 305, which intersects with Route 116. The shaded country road passes large farms and nice homes. There's also a University of Puerto Rico agricultural post here—a farm where experiments in growing crops and raising livestock are carried out.

Route 305 curves into Route 303. Turn right, taking it a short distance to make a left onto Route 101. This road eventually comes to Route 301, the road to Combate and the Punta Jagüey area at Puerto Rico's southwest corner, on which sits the Cabo Rojo Lighthouse.

Immediately after the turn onto Route 101, you'll pass the entrance to the **Boquerón Refugio de Ares** (Bird Refuge), run by the Department of Natural and Environmental Resources (DNER), where you'll find rare migratory and local birds as well as some walking trails. Fishing (tarpin and snook are common) and hunting (most commonly hunted are ducks) are allowed. Call for specifics (787–851–4795). Open 8:00 A.M. to 4:00 P.M., closed Monday.

Boquerón

Continue about 5 miles through the Penones de Melones area along Route 101 to get to Boquerón, which is a must-visit for every traveler to this region. As you come into town, the turnoff to your left will take you to the **Playa Boquerón,** the *balneario* and adjacent cabins. Many say that this is the best beach in Puerto Rico, and there's no doubt

Cabo Rojo Lighthouse

that it's a contender. The wide white beach is lined with palms and arcs around a clear blue bay protected by coral reefs. It also has some of the best facilities of any public beach on the island, with showers, lockers, rest rooms, and a good snack bar. If you bring a hammock, you'll likely get a nice spot in the shade between two coconut palms. There are also picnic tables and barbecue pits.

The adjacent accommodations at the *Centro Vacacional de Boquerón* (787–851–1900), sometimes fill up weeks or even months in advance; call the office for reservations (787–622–5200). There are rustic lodgings at the ocean's edge off to the far end of Boquerón Beach. With a few creatively strung tarps, you can dramatically increase your living space, not to mention your privacy.

Continuing straight along Route 101 will take you into *Boquerón.* The town is experiencing some growing pains because of recent development, but the funky beach-town quality is still there. Boquerón Bay has also been a favorite stopping point for boaters who can dock for free. This policy is responsible for the international feeling to the town, which is filled with boaters from around the world.

Side Trip: Cabo Rojo Lighthouse

*From Route 101 (the road to Boquerón), bearing left onto Route 301 will take you out to the southwest corner of the island. The road descends to sea level, and the twisted arms of the mangrove swamp tumble along the shoreline. The road will eventually lead to the **Cabo Rojo National Wildlife Refuge**, run by the U.S. Department of Fish and Wildlife (787–851–7219). The visitor center features a nature exhibit that includes freshwater shrimp, mangrove sea turtles, and displays on the area's fauna. Rare migratory birds spotted here include the yellow-shouldered blackbird (native to Puerto Rico) and the flamingo. Open 9:00 A.M. to 5:00 P.M.; closed Monday. Free admission.*

The park recently acquired the adjacent (and eerie) salt flats, which house a salt mining enterprise. A musty odor usually hangs over the long mounds of salt, but it quickly dissipates as the road continues toward the coastline.

*Drive beyond the end of Route 301, which turns into a hard-packed dirt road. You'll travel over a strip of land that passes between the Salinas and Sucia Bays. Watch out for rocky and wet patches. Brave the drive to its rocky and increasingly trail-like conclusion, and you'll come to the **Cabo Rojo Lighthouse** (not open to the public) overlooking a beautiful white-sand beach, Playa Sucia, in a reef-protected cove along Bahia Sucia. By all means, take a swim here, and bring snorkeling gear if you have it. If the waves aren't coming into the bay from the south, snorkeling is great here.*

*The lighthouse was built by the Spanish in 1877. It's set atop dramatic **Punta Jagüey**, a flat-topped headland jutting out into the Caribbean and offering commanding views on every side as it drops down to sea level in sharply etched cliffs. The lighthouse has equal west–east exposure, and is at its most beautiful in the early morning and during the last rays of the day. Despite its rundown condition, the lighthouse is a fine example of colonial architecture.*

The road passes a charming plaza and then comes to a 90-degree curve at *la esquina* (the corner), the place to while away the hours sipping cool drinks and shooting the breeze at one of the open-air establishments. Try the eighty-plus-year-old **Shamar Bar.** It's one of the few legal establishments on the beach, since the land title stems from the Spanish crown and predates U.S. rule. Rooms are available for rent above the bar. **Wildflowers Antiques, Cafe & Inn** (787–851–1793) is located in a charming house across from the plaza. The rooms are decorated with antiques the owners collected throughout New England, and the details, from the bedposts to the bathroom fixtures, have all been tended to. Nice breakfasts and lunches are served in the quaint cafe. A sports and music bar, **Guillermo's Econdite Pub** (entrance in the back), is also located in the building.

The best spot to eat in town is easily **Galloway's Bar & Restaurant** (787–254–3302), a restaurant on a porch out on Boquerón Bay. It has daily specials that range from homemade meat loaf and roast turkey to Italian specials and fresh seafood. The bar area draws an interesting crowd, which usually makes for entertaining and informative conversation. Food is served until 10:00 P.M. on weekdays (closed Wednesday), weekends until 11:00 P.M.

The **Parador Boquemar** (787–851–2158 or 888–634–4343; www.boquemar.com), directly down the road that circles back out of town in front of Galloway's, is a comfortable *parador* with a pool. The rooms are comfortable but not great. The restaurant, **La Cascada**, has a distinct decor; the service is wonderful and the food is great.

In Boquerón, you can rent kayaks at **Kaipo Kayak Rentals** (787–254–3413) and play golf—nine holes—at **Club Desportivo de Oeste** (Routes 102 and 308; 787–851–8880).

Take Route 307 up the west coast to go through Boca Prieta, Buyé, and La Mela Beaches. Buyé Beach is lovely and often described as "a gem." Farther along, about 4 miles north, you climb over another pine-covered mount that overlooks **Puerto Real Bay.** Puerto Real is worth seeing, a small working harbor for pleasure and fishing boats. A good watersports operator, the **Caribbean Reef Dive Shop** (1158 Main; 787–254–4006), is located in Puerto Real. The shop offers day trips for scuba and snorkel enthusiasts of all abilities.

Playa Joyuda is a coastal town known for its beachfront restaurants—thirty-five of them. Almost all are good, so just pick one that feels right. The town's beach isn't particularly nice because it has eroded substantially. The best move is to stay elsewhere and drive into town one evening for a good waterfront meal. There are a few places to stay here, including the *paradores* **Pirichi's** (Route 102, km 14.3; 787–851–3131 or 800–435–7197) and **Joyuda Beach** (Route 102, km 11.7; 787–851–5650 or 800–981–5464).

The San Germán Region

Sabana Grande and San Germán can be reached by driving out along Route 116, but the most direct route is to continue along Highway 2 after Yauco past the Route 116 exit to Guánica. This route tumbles through the farmland of Sabana Grande, with cattle grazing in the rolling fields planted with sugarcane, *plátanos,* and other crops.

Lola Rodríguez de Tió

*B*orn on September 14, 1843, in San Germán, Lola Rodríguez grew up with family support for her interests as a writer and an intellectual. Her father was a highly respected lawyer and one of the founders of the Puerto Rican College of Lawyers. Her mother, a descendant of the aristocratic Ponce de León family, valued literature, art, and spirituality.

Rodríguez was homeschooled, and as a youth began to write poetry. At age twenty she married Bonocío Tió Segarra, also well educated, a writer, and of liberal politics. She and her husband both campaigned for Puerto Rico's independence from Spain. In 1867, Rodríguez wrote new lyrics to the popular Spanish danza song "La Borinqueña." She changed the words from an ode to a "beautiful island," as exclaimed by Columbus the conqueror, to words exhorting islanders to claim freedom for their "bellísima Borinquén."

The song gained popularity as Ramón Betances developed a movement toward liberation, leading to an uprising in Lares in 1868. In 1877, the Tiós were forced to leave Puerto Rico because of their political activities, but they returned from Venezuela to Mayagüez a year later. Again in 1889 they had to leave, moving to New York and later Havana, Cuba. Here too they worked on behalf of independence from Spain. Forced into exile in New York again, they were able to return triumphantly to Cuba when independence was won in 1898.

Rodríguez visited Puerto Rico twice more, but made Havana her home, where she died and was buried in 1924. Her three published volumes of poetry and lifelong political work have given her a place of respect as a Puerto Rican author and intellectual. Every year at the time of her birthday, her life is celebrated over several days with a festival in San Germán.

Sabana Grande, which means "large plain," is best known as the place of the *Santuario de la Virgen del Pozo* (787–873–0450), where the Virgin Mary was reportedly sighted here by Juan Angel Collado and a group of other children in 1953. Every year religious pilgrims from across the island come here to pay homage to the Virgin Mary and pray for miracles at the mountainside chapel built in her honor. Route 120 (which brings you into the Sabana Grande mountains) leads to the smaller Road 364, which leads to the chapel. Open daily 5:00 A.M. to 11:00 P.M.

Farther along Highway 2 is *San Germán,* Puerto Rico's second-oldest town. Founded in 1573 by the Spanish, this sun-bleached historical gem is set between the foothills of the Cordillera Central and the beautiful southwestern coast. Although the city is set back from the coast, most of the beaches discussed in this section can be reached in less than thirty minutes by car, and all the drives are pretty.

The best way to explore the city is to pick up the concise, one-page map and guide of San Germán prepared by Jorge Lamboy Torres. Copies are available at the wonderful old *Hotel Parador Oasis* (72 Luna; 787–892–1175 or 800–942–8086). A pool and adjacent restaurant dining area are located in the huge courtyard. Meals here are also recommended.

The town's appeal is boosted by the presence of *Interamerican University,* which is located above the historic zone on the western edge of the city. Founded in 1912 as the Polytechnic University, the campus is beautiful. More importantly, the student body and the faculty add immensely to the town's cultural life.

It's a nice trek up Calle Dr. Santiago Veve, which passes historic homes on the way to the main plaza. Here is *Porta Coeli Church,* now known as the Porta Coeli Museum of Religious Art (787–892–5845). Built in 1606, it is one of the oldest churches in the Americas. The church's name in Latin means "Heaven's Gate." The squat structure, sitting atop a stone staircase, opens up in a massive arcing doorway, which is made from *ausubo,* a once common hardwood tree in Puerto Rico.

No longer used as a church, it is run by the Instituto de Cultura and presents objects of religious art. It is open Wednesday through Sunday

Porta Coeli Church

8:30 A.M. to noon and 1:00 to 4:00 P.M. The church's impressive carved wooden altar was made in Puerto Rico during the seventeenth century and brought to the church in the 1930s after originally being placed in Old San Juan's San José Cathedral. Surrounding the altar are Dutch tiles that depict biblical scenes. The tiles were first placed in Old San Juan's San Francisco Church. Two icons inside the church honor Nuestra Señora de Monserrate, a revered saint in Puerto Rico since she appeared to island settlers in the sixteenth century. There are also examples of the religious wood carvings known as santos, which have become a specialty in Puerto Rico over the centuries.

The Victorian *Casa Morales* (not open to the public), right outside the church, is spectacular in its own right and a good example of the North American influence on Puerto Rican architecture in the early part of this century.

Continuing up the hill takes you to *Plaza Santo Domingo,* which is lined with the busts of prominent San Germán citizens, many of them nationally recognized for their patriotism or for their successes in various endeavors. Also here is the town's other great church, the *Catedral de San Germán de Auxerre* (787–892–1027), named for the French saint who is the town's patron. The church was constructed in 1739 but underwent so many substantial changes over the next one hundred years that today it mixes styles from many different time periods. Its lit, stone-washed walls are particularly impressive at night. Open daily for Mass.

The historic zone is filled with businesses and residences that are every bit as intriguing as the more frequently visited Ponce and Old San Juan. Many of the residences in town date from the late 1800s and were built by rich local families. Favorite buildings include the *Domínguez Pharmacy* (Calle Cruz off Dr. Veve) and *13 Calle Dr. Santiago Veve,* the home of the poet Lola Rodríguez de Tió (now a private residence).

PONCE

Colonial Guest House
33 Marina
(787) 843-7585

Holiday Inn Ponce
3315 Ponce By-pass off
Highway 2, km 255
(787) 844-1200 or
(800) 981-2398
www.holidayinn.com

Hotel Bélgica
122 Villa
(787) 844-3255

Hotel El Cacique
Route 368, km 10.3
(787) 856-0345

Ponce Inn
103 Mercedita
off Highway 52
(787) 668-4577 or
(800) 981-7188

Texan Guest House
Route 1, km 24.2
(787) 843-1690

GUÁNICA
Gilligan's View
27 San Jacíinto (Route 333)
(787) 821-4901

THE COASTAL HIGHWAY
Andino's Chalet and
Guest House
133 Eigth Street,
La Parguera
(787) 899-0000

Cayo Laurel Court
Avenida Pedro Albizu
Campos, La Parguera
(787) 899-2298

Centro Turistico
Mojacasabe
North end, Cabo Rojo
(787) 254-4888
www.mojacasabe.com

Combate Beach Hotel
Road 3301, km 2.7,
Cabo Rojo
(787) 254-2358
www.combatcbeach
hotel.com

Estáncia La Jamaca
Route 304, km 3.3,
La Parguera
(787) 899-6162

Guesthouse Viento y Vela
Route 304, km 3.2,
La Parguera
(787) 899-3030

Hostal Casa Blanca
Route 304, km 3.5,
La Parguera
(787) 899-4250

Hotel Parador Villa del Mar
3 Albizu Campos,
La Parguera
(787) 899-4265
www.pinacolada.net/
villadelmar

Lighthouse Inn Hotel
Route 102 at Route 100,
Cabo Rojo
(787) 255-3887
www.lighthousehotel.net

Nautilus Hotel
238 Route 304, La Parguera
(787) 899-4004

Parador Bahía Salinas
Route 301, km 11.5,
Cabo Rojo
(787) 254-1212 or
(877) 205-7507
www.bahiasalina.com

Parador Highway Inn
Route 100, km 8, Cabo Rojo
(787) 851-1839
www.paradorhighway
inn.com

Parador Posada Porlamar
Route 304, km 3.3,
La Parguera
(787) 899-4015 or
(800) 223-6530
www.posadaporlamar.com

Parador Villa Parguera
Route 304, La Parguera
(787) 899-7777 or
(800) 443-0266
www.villaparguera.com

Punta Aguila Resort
Route 301, km 12.0,
Cabo Rojo
(787) 254-4954 or
(866) 624-8452
www.puntaaguila.com

BOQUERÓN
A Boquerón Bay Guest
House
10 Quintas del Mar
(787) 255-0224
www.boqueronbay.com

Adamari's Apartments
Calle de Diego
(787) 851-6860

Boquerón Beach Hotel
Route 101, km 18.1
(787) 851-7110
www.boqueronbeach
hotel.com

Buyé Beach Resort
Route 307, km 4.8
(787) 255-0358

Cofresí Beach Hotel
57 Muñoz Rivera
(787) 254-3000
www.cofresibeach.com

Cuestamar Hotel
Route 307, km 7.4
(787) 851-2819
www.ihppr.com

Hotel Buena Vista Bahía
Route 307, km 6.6
(787) 255-2255

Hotel Tropical Inn
Route 101, km 18.7
(787) 851-0284

Joyuda Plaza Hotel
Route 102, km 14.7,
Playa Joyuda
(787) 851-8800

Moreau's Inn
Route 102, km 9.8,
Playa Joyuda
(787) 255-3861

Papa Alberto Resort
Route 307, km 7.5,
Villa Taina
(787) 851-2900

Shamar Bar-Restaurant
Calle de Diego
(787) 851-0542

Wildflowers Antiques,
Café, and Inn
Calle Principal on the Plaza
(787) 851-1793

SAN GERMÁN REGION
Villa del Rey Country Inn
Route 361, km 0.8
(787) 642-2627

PLACES TO EAT IN PONCE AND THE SOUTH

SOUTH OF SAN JUAN
Costa Marina
Marina de Salinas
Route 701, G-8 Chapin,
Salinas
(787) 824-6647

Ladis
Route 708, Playa Salinas,
Salinas
(787) 824-2035

Puerta al Sol
A-44 Principal,
Playa Salinas, Salinas
(787) 824-1133

PONCE
Café de Tomás
56 Isabel
(787) 840-1965

Canda's Restaurant
Bonaire at Alfonso XII,
Playa Ponce
(787) 843-9223

Criollisimo
1233 Hostos
(787) 840-0818

El Ancla
9 Hostas, Playa Ponce
(787) 840-2450

El Bohío
22 Coto Canas
(787) 844-7825

El Mesón de René
17 Ferrocarril
(787) 844-6110

La Monserrate Sea Port
Highway 2, km 2.18, Sector
Las Cucharas
(787) 841-2740

La Terraza
Ponce Hilton
1150 Caribe
(787) 259-7676

Las Cucharas Seafood
Restaurant
3738 Ponce By-pass, sector
Las Cucharas
(787) 841-0620

Lupita's Mexican
Restaurant
60 Isabel
(787) 848-8808

Pizza Heaven
8023 Concordia
(787) 844-0448

Puerto Santiago
Paseo Tablado La Guancha
(787) 840-7313

Victor's
20 Las Américas
(787) 841-8383

Willie's Sea Food
947 Hostos, Playa Ponce
(787) 840-7060

Yeyos Seafood
Highway 2, km 252.1,
sector Las Cucharas
(787) 843-7629

Zambumbia
39 Luna
(787) 984-1125

GUÁNICA
Alexandra
Copamarina Hotel and
Beach Resort
Route 333, km 6.5
(787) 821-0505, ext. 766

Guánica Seafood
Route 333,
Ochoa at 13 de Marzo
(787) 821–3000

La Ballena
Route 333, km 6.5
(787) 821–0505

La Concha
Playa Santa
C–4 Principal (Route 325)
(787) 821–5522

THE COASTAL HIGHWAY
Annie's Seafood Restaurant
Route 3301, km 2.9,
Cabo Rojo
(787) 254–0021

Combate Beach Hotel
and Restaurant
Route 3301, Cabo Rojo
(787) 254–7053

La Jamaca Restaurant
La Jamaca Guest House,
Route 304, km 3.3,
La Parguera
(787) 899–6162

La Pared
Posada Porlamar
Route 304, km 3.3,
La Parguera
(787) 899–4015, ext. 151

Los Balcones
Route 304, La Parguera
(787) 899–2145

Lucy's Steak House
Parador Highway Inn
Route 100, km 8, Cabo Rojo
(787) 851–6833

Restaurante El Náutico
7 La Parguera, Playita
Rosada, La Parguera
(787) 899–5237

BOQUERÓN
Cuesta Blanca
Route 307, km 5
(787) 851–6899

El Bohío
Route 102, km 9.7,
Playa Joyuda
(787) 851–2755

La Bahía
210 José de Diego
(787) 851–0345

Perichi's Restaurant
Parador Perichi's
Route 102, km 14.3,
Playa Joyuda
(787) 851–3131

Pika-Pika
224 Estación
(787) 851–2440

Tino's Restaurant
Route 102, km 13.6,
Playa Joyuda
(787) 851–2976

Tony's Restaurant
Route 102, km 10.9,
Playa Joyuda
(787) 851–2500

Vista Bahía
Route 102, Playa Joyuda
(787) 851–4140

SAN GERMÁN REGION
Botica
33 Dr. Veve
(787) 892–5790

Cilantro's
Cruz at Dr. Veve
(787) 264–2735

Del Mar y Algo Mas
Plazuela Santo Domingo at
Calle Carro
(787) 636–4265

Galería Lubben
9 Luna
(787) 892–7420

The North Coast and West

ighway 22, also known as Expressway De Diego, holds the key to Puerto Rico's western spirit as it runs along the north coast and then leads to roads that wind around the island's magnificent northwest coast. There's much to be seen on this route, from one of the most interesting observatories in the world to one of the most intricate underground cave systems. Beautiful beaches spread out in two stretches along this route; the first starts just west of San Juan, and a second stretches from Camuy on the north coast down to Mayaguez, Puerto Rico's third largest city, known as the Sultan of the West.

West of San Juan

here are two common ways to pick up the westbound Expressway De Diego (Highway 22) out of San Juan. One way is to travel west on Kennedy Avenue (Highway 1) on the traffic-clogged route to Bayamón, and the other is by taking Las Américas Expressway south of San Juan.

As you're passing out of Bayamón, to your left you'll notice something that looks like a huge set of colorful plastic blocks and a metal Erector Set. Above it are real NASA rockets, but from this distance they look like plastic models. This is the **Luis A. Ferré Science Park** (exit south from Expressway to Route 167; 787–740–6868 or 787–740–6878), with an aerospace museum, a small zoo, archaeological exhibits of Taíno artifacts, and a space-flight simulator (a hit with school groups). There are also art, transportation, physics, electric energy, and natural history exhibits here. The newest installation is a planetarium. The park has plenty of picnic areas, and paddleboats are available for rent at an artificial lake. From its perch at 300 feet above sea level, the science park overlooks sprawling San Juan. Open Wednesday through Friday 9:00 A.M. to 4:00 P.M., Saturday and Sunday 10:00 A.M. to 6:00 P.M. Admission is $3.00 for children (two to twelve years old), $5.00 for adults, and $2.00 for senior citizens.

Immediately past the second toll booth is the exit for Toa Baja and **Dorado,** about forty minutes west of San Juan. Route 165 exits the highway on the site of an old sugar plantation surrounded by big palms and

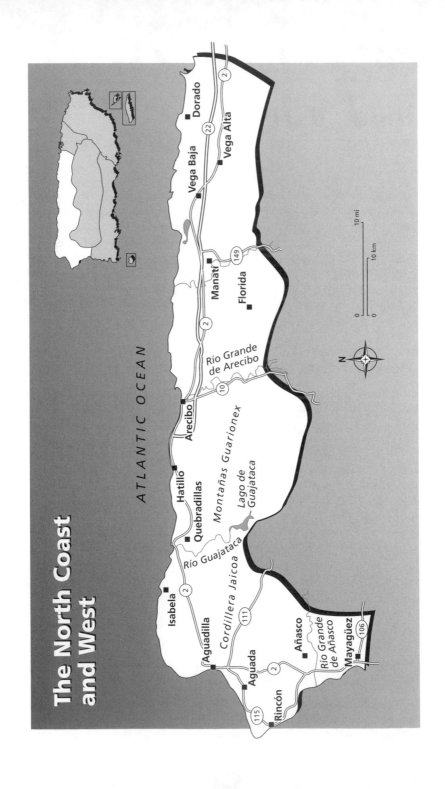

The North Coast and West

ATLANTIC OCEAN

Dorado
Vega Baja
Vega Alta
Manatí
Florida
Río Grande de Arecibo
Arecibo
Hatillo
Quebradillas
Montañas Guarionex
Lago de Guajataca
Río Guajataca
Isabela
Aguadilla
Cordillera Jaicoa
Aguada
Añasco
Río Grande de Añasco
Mayagüez
Rincón

10 mi
10 km

N

THE NORTH COAST AND WEST

tall flowering trees. Dorado may be growing as a tourist and residential community, but there's still a hometown feel to its downtown area (which boasts one of the few full-service libraries on the island). The road to Dorado twists through the downtown area right beyond the bridge. It's a good place to stretch your legs or grab a bite to eat. The downtown is loaded with little pizzerias, delis, and restaurants specializing in local fare. Park near **Dorado City Hall** (on your right, beside the plaza, as you enter town).

As quickly as it enters town, the road (which has become Route 698) leaves again after climbing a short hill. Soon you are driving through the shade of the massive trees and coconut palms that line the rural roadway. This road leads to a former plantation that was bought by the Rockefeller family, which it converted to two RockResorts, one in 1958 (the Dorado) and one in 1972 (the Cerromar). Both were acquired by the Hyatt Corporation in 1985. Guests could use the facilities at both hotels, including four top-notch 18-hole golf courses and a swimming river at Cerromar.

The Hyatt Regency closed the 506-room Cerromar Beach Resort and Casino in July 2003. The golf, pool, and club member facilities remain open. The 206-room **Hyatt Dorado Beach Resort and Country Club** (Route 693; 787–796–1234; www.doradobeach.hyatt.com) stands as the flagship hotel. In addition to the original plantation house that is used as a restaurant, the Dorado offers a casino, pools, spas, fitness center, restaurants, bars, and a children's program.

A number of independent water-sports operators in town undertake everything from scuba trips to deep-sea fishing expeditions. Try the **Great Lady** (787–796–1242). Dorado's public beach, Playa Sardinera, is just one of the beaches making up what locals call **Playa del Dorado,** a string of about six white-sand beaches. There are plenty of good seafood restaurants here, including **El Malecón** (Route 693, km 8.2; 787–796–1645), an unpretentious family-run place serving up good seafood and Puerto Rican cuisine.

Also on Route 693 is **Tropical Paradise Horseback Riding** (787–720–5454), where horses are available to ride through nearby forest or the beaches.

West of Dorado is the balneario **Cerro Gordo,** at the end of Route 690 off Route 22. Its attractive beach is lined with rows of palms and has

AUTHOR'S FAVORITES

Rincón beaches, Rincón

Río Camuy Caves, Arecibo

Caguana Indian Ceremonial Park, Arecibo

Beaches of Isabela and Aguadilla

Beaches of Barceloneta, Manatí, and Dorado

interesting rock formations and cliffs. This gets crowded on weekends. Continue west along Highway 2 or 22 to Vega Baja's other beautiful beaches, including Los Tubos, with surfable waves most of the year, Playa de Vega Baja, with great surf when it's up, Playa Puerto Nuevo, and Playa Kahlua. *Los Tubos* is the site of an outdoor music bash at the Festival Internacional Playero de Los Tubos every Fourth of July, featuring rock, salsa, and merengue bands.

The Route 687 exit leads to the *Laguna Tortuguero Nature Reserve,* run by the Department of Natural and Environmental Resources. There is a new Ecotourism Center here (787–858–6617). The lagoon is a freshwater spring-fed lake that empties into the ocean. It has become a home to caimans, once imported from Central and South America as a trendy pet. As the caimans grew up and were no longer "cute," they were discarded by households. This alligator population now numbers over 2,000. Local residents see them as a mixed blessing. Cooked, they are considered a delicacy, reminiscent of rabbit or lobster. Stuffed, they are sold as curios. But live, they prey ferociously on dogs, cats, and other domestic and wild animals. They grow to 6 or 7 feet long and survive up to twenty years. One souvenir to avoid taking home is any injury from getting too close to one. Caimans are nocturnal, and the night action includes hunters out to bag them, more ferocity to avoid. Use the fishing area at its east end off Route 687 for a view.

Across from the lagoon is a beach, *Playa Tortuguero,* which stretches for a mile. A new *balneario* is located here. This spot has been decorated with garishly painted concrete animals, provoking some criticism. *Playa Mar Chiquita* is 5 miles west of Tortuguero on Route 685, or 2

Save a Sato

*C*oncerned volunteers in Puerto Rico routinely catch homeless dogs and cats and help find adoptive families. Two organizations on the island are Save a Sato (the Spanish word sato *describes mixed-breed "mutts") and Puerto Rican Animal Welfare Society, known as PAWS. These animals, primarily dogs from beaches or urban areas, are cleaned up and given a medical evaluation as well as some socialization before* *being flown to the United States to shelters participating in the programs. Rather than crowding American facilities with more unwanted dogs, these fill a special need. Homeless Puerto Rican dogs tend to be mixed breeds that are smaller and younger than American strays; those are desirable qualities to many adoptive families. More information on this can be found at* www.saveasato.org.

TOP ANNUAL EVENTS

Whale watching, January through March, Rincón

Cinco Dias con Nuestro Tierra, second week in March, Mayagüez

Copa Dorado Mininquilan, third week of April, Dorado

Puerto Rico Country Fair, early May, Hatillo

Festival del Tejido, early May, Isabela

Crash Boat Summer Festival, last week of May, Aguadilla

Festival Internacional Playero de Los Tubos, July 4, Manatí

Hormigueros Patron Saint Festival, second week of September

Discovery of Puerto Rico Day, November 19, Aguada

Masks Festival, December 28, Hatillo

miles north of Manatí off Highway 22. This lovely beach has something for everyone. Usually calm, there is a shallow inlet perfect for wading. When the surf kicks up, it surges in with good waves. A coral reef invites snorkelers. The undertow is strong here, so swimmers take caution. Mar Chiquita is one of those beaches whose parking area serves as home to a band of stray dogs, timid and hungry, who check every car for possibilities.

Manatí is the location of 2,265-acre *Hacienda La Esperanza* (787 854-2679), owned and currently being refurbished by the Conservation Trust of Puerto Rico to showcase the island's sugar plantation past. Although the manor house and mill, both from the nineteenth century, are not restored yet, on Fridays, Sundays, and holidays you can walk the grounds and the beaches along its 5 miles of coastline. Take Route 685 north from Manatí to Route 616.

From Manatí into Barceloneta are more beaches, including Pescadora de la Boca on Route 684 and Hallows, farther on Route 681. Past Hallows off Route 681 is Punta Caracoles, where *Cueva del Indio* is located, a cave with paintings believed to be Taíno. A gas station is across the road from it, about 2 miles east of the Arecibo lighthouse (Faro de los Morrillos). A little farther west is La Pozita, a beach also referred to as La Poza del Obizpo. Rocks here create a small enclosed pool.

Besides being home to many small pockets of quiet beaches, Manatí and Barceloneta are also home to major pharmaceutical firms. Products manufactured here include Viagra, Valium, Claritin, and Oxycontin.

Arecibo

Approach Arecibo from Route 681, the coastal route, to see the city at its best. At Punta Morrillos, on the waterfront, is the *Arecibo Lighthouse and Historical Park* (787–880–7540). Part of a recreation area with two beaches and a children's play area, there are great views from here. Built in 1898, the museum in the Punta Morrillos Lighthouse

Best Beaches for Surf

*T*he best surfing on the north coast is in winter (November through March). Below is a sampling of the towns in the area, along with their beaches.

Dorado: El Único, Kikitas, El Puerto

Vega Alta: Las Pasas, La Peinilla

Vega Baja: Sarapa, Boquetes, Cibuco

Manatí: Los Tubos, Sarapa, Palmas

Barceloneta: Hollows, Machucas

Arecibo: Peñon de Mero, Margara, La Marginal, Cueva del Indio, Cueva Vaca, Caza y Pesca, Mingo's Wedge

Hatillo: Las Cabras, La María

Camuy: Los Almendros, El Peñon

Isabela: Los Jobos, Golondrinas, Middles, Surfer Beach, Table Top, Secret Spot, Shacks, Shore Island, Sal Sí Puedes, Crica de Marta, Montones

has a permanent exhibit of paintings, stamps, and handmade sculptures and ceramics. Open Monday through Thursday 9:00 A.M. to 6:00 P.M. and Friday through Sunday 9:00 A.M. to 9:00 P.M.

Although the town's once-thriving historic district is now past its prime, it still holds on to some of its charm. Arecibo was founded in 1515. In 1606 it was officially recognized as a town. Near the historic plaza and Paseo Victor Rojas stands **Casa Ulanga** (7 Gonzalo Marín). This venerable structure has been used as everything from a home to a hospital to a bank, town hall, prison, and courthouse. The building takes its name from Francisco Ulanga, a Spaniard who came to Puerto Rico in 1810 and ordered the building's construction in 1850. It holds the distinction of being the first three-story building in Arecibo. Today Casa Ulanga houses a regional office of the **Puerto Rican Institute of Culture** (787–878–8020).

Karst Country

*P*uerto Rico's Karst Country is home to some of the world's most unique geographic formations—a dramatic landscape of limestone, haystack-shaped hills (called *mogotes* by the locals), underground rivers and caves, and large conical sinkholes. The region stretches from Manatí to Isabela, with some of its most prominent traits found in the foothills and hills of the Guarionex mountain chain, just south of Arecibo. Much of Karst Country is still an almost impenetrable maze of hills and thick forest.

This geography was formed over millions of years by an underground river system in the limestone terrain. There are only a handful of places in the world with geography similar to this, including one area across the Mona Channel in the Dominican Republic.

These sharply etched hills are formed by land masses that have yet to sink into the porous limestone terrain. The surrounding depressions are a result of the gradual process of water pouring through limestone over millions of years. This process creates sinkholes, which form more and larger sinkholes, until at last the surface level of the area is pulled down. Sharp drop-offs, which have the dramatic thrust and form of mountains, stand at heights of as little as 100 feet. This lack of height allows the area's lush green growth to cling to and cover the hills. The effect gives you the feeling of being a giant in a miniature world.

The region can be most intimately explored by descending into the extensive cave system carved out by Río Camuy, the world's third largest underground river. The underground cave network stretches for miles in the island's northwest region. The easiest way to explore it is to go to the 268-acre **Río Camuy Cave Park** (Route 129, km 18,3; 787-898–3100), located north of Route 111. The park is open from 8:30 A.M. to 3:45 P.M. Wednesday through Sunday. Facilities include a snack bar, souvenir shop, displays, picnic areas, and hiking trails. Guided tours go through tropical vegetation and into caves where sinkholes, subterranean streams, and giant stalactites abound. The stalactites look like delicate crystals, and the cave walls are as beautiful as carved stone tapestries. The caves are 45 million years old, and the ancient tropical Río Camuy that formed them still rages through them, like the main artery to the cave system's heart.

The park's trolleys carry visitors to the major sites, and the caves have been developed, with lighting and comfortable walkways stretching throughout. Since 1989 visitors here have been thrilled by **Tres Pueblos Sinkhole,** located on the borders of the Camuy, Hatillo, and Lares municipalities (which is how it got its name). This natural wonder widens to 65 feet in diameter and plunges 400 feet down through the soft limestone terrain into the Río Camuy. Visitors can view it from two different platforms: one overlooking the town of Camuy and the other overlooking Tres Pueblos Cave and the river. The other major sinkhole within the park is **Cueva Clara de Empalme.**

New in 2003, visitors can rappel 150 feet down into a cave containing forty Taíno petroglyphs. Then a hike through interlinked caves leads to the valley floor and a return to the canyon rim. Equipment and instruction are included. Trips are subject to weather conditions; rain may force cancellation. Advance reservations are required; call (787) 898–3100.

Río Camuy Cave Park

Despite its popularity and development, much of the underground cave system remains unexplored and undeveloped. A number of companies on the island give tours in areas beyond the park.

The almost 4,000 acres of protected land in Karst Country is divided into four commonwealth forests: Cambalache, Guajataca, Vega Alta, and Río Abajo, which is the largest, accounting for more than half the total land area. Like Puerto Rico's other public forests, each features picnic areas, nature exhibits, and numerous hiking trails (be sure to first pick up a map at each area). Camping is also permitted in these forests (at a cost of $4.00 per night), but permits must first be obtained from San Juan–based Department of Natural and Environmental Resources Miramar Division

THE NORTH COAST AND WEST

(787–724–3647 or 787–724–3724). The public forests are open from 8:00 A.M. to 5:00 P.M. Tuesday through Sunday, and are closed Mondays.

Cambalache Forest (787–881–1004) features two camping areas. It's reached by exiting Highway 22 onto Highway 2 east of Arecibo and then taking Route 682. The entrance is at km 6.3. Open 9:00 A.M. to 5:00 P.M. daily, it features hiking and a 2-mile mountain bike trail. *Guajataca Forest* has an 8-mile hiking trail, mountain bike trail, and a lakefront beach. Take Highway 2 west of Arecibo. After the road crosses Río Guajataca, exit left on Route 446, which leads to the forest entrance.

The lake here was created in 1929 with a dam on the river. It is great for fishing, bird-watching, and hiking. On the lake on Route 453 is *Vista de Lago* (787–637–4534) with live music in a large dance hall every Saturday and Sunday and a menu of *comida criolla*.

> ## Spelunking
>
> *Cave explorers say that the system at **Río Camuy Cave Park** presents some of the most enjoyable spelunking spots in the world. Although much of the system remains unexplored, it has been known to locals for years. When official exploration of the caves began in 1958, local boys had knowledge of the cave system from years of hiking through parts of it. In fact, the boys served as guides for the explorers. There's even evidence of Taíno remains in some of the caves.*

Río Abajo Forest has a camping area. Exit Highway 22 by turning left on Highway 10. At km 70.3, take a right on Route 621. At km 4.4 lies the access road to the forest. *Vega Alta Forest* is one of the smaller camping areas in the system. It's located at km 1.5 on Route 676, alongside the municipal cemetery.

Several attractions lie south of Arecibo. More than 800 years ago, the Taínos built the ceremonial grounds of the *Caguana Indian Ceremonial Park* (Route 111, km 12.3; 787–894–7325). The thirteen-acre park contains ten Taíno *bateyes* (ball courts) lined with stone monoliths. There are carved petroglyphs on them, the most famous showing a fertile "earth mother" figure. When the Taínos played their game of *batey*, they used a hard ball made of rubber. The players wore protective padding and could not touch the bouncing ball with their hands, but used their heads, shoulders, arms, hips, or legs to hit it. Other contests held here, all with religious and political significance, included foot races, archery, and song and dance. The Taínos were an equal-opportunity community: Women participated as much as men in the competitions. The park includes a small museum exhibiting Taíno artifacts, as well as a gift shop with reproductions.

> ## Cave of the Wind
>
> *If you hike in Guajataca Forest, wear sturdy shoes and bring a flashlight. You can descend on a ladder into Cueva del Viento (Cave of the Wind), where stalagmites, stalacites, and other sediment formations exist.*

Open daily 9:00 A.M. to 4:00 P.M.; no admission charge. In this quiet, lushly forested setting, you could feel you have stepped back in time, connecting with the island's ancestors in a sacred space.

Here also is the awesome **Arecibo Observatory** (end of Route 625; 787–878–2612; www.naic.edu), home to the world's largest radar/radio telescope. The telescope is 305 meters in diameter and is dramatically set in a depression surrounded by a ring of the stunted limestone mountains of Karst Country. Cornell University scientists operate the facility to search for radio emissions from across the galaxies. To follow their work more closely, visit their Web site, which has links to the observatory, Cornell University, and the National Science Foundation. Portions of the famous SETI project, a search for intelligent life in the universe through the sending of radio signals, were conducted here. It was also the setting for much of the movie *Contact,* in which Jodie Foster contacts an alien presence.

The approach to the observatory is one of the most dramatic you're likely to see—a science fiction movie prop set against the lush green and twisted hillsides. The **Angel Ramos Foundation Visitors' Center** makes the observatory more accessible than ever. Through exhibits, videos, telescopes, and other presentations, the observatory puts you on intimate terms with the solar system and the universe. The observatory is open Wednesday through Friday noon to 4:00 P.M.; Saturday, Sunday, and holidays, 9:00 A.M. to 4:00 P.M. Admission is $3.50 for adults, $1.50 for kids and seniors. To get there take Route 129 to Route 134. From Route 134, take Route 635 and then Route 625, which ends at the observatory.

The North Coast

As Highway 22 joins Highway 2, you'll know you've reached **Hatillo** when you see the statue of a guy with a pig (*el jíbaro,* a rural person caricatured as a hillbilly). There's a *parador* right on Highway 2, **El Buen Café** (km 84; 787–898–1000; www.elbuencafe. com) with a *mesón gestrónomjco* restaurant of the same name. Open daily 5:30 A.M. to 10:00 P.M. The **Municipal Vacation Center Luis Muñoz Marín** (787–820–0274) offers cabañas, campsites, and activities for children at Punta Maracayo.

Farther west lies **Quebradillas,** a stunning cliffside town with a seafaring and pirate past. You'll pass **Parador El Guajataca** (Highway 2, km 103.8; 787–895–3070 or 800–964–3065; www.elguajataca.com), which overlooks the northern coast on a bluff at the point where the Guajataca River empties into the Atlantic. There are tennis courts, a pool, and a restaurant here. Also nearby is *Parador Vistamar* (Highway 2, km 7.3; 787–895–2065 or 888–391– 0606; www.paradorvistamar. com), another hilltop *parador* with a pool, tennis and dining areas, and weekend entertainment set into the hillside, the grounds are nicely landscaped. You'll also pass the oceanfront *Pedro Albizu Campos Recreation Area,* a wonderful place to stop for great views of both the cliffs and water. For a good look at the dramatic north coast scenery, pull over at one of the rest stops off Highway 2.

Quebradillas is known for *Guajataca Beach.* There's a public beach here and the surf is fierce, but the white sand makes it a great beach to stroll and beachcomb. It is located alongside what is called *El Túnel,* a railroad tunnel for a train that ran from San Juan to Ponce from 1907 until the mid-1950s. El Túnel has an eatery and picnic area bordering the beach.

Quebradillas is home to two collections of pop culture memorabilia. *The Burbie Museum* (Route 482 at Highway 2; 787–895–1646) is open weekends only. *Wenchy's* (Route 482, km 1.0; 787–895–1782) exhibits a collection of Hot Wheels cars as well as providing a restaurant and mini golf. Closed Mondays. This combination could keep the kids happy.

Puerto Rico's Northwest Corner

eyond Quebradillas, visitors who want to see one of the most beautiful and undeveloped coastal areas in the Caribbean will take the exit for Route 113 and *Isabela.* Immediately after leaving the highway, the roadway cuts through dense forest. Butterflies flutter between the branches of the almond trees, and greenery surrounds.

The forest quickly gives way to a strip of farmland, residences, and scattered commercial establishments. The next commercial area at *Playa Jobos* is a good forty-minute drive down this double-lane country road, which soon turns into Road 4466, a hardened dirt roadway that passes rows of beautiful but deserted beaches.

Isabela has been hit by more than its fair share of natural disasters, including a 1918 earthquake that destroyed the town. In the town's Aresnales sector, there are many *paso fino* horse farms. Before turning into an undeveloped coastal area, the roadway comes to Isabela's town plaza. In general, stay to your right and try to exit the town center going downhill toward the coast.

Just down the coastal road out of town is the **Costa Dorada Beach Resort** (900 Emilio González; 787–872–7255; www.costadoradabeach.com), a great setting on a mile-long beach. One of Puerto Rico's best locally run small hotels, all fifty-two rooms face the ocean. You'll also find pool areas, tennis and basketball courts, bars, and restaurants here.

Beyond this resort the roadway leaves its asphalt behind and becomes hard-packed sand as you move into some of Puerto Rico's most pristine, isolated areas. Here you'll find miles of undeveloped beachfront property, much of it fronted by agricultural fields, with wild cotton plants blooming along wooden fences backed by towering trees.

As you approach the colorful beach cottages of **Villas Del Mar Hau** (Road 4466, km 8.3; 787–872–2045; www.villahau.com), you'll be struck by its Shangri-La-like appearance, since this thriving but low-key resort surrounded by towering casuarina pines lies in the middle of desolate beachfront. Located at **Playa Montones,** a beautiful white-sand beach, the colorful cottages are built in the traditional Puerto Rican *casita* style (with a wide front porch) and are linked by a boardwalk that runs across the edge of the beach. Just about everything is here, from a convenience store to fax and photocopy services. There are game rooms, laundry rooms, basketball and volleyball courts, a pool, as well as scuba, snorkeling, and horseback riding tours. There's also a cocktail lounge and restaurant. If you're camping with a tent, ask about sites on the beach to rent here.

Playa Jobos, about a mile west of Villas Del Mar Hau, became famous after hosting the 1989 world surfing championships. When the water is

The Train

*E*l **Túnel** is one of the best-kept remains of the famous and notoriously slow train that ran from San Juan to Ponce from 1907 until the mid-1950s. The train line, originally commissioned in 1888 by the Spanish crown, was not completed until after the American invasion of 1898. It was purchased by the American Railroad Company in 1910 and subsequently grew to include 420 miles of track.

For most of its history, the train line was primarily used to ship agricultural products such as sugarcane from the farm to the mill and from the mill to the ports. Because it lacked restaurant cars, people debarked at train stations to buy food from vendors. As a result, towns began to develop reputations for the particular types of food served at their train stops.

Paso Fino

flat here, it is exceptionally clear for snorkeling and scuba diving. *Playa Shacks* is highly regarded as a destination for both surfing and seclusion, a beach so wide and long that it always feels quiet and uncrowded. It is also internationally renowned for windsurfing. A place to rent or buy gear or get a ding repaired is *Hang Loose Surf Shop* (Road 4466, km 1.2; 787–872–2490); closed Mondays.

Puerto Rico is famous for long-maned, strong-legged **paso fino horses.** *The name paso fino literally translates to "fine step," a reference to the graceful, dancelike movements of well-trained members of the breed.*

Ocean Front Hotel and Restaurant (Road 4466, km 0.1; 787–872–0444; www.oceanfrontpr.com) has a rooftop deck for sunset viewing, and the restaurant serves good seafood. Thursday through Saturday nights you can catch classic and Latin rock played live on the deck. *Villa Montaña* also offers accommodations (Road 4466, km 1.9; 787–872–9554 or 888–780–9195; www.villamontana.com), with sixteen oceanfront villas on 2 miles of quiet beach. There are tennis courts, a pool, a bar, and *Eclipse,* a restaurant serving gourmet fare (787–890–0275). Also here is *Happy Belly's on the Beach* (787–830–2457) offering food in a rustic setting and live salsa and Latin rock on weekend evenings. Nearby is *Tropical Trail Rides* (787–872–9256; http://home.coqui.net/barker), with horses available for trail rides twice daily at 9:00 A.M. and 4:00 P.M. Each trip lasts two hours and is the perfect way to see the shore.

Road 4466 joins Route 110 as Isabela passes into *Aguadilla.* Heading into Aguadilla, you see how built-up this area has become. During the Cold War era, Ramey Air Force Base had been an important presence, with a B-52 bomber squadron of the Strategic Air Command. The base included extensive housing, the longest runway in the Caribbean, and a golf course, which all continue to be used today. When the base was deactivated in 1973, islanders were given the opportunity to take over the residences. *Punta Borinquen Golf* (787–890–2987), the eighteen-hole course favored by General Dwight D. Eisenhower, is now open to the public from 7:00 A.M. to 7:00 P.M. daily, offering the island's least-expensive greens fees. The 2-mile-long landing strip—now the *Rafael Hernandez Airport* (787–891–2286)—is used for commercial cargo flights and passenger flights, including connections with Newark (New Jersey) and San Juan. The U.S. Coast Guard operates search-and-rescue missions from here. Visitors can enter the base through Gate 5 off Route 110 and explore this military ghost town.

While suburbanization is clearly gaining in Aguadilla, its coastline holds some of the island's best beaches, with many empty stretches. Excellent surfing can be found at Crashboat, Bridges, Gas Chambers,

Rafael Hernández

Rafael Hernández, whose prolific output has been called the "highest expression of Puerto Rican popular music," was born in Aguadilla in 1891. Hernández's musical talent was evident at an early age, and as an adolescent he penned his first melody, "Mi Provisa." He went on to compose hundreds of songs, many of which have been etched into Puerto Rico's popular culture, including "Preciosa," "Lamento Borinquen," and "Cumbanchero."

Many of Hernández's songs have been reinterpreted by a new generation of musicians, in styles as varied as salsa, rap, reggae, and rock. Hernández died in 1965. His life is celebrated every year with a festival in October.

Wishing Well, Wilderness, Hole in the Wall, Surfer, Pressure Point, Mix, and Wildo. For any kind of equipment to enjoy this wild part of the coast, *Aquatica Dive Shop* (Route 110, km 10; 787–890–6071; www.aquatica.cjb.net) can help with sales, rentals, and lessons. *El Rincón Surf/Beach Shop* (787–890–3108) is at 703 Belt Road at Ramey. The surf is best in the winter, November through March.

You might guess that water is an important motif in this locale. So of course, the largest water-oriented theme park in the Caribbean is located here. *Parque Acuatico Las Cascadas* (Highway 2, km 126.5; 787–882–3310) has giant water slides, a wave pool, an aquatic tunnel, a magic fountain, and other delights. Open March through September, weekdays 10:00 A.M. to 5:00 P.M. and weekends 10:00 A.M. to 6:00 P.M.

The town has historical importance for its fresh water from the Ojo de Agua underground springs. This source is enshrined at the town's plaza, El Parterre. It is said that Christopher Columbus first came ashore on Puerto Rico here in 1493, looking for drinking water for his crew. Aguadilla claims he found it here. A statue, *La Cruz de Colón,* commemorates this event. Aguadilla is also known for its tradition of *mundillo,* a delicately woven bobbin lace with Spanish roots that is still produced here. Every April a weaving festival, the *Festival del Tejído,* is held in Aguadilla.

There are some accommodations worth noting. Located inland, *Parador El Faro* (Route 107, km 2.1; 787–882–8000 or 888–300–8002; www.ihppr.com) has posh landscaping and a pool you'll enjoy. *Hotel Cielo Mar* (84 Montemar; 787–882–5959; www.cielomar.com) has a breathtaking view over the water, and every room has a balcony. *Hotel Hacienda El Pedregal* (Route 111, km 0.1; 787–891–6068 or 888–568– 6068; www.hotelpedregal.com) is built on the former estate of General Esteves, the first Puerto Rican to make the rank of general in the U.S. armed forces. The hotel offers great sunset vistas over the water. Other lodging includes *La Cima Hotel* (Route 110, km 9.2; 787–890–2016), *Parador Borinquén* (Route 467, km 2; 787–891–0451), and *Hotel Villa Forín* (Route 107, km 2.2; 787–882–8341).

Columbus's First Stop

Aguadilla and neighboring Aguada have a running historical argument over where Christopher Columbus actually landed on Puerto Rico in 1493. Aguadilla residents argue that Columbus and his crew first stopped to get water from a spring that is now the site of Parque El Parterre. To back its claim, Aguada erected the **Parque de Colón** *in the center of the 2,500-foot Playa Espinar.*

Just inland from Aguadilla is *Moca,* reached by Routes 111 and 110. In the nineteenth and early twentieth centuries, it was an important center for sugarcane. Three mansions here illustrate that chapter of the area's history. *Hacienda Enrique,* on Route 111, is privately owned, although sometimes the owner offers tours. On Route 110 is *Los Castillos Meléndez,* looking like a medieval castle. A French Provincial–style mansion, *Palacete Los Moreau,* has just been opened to the public after restoration due to a fire. Call (787) 830-2540 for hours. The house is best known as the site where Puerto Rican novelist Enrique A. Laguerre wrote and situated his 1935 book *La Llamarada,* about life on sugarcane plantations. His fictional family was the Moreaus, for which the house is now known. His personal library is on view here.

Mundillo lace is also woven in Moca and sold at two locations, *Tienda Bazaar Maria Lasalle* on the plaza, and *Leonides,* at 114 Ramos Antonini. Moca's *mundillo* festival is held every year at the end of November.

Aguada and Rincón

Back on the coast around *Aguada,* good surfing can be found at several beaches on the coastal road, Route 441: Espinar, Table Rock, Bridges, and Punta Río Grande. There's a nice public beach with facilities at Pico de Piedra. Unless you're in a rush south on Highway 2, you can see Aguada's town center by driving in on Route 115.

Downtown Aguada is one of those superclean, small Puerto Rican towns that seems so far away from San Juan. This isn't a bad spot to grab some lunch. *El Túnel Pizzeria* (214 Colón; 787–868–5430), just north of the plaza, is a busy, unpretentious place that draws a loyal local clientele. As you enter town there is a public parking lot right behind the main plaza, so park there if you don't find a spot along the street. The plaza, fronted by *Iglesia San Francisco de Asís,* is a nice place to stroll. A former train station that has been converted to a museum, *Museo de Aguadia* has Taíno and African artifacts and relics of the sugarcane era. Open Monday through Friday 8:00 A.M. to noon and 1:00 to 5:00 P.M., weekends by reservation; call (787) 868–6300.

Aguada is known for its grand parade every November 19 when the town observes "Discovery of Puerto Rico Day." The big celebration and a big statue of Columbus seem to be proof of how strongly Aguada feels about its claim that Columbus landed there first (and not in Aguadilla).

Aguada has accommodations at *Parador JB Hidden Village* (Route 102 at Road 4416; 787–868–8687) and a *mesón gastronómico, Las Colinas* (Highway 2, km 1.9; 787–868–8686).

Beyond town, the road to Rincón passes through a hilly forested area that stretches out to the coast. Look for *Cheers & Beers* (Route 115, km 21.4; 787–484–5922), a huge nightclub with outdoor huts and bars, run by merengue sensation Elvis Crespo.

The approach to *Rincón* may be disorienting for two reasons: The town's main road runs in a circle, and there's water on all sides, making it difficult to tell north from south and east from west. It's a good idea to pick up a Rincón tourist map, available for $1.00—or sometimes free—at many of the town's restaurants and guest houses. It's an excellent guide to town and is sure to save you many hours of aimless wandering.

The town is located on a flat peninsula of *La Cadena Hills,* the most western offshoot of the Cordillera Central that runs through Puerto Rico. The dramatic meeting of mountain and coast makes for awesome views all around town, and the white-sand beaches that surround the town are just as beautiful.

Rincón has a worldwide reputation for its powerful waves, and it's been a haven for surfers since at least 1968, when this small town was the host of the World Surfing Championship. The town continues to be the surfing capital of the Caribbean and boasts a lively nightlife.

While beachfront guest houses have long catered to the surfer culture by offering basic accommodations at rock-bottom prices, Rincón has become a haven for vacationing families, and the quality of the restaurants and lodgings within town have dramatically improved in recent years. With so many water-oriented activities to watch or participate in, it's hard to imagine kids being bored here. Long used to English-speaking tourists, Rincón is accessible, has a range of prices and styles, and food for all tastes. To enter Rincón, get off Route 115 with a right turn onto Route 413, Rincón's main road, which winds through the center of the municipality on the back of a rising hillside. To keep your bearings, think of Rincón as a circle that spreads out from this road. You may get the sense that you are leaving Rincón as the road winds its way into increasing heights, but you're actually entering its elusive heart.

Off to the right is the gorgeous *Sandy Beach* area, which can be accessed by taking any one of the turnoffs on the right side between the Velázquez Shell Station and the Nieves Mini-Market and Puntas Bakery. This beach is often quiet and is a good place to stroll, combing the beach for sea glass. If you take the road straight until it drops off to your left, you'll get to the lighthouse area or the low road into the town proper and its equally pretty southern end.

Taking the first turn after the gas station will allow you to take the entire beach road. The first stop of note is *The Landing* (Sandy Beach Coast Road; 787–823–3112), a sprawling bar and full-service restaurant that is one of the best and most reliably open restaurants in town (from 11:30 A.M. to 11:00 P.M.). Surf, turf, jerk chicken sandwiches, and inventive appetizers such as the "exploding onion" are served here. The wooden interior is decorated with a seafaring and mariner theme, and it looks as if it could be located in any New England coastal town until you walk out onto the huge back porch overlooking a nice stretch of palm-lined beach. There's live music on weekends: rock Friday and Saturday, jazz on Sunday.

Going past the restaurant, the road passes a cutoff that leads to the *Rincón Surf & Board Caribbean Surfari Guest House* (787–823–0610 or 800–458–3628), which boasts a backyard jungle. Farther along the lower road that runs along Sandy Beach is the *Beside the Pointe Guest House* (787–823–8550; www.besidethepointe.com), which must be one of the most charming, affordable guest houses in the Caribbean. Room No. 8, which has an ocean view, is particularly nice. Room No. 7, with a small kitchenette and deck, isn't bad either. The guest house also includes the Tamboo Tavern, which hops on many nights. The bar and accommodations score high as a fun place to be.

Beyond Nieves Shell Station and the Brisas Bar cutoff, Route 413 continues to climb high, lined with beautiful homes and small businesses. *The Lazy Parrot Inn & Restaurant* (Route 413, km 4.1; 787–823–5654 or 800–294–1752; www.lazyparrot.com) is a restored home on a hill with views of the water all around. Each room has a different tropical theme and a small outdoor deck. The restaurant has outdoor and indoor eating areas, and the inn opens up onto a lovely waterfall pool set on the hill. Next door is a good bakery, *Punta Mar.*

Route 413 then drops down. Turning right will take you to the 1892 *Punta Higuera Lighthouse,* which is open to the public. El Faro Park fronts the restored lighthouse. Off the western coast of Puerto Rico is the winter playground of humpback whales, which come from as far as

For your interests in surfing, boogie boarding,
windsurfing, diving, snorkeling, kayaking, fishing,
whale-watching cruises,
sailing a Hobie cat, or seeing Isla Desecheo, check
these Rincón businesses.

Taíno Divers
Black Eagle Marina
(787) 823–6429
www.tainodivers.com

**Desecheo Dive and Surf
Shop**
Route 413, km 2.5
(787) 823–0390

West Coast Surf Shop
2-E Muñoz Rivera (on plaza
in town)
(787) 823–3935
www.westcoastsurf.com

Hot Wavz Surf Shop
Route 413, km 2.5
(787) 823–3942

Moondog Charters
(787) 823–3050
www.moondogcharters.com

Oceans Unlimited
Route 115, km 12.2
(787) 823–2340
www.oceans-unlimited.com

West Coast Surf Charters
Black Eagle Marina
(787) 823–4114

Newfoundland and New England to frolic and mate in the warm Caribbean waters. In the winter bring your binoculars to see whales breaching off the coast. Whales can be seen from late December to late March, but the peak time is January and February. Also visible offshore is 360-acre **Isla Desecheo,** a federal wildlife reserve located 13.3 miles off the coast of Rincón, described later in this chapter.

The road continues past a forested area of towering pine and palm trees as it approaches the **B.O.N.U.S. Thermonuclear Energy Plant,** Latin America's first nuclear power plant, which was decommissioned in 1974. The dull turquoise-domed structure cuts an eerie presence on this majestic coastline. The adjacent **Domes Beach,** one of the more popular with surfers, draws its name from the reactor. The empty structure may become a science museum in the future. Some locals interested in reviving it have suggested painting it with bright stripes to look like the world's largest beach ball.

On the southern end of town off Route 115 is the cutoff for Route 429, a beautiful coastal road with some of this town's better lodging options. The landscape here evokes the Mediterranean, which must have been an inspiration to the owners of the **Horned Dorset Primavera Hotel** (Route 429; km 3; 787–823–4030 or 800– 633–1857; www.horneddorset.com), one of the Caribbean's most luxurious resorts. You might think you're lost as you drive through a rural barrio, but the hotel's discreet entrance lies farther along the road. The resort is built in the style of a Spanish villa, complete with seaside terraces, hand-painted tiles, and blooming gardens. The grounds are lush, filled with birds and coquís, Puerto Rico's famous singing tree frogs. The resort's restaurant is regarded as the best in western Puerto Rico, and it attracts diners from across the island. Although staying at the resort or eating at the restaurant will cost you a bundle, it's well worth it.

For more reasonably priced accommodations, try **El Quijote Beach Cabañas** (Route 429; 787–823–4010), which has fully equipped

B. O. N. U. S. Thermonuclear Energy Plant

oceanfront beach units for rent. There's a beachfront area with hammocks and barbecue pits. The restaurant here, open Friday through Sunday, specializes in Spanish and Puerto Rican food, with good paella, tapas, and sangria.

Beyond this, Route 429 hooks back up to Route 115. This is the quickest way back to Highway 2. If you're continuing on to Mayagüez, turn right on Route 115.

One last spot you should get to in Rincón is *Pico Atalaya,* also known as *La Bandera,* a mountaintop from which rugged Mona Island can be seen. While you're here, stop by *La Cima Burger* (on Route 411), a restaurant with a view, serving *mofongo,* steak, seafood, burgers, and sandwiches.

Añasco

As you head south on Route 115, the next town is Añasco. On Playa Almirante is the new *Rincón Beach Resort* (Route 115, km 5.8; 787–589–9000 or 866–589–0009; www.rinconbeach.com) with a pool, fitness center, meeting facilities, beach, restaurant, bar, and other amenities. And at the other extreme of accommodations, if you're camping with a tent or RV, you can stay at the *Balneario Tres Hermanos* right on the beach (Route 401, km 1; 787–826–1610) or rent a rustic cabana or villa at the ***Centro Vacacional Villas de Añasco*** (Route 401, km 5; 787–826–1610; reservations, 787–724–2500).

Mayagüez

Mayagüez, the island's third largest city, is known as *La Sultana del Oeste* (the Sultan of the West). Its name is derived from a Taíno word meaning "place of many streams." The main river, the Río Yagüez, runs through town, and much of Mayagüez is open to the sea as it sits on its wide-mouthed bay.

Mayagüez isn't the tourist town you think it might be, located as it is halfway down Puerto Rico's enviable west coast. There is no beach here (although plenty surround the city), and many visitors probably stay elsewhere. Several hotels here offer pools, ballrooms, casinos, and other amenities, so that a stay here has that feeling of getting away to a resort.

Entering Mayagüez from Highway 2 south takes you past its two most

Beaches of Rincón

*T*he best surfing can be found at these beaches on the north side of Rincón:

Punta Higüero, *also known as* Antonio's

Sandy Beach

Spanish Wall

Domes

Indicators

Marías

Pools

Puntas

For surfing in winter, visit these beaches to the south:

Tres Palmas

Steps

Dogman's

Little Malibu

The following beaches on the south side of Rincón offer the best swimming, windsurfing, and scuba diving:

Barrero *(good kayaking in the summer)*

Dogman's

Tres Palmas

Steps *(good snorkeling in the summer)*

Little Malibu

Córcega

Almendros

established hotels. The *Holiday Inn Mayagüez* (2701 Highway 2, km 149.9; 787–833–1100; www.holiday-inn.com) lies a mile from downtown. The hotel bar and disco are jammed on weekends, and behind the hotel is a lively string of bars and restaurants that fill up for weekend happy hours. The best place to stay if you're looking for a big hotel is the recently renovated *Mayagüez Resort & Casino* (Route 104; 787–832–3030; www.mayaguezresort.com). The hotel features a casino and restaurant and sits on a clifftop overlooking Mayagüez Bay on more than twenty acres of tropical gardens. It's right off Highway 2 on the way into town. *Parador Hotel El Sol* (9 Palmer; 787–834–0303), with fifty-two clean, modest rooms and a pool, is located two blocks from the center of town and is much cheaper than the name-brand hotels. Another inexpensive choice with local character is *Colonial Hotel* (14 Iglesia; 787–833–2150; www.hotel-colonial.com), formerly a convent and now a twenty-nine-room bed-and-breakfast.

Mayagüez's elegantly tiled *Plaza Colón* is dominated by a monument to Christopher Columbus. There are several architecturally interesting buildings on the central plaza, including *La Alcadía,* Mayagüez City Hall. Other historic sites include the Art Deco *Teatro Yagüez* and the post office, both of which are located on McKinley Street.

If Mayagüez isn't steeped in visible history, what it does have is the energy of a college town. There's streetlife here that enlivens the city. As you might suspect, the nightlife reflects that influence too. There's a neighborhood called *Barrio Paris,* north of Plaza Colón, with bars, bistros, boarding houses, and bookstores.

Mayagüez is where you'll find the campus of *Recinto Universitario Mayagüez,* a branch of the University of Puerto Rico. A convenient city trolley runs between downtown sites, the university, a municipal

Mayagüez's Unique Architecture

*A*lthough Mayagüez was founded as a Spanish settlement in 1763, aside from the small historic district surrounding the plaza, this west coast town is filled with the sunburned hulks of pre-1930s wooden homes. Not known for its historic districts, Mayagüez owes its unique architecture to a series of disasters that led to successive rebuildings of the town. First there was the Great Fire of 1841 and, in 1862, a second fire ravaged the city's waterfront district. These two disasters were but preludes to 1918, when a large earthquake destroyed most of the town.

¡Viva Sangria!

Something notable about Mayagüez is the significance of sangria here. Wilfredo Aponte Hernández put his recipe and establishment on the map with "La Sangria de Fido's." If you haven't tried this punch that combines liquor, wine, and fruit, you might raise a glass in Mayagüez. The island version blends its local fruit with rum and wine. Here's one typical recipe:

1 bottle dry red wine (an inexpensive one is fine)
1 cup Puerto Rican dark rum (or more, to taste)

1 cup sugar
1 cup orange juice
½ cup lime juice

Combine all ingredients in large glass bowl or pitcher, stir well to dissolve sugar, cover and refrigerate for four to six hours or overnight.

Before serving, add any of these fruits, thinly sliced: oranges, apples, peaches, grapes, strawberries, lemon, lime. (Feel free to experiment!) Pour over ice in tall glasses.

stadium, and the city zoo. The campus grounds, located near the roadway heading up into the western mountains, are beautiful, and the university itself easily mixes modern and neoclassic styles. Next door to the campus are the beautiful botanical gardens of the **Tropical Agriculture Research Station** (787–831–3435), which feature wild fruit trees, bamboo, ornamental flowers, and timber trees. Free maps are available at the station. The research station is open 7:00 A.M. to 4:00 P.M. weekdays only; no admission charge. Across the street is the pretty Patriots Park. A budget hotel on campus, **Hostal Colegial** (787–265–3891), is the best deal around for visiting students and educators.

The forty-five-acre **Mayagüez Zoo** (787–834–8110), nearby on Route 108, has 300 species and includes an African savannah with lions, giraffes, hippos, rhinos, and large reptiles. A Caribbean exhibit with jaguars, pelicans, and flamingos is also in the works. Open Wednesday through Sunday 8:30 A.M. to 4:00 P.M.; $3.00 admission.

Mayagüez has a regional airport, off Highway 2 north of town. Also, you can take a ferry from the waterfront to cross the Mona Passage and land at Santo Domingo, capital city of the Dominican Republic, eleven hours away. Check with **Ferries Del Caribe** (787–832–4800) for current schedule and prices.

Just south of Mayagüez is **Hormigueros,** a pretty town in the hillsides of the west coast. Its **Basílica Nuestra Señora de la Monserrate,** with its ivory columns and crimson-domed top, is a simple yet forceful presence rising above the town. Every September during the patron saint celebration of the church's namesake, thousands of pilgrims travel here for a religious procession. The church is named after the Virgin of Montserrat, a saint who intervened and saved a farmer's life when he was about to be gored by a raging bull. The dark-skinned virgin is popular throughout the Spanish Caribbean.

The Natural Islands

oth Isla Desecheo, 13.3 miles off the west coast, and Isla Mona, 48 miles southwest of Rincón, are protected wildlife reserves with only rustic accommodations for overnight stays. While Desecheo can be visited for an afternoon of snorkeling, visiting Mona requires an expedition.

Isla Mona has been called the Caribbean Galapagos, a natural reserve in the middle of the rough Mona Channel. Although the island is uninhabited today (except for transient and hardy campers and rotating personnel from the Department of Natural and Environmental Resources), it was settled centuries ago by the Taíno Indians, as the petroglyphs and ancient ceramic shards in the ruins of ceremonial ballparks attest. When

Puerto Rico's Pirate Past

*W*hen Spain all but stopped trading with Puerto Rico from 1640 to 1750, the island experienced a minidepression. To compensate, islanders began illegally trading food products and other goods with Spain's enemies, including the neighboring French, Dutch, and British islands. Coastal towns bustled in contraband goods, and the booming trade attracted not only trading partners, but rogues and pirates as well.

Many pirates used Puerto Rico as their base of operations or sold their loot on the black market on the island's east coast. Many also took refuge from their high-seas adventures on the island's shores.

The offshore island of Mona, in the Mona Channel between Hispaniola and Puerto Rico, was a favorite place to lie low. In fact, in1698 **Captain Kidd** *hid here. Kidd's biggest hoist had occurred earlier that year, when he captured the* Quedagh Merchant, *an Armenian ship bound for Bengal with a hull full of silk, guns, spices, and valuable metals.*

Kidd was eventually hanged for his crimes, but the whereabouts of much of the Quedagh Merchant *loot remains a mystery. Some speculate it might still be buried on Mona Island or on the neighboring island of Hispaniola (the Dominican Republic and Haiti).*

Columbus and Ponce de León stopped here, in 1494 and 1508 respectively, both encountered a well-established Taíno community. In later years, pirates used the island as a base. Captain Kidd used it as a hideout, and the famous Puerto Rican pirate Roberto Cofresí also operated from here.

The lure of still-buried treasure continues to attract an assorted mix of fortune hunters. For a time the island was home to settlers who mined for guano, a mixture of limestone and bat manure used as fertilizer. Today the nature reserve attracts campers, spelunkers, scuba aficionados, and nature buffs. Teams of researchers and scientists also use it as a natural laboratory.

Most visitors' first glimpse of the island is **Playa Sardinera.** This is the first stop for many boats, as it has a lighthouse and primitive showers. The beach also is home to an old colonial jail and a cave. Here you'll find some of the calmest waters on Mona.

Two-hundred-foot-tall limestone cliffs ring the island, which also has thick mangrove forests and what is thought to be one of the largest ocean-formed cave systems in the world. The bean-shaped, 7-mile-by-4-mile island is home to 650 plant and tree species, including 78 endangered species. There are some twenty endangered animal species here, including three different types of sea turtles that nest on its shores. Left over from homesteading days, feral goats and pigs roam free, posing a hazard to turtles and tourists alike. A hunting season each year is one attempt to eliminate the problem. The island is filled with 4-foot-long iguanas, and flocks of seabirds, such as the red-footed booby. It is surrounded by coral reefs in waters teeming with marine life, including tropical fish, lobster, queen conch, barracuda, dolphin, tuna, and five different species of whale. Just offshore the ocean is filled with black coral and patch reefs, as well as underground caverns. Large sea sponges, spoor, and groove growth are found here. Visibility in the Mona waters stretches out 200 feet, which makes for great diving. In addition to abundant marine life, there are also eleven known shipwrecks, including old Spanish galleons, buried in the surrounding waters.

Basic camping, for which all necessities must be packed in and all garbage packed out, is still the only way to stay at the nature reserve. Drinking water, a compass, and bug repellent are vital. Camping permits are available through the Department of Natural and Environmental Resources (787–723–1616 or 787–721–5495). You must apply for the permit at least seven days in advance. A strict control on the number of visitors allows only one hundred people on the island at a time. Electricity for water, lighting, communication, and navigation beacons comes from solar panels erected on top of the *Mona Island Museum,* an outdoor permanent exhibit about the island's animal and plant life, and six other sites. Diesel and gas powered generators have been completely and successfully replaced.

Today scuba divers can make it out for a full-day dive in Mona's waters and back with no need to stay over. A number of private tour and travel companies organize trips here. Some will include providing your permits and provisions, or you can arrange for your drop-off and pickup. Depending on the number of people involved and the types of activities planned, a weekend trip can range in price from $300 to $1,000 per person. Because planes are no longer allowed to land on Mona, most people get here via a three-hour boat trip that travels at night when the water is calmest. Companies offering excursions to Mona include *Attabeira Educative Travel* in San Juan (787–767–4023); *Mona Aquatics* in Boquerón (787–851–2185); and *Taíno Divers* (787–823–6429) and *Desecho Dive and Surf Shop* (787–823–0390), both in Rincón.

A 4-mile road from the beach leads to *Playa Uvero,* where you can camp among low-lying trees running across the beachfront. A cave in the area, *Cueva de Doña Geña,* was named after a woman who lived in it for thirty-three years while working as a cook for guano miners. A small trail off Uvero leads to the ruins of ceremonial Taíno ball courts.

Isla Desecheo is much smaller than Mona and lies 13 miles off Puerto Rico's coast. Landing on the island is not permitted in order to protect the ecosystem. *Taíno Divers* (787–823–6429) and *Desecho Dive and Surf Shop* (787–823–0390), both in Rincón, and *Aquatica Underwater Adventures* (787–890–6071) in Aquadilla can take you out for a day of snorkeling or diving. There is underwater visibility up to 200 feet.

PLACES TO STAY ON THE NORTH COAST AND WEST

WEST OF SAN JUAN
Campomar Hotel and Restaurant
Route 165, Playa de Levittown, Dorado
(787) 784–7295

Costa de Oro Guest House and Restaurant
B-28 H Street, Dorado
(787) 278–7888
www.costadeoropr.com

Embassy Suites Hotel
Dorado del Mar Beach and Golf Resort
201 Dorado del Mar Boulevard, Dorado
(787) 796–6125
www.embassysuites.com

KARST COUNTRY
Posasa El Palomar
Route 119, km 7.5, Camuy
(787) 898–1060

THE NORTH COAST
Casa de Playa Restaurant and Country Inn
Highway 2, km 85.6, Hatillo
(787) 898–3850

Lane's Casa
721 Estación, Quebradillas
(787) 895–2131

PUERTO RICO'S NORTHWEST CORNER

Parador Villas del Mar Hau
Road 4466, km 8.3, Isabela
(787) 872-2045
www.villahau.com

Sonia Rican Guest House
Road 4466, Isabela
(787) 872-1818

AGUADA AND RINCÓN

Ann Wigmore Spa
Route 114, Aguada
(787) 868-6307
www.annwigmore.org

Cabañas el Palmer
Route 115, Aguada
(787) 868-6307

Casa Garcia
Route 413, km 4.7, Rincón
(787) 823-3877

Casa Islena Inn
Route 413, km 4.8, Rincón
(787) 823-1525 or
(888) 289-7750
www.casa-islena.com

Casa Vista del Mar
Route 115, km 11.4, Rincón
(787) 823-6437 or
(866) 887-0175
www.casavistadelmar.net

Coconut Palms Guest
House
2734 Calle 8, Rincón
(787) 823-0147
www.coconutpalmsinn.com

Desecheo Inn
Route 413, km 2.5, Rincón
(787) 823-0390

Lemontree Waterfront
Cottages
Route 429, km 4.1, Rincón
(787) 823-6452
www.lemontreepr.co

Parada Muñoz Guest House
Route 115, km 15, Rincón
(787) 823-4725

Parador Villa Antonio
Route 115, km 12.3, Rincón
(787) 823-2645
www.villa-antonio.com

Pino Mar
Route 115, Aguada
(787) 868-8269

Pípons Resort
Route 413, km 3.1, Rincón
(787) 823-5106
www.piponsresort.com

Pool's Beach Cabañas Verdes
Pool's Beach, Rincón
(787) 823-8135

Rincón del Mar Grand
Caribbean Hotel
Route 115, km 12.2, Rincón
(787) 823-6189 or
(866) 2-RINCON
www.rinconoftheseas.com

Sandy Beach Inn and
Restaurant
Route 413, km 4.3, Rincón
(787) 823-1146
www.sandybeachinn.com

Sunset Paradise Villas
Calle 10 off Route 115,
Rincón
(787) 823-7183 or
(800) 875-6399
www.sunsetparadise.com

Villa Cofresi
Route 115, km 12, Rincón
(787) 823-2450
www.villacofresi.com

Villa Ensenada Guest House
Route 413, km 2.2, Rincón
(787) 823-5807 or
(888) 779-3788

Vista Vacation Resort
Calle Vista Nuclear off
Route 413, Rincón
(787) 823-3673
www.vistapr.com

MAYAGÜEZ

Hotel El Embajador
111 Ramos Antonini, Este
(787) 833-3340

Hotel Mayagüez Plaza
67 Calle McKinley Este
(787) 891-9191 or
(888) 300-8002
www.ihppr.com

Paradise Guest House
Route 345, km 2.2,
Hormigueros
(787) 849-2679

PLACES TO EAT ON
THE NORTH COAST
AND WEST

WEST OF SAN JUAN

El Ladrillo
334 Méndez Vigo, Dorado
(787) 796-2120

El Navegante
385 Méndez Vigo, Dorado
(787) 796-7177

Jewel of China
Route 693, km 8.1, Dorado
(787) 796-4644

La Terraza
C-1 Marginal at Route 696,
Dorado
(787) 796-1242

Mangére
Route 693, km 8.5, Dorado
(787) 796-4444

Palma Dorado
2A Kennedy, Dorado
(787) 796-3152

Su Casa Steak House
Route 670, km 1, Manatí
(787) 884-0047

Zen Garden
Route 693, Dorado
(787) 796-1176

KARST COUNTRY
Casa del Playa
Highway 2, Camuy
(787) 989-3850

El Fogón de Abuela
Route 485, km 3.1, Camuy
(787) 262-0781

Johnny's Barbecue
Highway 2, Camuy
(787) 262-5059

Mesón Don Juan
Posada El Palomar
Route 119, km 7.5, Camuy
(787) 898-1060

THE NORTH COAST
Casabi
Parador El Guajataca
Highway 2, km 103.8
Quebradillas,
(787) 895-3070

Casa de Playa Restaurant
and Country Inn
Highway 2, km 85.6, Hatillo
(787) 898-3850

Histórico Puente Blanco
Road 4484, km 1.09,
Quebradillas
(787) 895-1934

**PUERTO RICO'S NORTHWEST
CORNER**
Olas y Arenas
Villas del Mar Hau
Road 4466, km 8.3, Isabela
(787) 830-8315

Sonia Rican Seafood
Sonia Rican Guest House at
Playa Jobos
Road 4466, Isabela
(787) 872-1818

Dario's Gourmet
Restaurant
Route 110, km 8.8,
Aguadilla
(787) 890 6143

New Golden Crown
La Cima Hotel
Route 110, km 9.2,
Aguadilla
(787) 890-5077

Tres Amigos
Parador El Faro
Route 107, km 2.1,
Aguadilla
(787) 882-8000

AGUADA AND RINCÓN
Aguada Seafood
103 Jiménez, Aguada
(787) 868-2136

The Black Eagle
Route 413, km 1, Rincón
(787) 823-3510

Brasas Restaurant
Rincón Beach Resort
Route 115, km 5.8, Añasco
(787) 589-9000

Calypso Tropical Café
Route 413, Rincón
(787) 823-4151

Capriccio
12 Manuel Malave, Añasco
(787) 826-3387

El Molino del Quijote
Route 429, km 3.3, Rincón
(787) 823-4010

El Rafael
Route 115, km 6.6, Añasco
(787) 826-5023

El Rincón Tropical
Route 115, km 12.3,
Rincón
(787) 823 7108

El Tapatío Mexican
Restaurant
Route 115, Aguada
(787) 868-1160

Sandy Beach Inn
Linda Vista off Route 413,
km 4.3, Rincón
(787) 823-1146

MAYAGÜEZ
Brazo Gitano
101 Méndez Vigo
(787) 832-0565

El Estoril
100 Méndez Vigo, Este
(787) 834-2288

Mesón Español
525 José Gonzalez
Clemente
(787) 833-5445

Panadería Ricomini
202 Méndez Vigo
(787) 832-0565

Restaurante Don Pepe
58 Méndez Vigo, Este
(787) 834-4941

Repostería y Cafeteria
Franco
3 Manuel Pirallo
(787) 832-0070

The Central Corridor

The *Cordillera Central* mountain range runs through the center of Puerto Rico in an east-west direction, ranging in height from 1,000 to 3,000 feet. Several peaks push their way higher, such as Cerro de Punta, Puerto Rico's highest point, at 4,398 feet.

Central Puerto Rico is a land of dramatic beauty rarely seen by most visitors. The people and their way of life here seem more traditional than their coastal counterparts. A few multilane highways pass through the *Cordillera Central* as quickly as possible, connecting major points to coastal cities such as San Juan, Ponce, and Arecibo. But the only real way to explore the region is via winding country roads. The central mountains are home to a rain forest, several lakes, state forests, and coffee and tobacco plantations. The countryside is lush and on many roads the vegetation forms a tall green canopy overhead, while dazzling views stretch to the dry south coast and the verdant north coast. Wooden homes and roadside businesses are perched precariously at the edge of steep drop-offs, and the rural roadways switch back and forth around mountains, dropping suddenly and then climbing again. Expect to see lots of dogs, chickens, goats, cattle, and horses. The folks you run into are quite friendly to visitors; you're sure to meet them in the rustic bars and eateries along the mountain roads.

The **Panoramic Route** *(La Ruta Panorámica)* is a tangled network of more than forty country roads that stretches some 165 miles and goes directly through much of the region. It can be driven at a leisurely pace over three days, from its beginnings outside the east coast town of Yabucoa on the Caribbean to its end in the damp cool of coffee country between Maricao and Mayagüez. Alternate routes through the mountains are also enjoyable, however, and it's possible to pick up portions of the Panoramic Route off of major roads, such as Highway 52 or Highway 10. Another good idea is to combine a trip to the mountains with a visit to a beach town on the coast near that mountain region. This chapter follows, more or less, the Panoramic Route, although it detours to points of interest off the route.

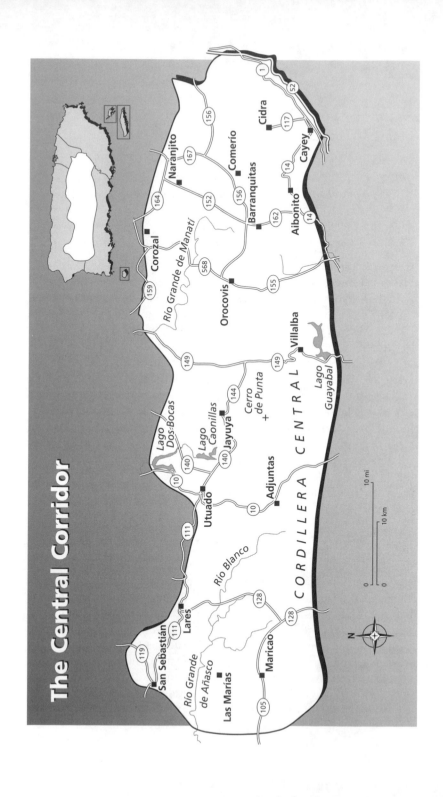

The Central Corridor

1

52

156

Cidra

117

167

156

Naranjito

Comerío

Barranquitas

Cayey

14

164

152

156

Aibonito

14

162

Corozal

Río Grande de Manatí

568

159

Orocovis

155

149

149

Villalba

CORDILLERA CENTRAL

Lago Guayabal

144

Lago Dos-Bocas

Lago Caonillas

Cerro de Punta

140

Jayuya

140

10

Adjuntas

Utuado

10

111

Río Blanco

128

111

Lares

128

San Sebastián

119

Río Grande de Añasco

Maricao

Las Marías

105

N

10 mi

10 km

0

0

Although lodgings are not as abundant as on the coast, several comfortable country inns are scattered throughout the mountains. The region is a perfect lure for the more low-key traveler, who may be genuinely surprised by how much the Caribbean can feel like New England, even if it is a wild, tropical New England.

> **AUTHOR'S FAVORITES IN THE CENTRAL MOUNTAINS**
>
> *Guavate's lechoneras,* Cayey
>
> *Museo Cemí and La Piedra Escrita,* Jayuya
>
> **Hiking and exploring** the area's caves, waterfalls, and forest trails
>
> *La Ruta Panorámica*

The Eastern Mountains

The Panoramic Route begins right outside the city of *Yabucoa,* where steep cliffs rise up out of deep blue water, their vast undersides eaten away by the glaring sun, the wind, and the pounding of sea and salt. A center of the sugar industry in its heyday, this city on a hill is beautiful. A new expressway, Highway 53, is your quickest route from Fajardo. From San Juan take Highway 52 to Highway 30; at Humacao, you can catch Highway 53 or Highway 3 south to Yabucoa.

The road quickly heads away from coastal Patillas into its beautiful hilly and forested region. As on much of its length, the road here is shaded in a tunnel of trees and towering bamboo. The Panoramic Route then segues into Road 7740.

From Patillas, heading north up Route 184 toward Cayey, *Las Casas de la Selva* is a private reserve offering camping and hiking on a limited basis. Set on 1,000 acres of secondary rain forest, the site is owned by Global Ecotechnics (www.ecotechnics.edu), a corporation that includes former members of the Biosphere2 crew who in 1991–93 lived in a giant greenhouse in Arizona in an effort to study how life could be sustained if humans lived on Mars. For this project, Ecotechnics is interested in sustaining a rain forest that protects a large tract of endangered ecosystem and is economically profitable without clear-cutting for timber or agricultural use. Researchers have planted mahogany—a valuable hardwood that will be harvested—amid the native trees. Volunteers help measure growth and record data, as well as work on infrastructure improvement. Visitors can hike, camp, and volunteer. Prices for activities vary. Sites and tents are available for camping, with access to kitchen and bathroom facilities (yes, flush toilets and hot showers). Meals, often with fruits and veggies grown there, can also be arranged. All visits need to be scheduled ahead; call Kathy Carrasquillo, the site manager, at (787) 839–7318, or e-mail Sally Silverstone at http://ssilverstone1@cs.com.

The Panoramic Route next takes you to the **Reserva Forestal Carite** (Route 184, Cayey), a 6,000-acre nature reserve with picnic and camping areas and 25 miles of hiking trails. To reserve a campsite, contact the Department of Natural and Environmental Resources in San Juan (787–724–3724). Two areas accommodate sixteen tents and have bathroom facilities. The reserve's main feature is **Charco Azul** (Blue Pond), a natural pool named for the color of its water. It's an easy mile hike from the parking area alongside the road to the pond. The roadside picnic area has a nice stream running through its grounds.

Homegrown

*T*he Taínos probably brought tobacco to Puerto Rico. The higher altitudes provided a perfect climate and soil for growing it. They dried it, rolled it, wrapped it, and smoked it, inhaling through their noses and exhaling through their mouths. When Christopher Columbus showed up, he and many Spaniards tried cigars and liked them. Tobacco was on the island to stay. Tobacco growing and cigar making have been elevated to an art, but not without a history of ups and downs similar to that of other agricultural crops on the island, dependent on colonizers' interests. From the 1600s into the early twentieth century, tobacco was one of the prime crops cultivated on the island, but there were several limitations to its corporate profitability. Less area was available to cultivate it for large-scale production, given the island's size. Laborers were organized in demands for reasonable working conditions and pay. By 1930, American companies stopped buying Puerto Rican tobacco for cigarettes. After that, small farms concentrated on growing tobacco for cigars.

When the Cuban revolution in 1959 made that country's tobacco unavailable to the United States, companies again looked to Puerto Rico. Some Cuban tobacco growers and cigar makers moved to the island, bringing their passion and expertise with them. In the 1960s, one hundred cigar factories were operating, using Puerto Rican and Dominican tobacco with wrapper tobacco from the Connecticut River Valley of western Massachusetts and Connecticut.

Although the island's economic base has shifted from agricultural to industrial, first with factories and now with high-tech industries, some cigar production, as with coffee, does hang on.

Today, the pharmaceutical industry dominates. These companies, with government incentives, produce 20 percent of the world's drugs. Ironically, 90 percent of the food consumed on the island is now imported, yet 60 percent of farmable land lies fallow. A toast is in order to the stubborn agricultural successes of the island, those sinful pleasures of coffee, tobacco, and sugar. A world without café con leche, *rum*, or *cigars* would be a different place.

THE CENTRAL CORRIDOR

The forest, with mahogany and *yagrumo* trees, towering ferns, and sierra and royal palms, is full of trails. **Carite Lake** is also in the reserve, just down Route 742. The artificial lake is stocked with bass and other fish. Another picnic area with rest rooms, barbecue pits, and covered eating areas sprawls out across a hilly stretch of forest farther along the roadway, right before the Ranger's Office.

Just south of the Carite Forest Ranger Station, along Route 184, is a string of *lechoneras* in *Guavate* (actually part of Cayey). Many trek here regularly from the San Juan area to enjoy roasted pig, and eating at these open-air restaurants is a memorable experience for visitors. Those looking for a more formal dining experience might try **La Casona de Guavate** (Route 184, km 28.5; 787–787–5533). The place is a hodgepodge of architectural styles, and the food can be just as inventive. There's very good basic Puerto Rican and Spanish fare, but the kitchen also experiments: for example, Filete Tropical, a filet mignon stuffed with lobster.

This is one of the quickest and easiest trips to the mountain region from San Juan and is easily accomplished in a single afternoon. The Guavate exit is about forty minutes south of San Juan on Highway 52.

> **TOP ANNUAL EVENTS IN THE CENTRAL MOUNTAINS**
>
> *Coffee Harvest Festival,* mid-February, Maricao
>
> *Festival de La China Dulce,* second week of March, Las Marías
>
> *Festival Típico Criollo,* first week of June, Caguas
>
> *Festival de Guineo,* second week of June, Lares
>
> *Aibonito Flower Festival,* late June and early July
>
> *Feria Nacional de Artesanías,* second week of July, Barranquitas
>
> *Anniversary of El Grito de Lares,* September 23, Lares
>
> *Festival Indígena de Jayuya,* third week of November, Jayuya
>
> *Pasteles National Festival,* late November, Orocovis

North of Guavate and directly south from San Juan on Highway 52 are a few other mountain towns of note. The first one is **Aguas Buenas,** just south of Caguas, the southern border of the San Juan metropolitan area. Route 156 begins climbing immediately after leaving Caguas on this northeastern shoot of the Cordillera Central. This town brings the mountains very close to San Juan, and many *sanjuaneros* who work in the city live here. The town is also home to the **Aguas Buenas Caves.** Although the Department of Natural and Environmental Resources no longer runs tours through here, it is still a favorite spot of experienced spelunkers. There's a story that the chupacabra (a Puerto Rican mythic werewolf) and the UFO it arrived in are hiding here. In the 1970s biologists detected the presence of a fungus, *Histoplasma capsulatum,* in a passage of the cave system. This fungus can grow where damp soil has

157

been contaminated with bat or bird droppings. When disturbed, the spores can be inhaled and develop into a lung infection that, untreated, could lead to a serious disease. If you wish to explore the dry caves in this area, contact one of Puerto Rico's speleological organizations.

A bit south, along Route 172, is **Cidra**, a small mountain town that is one of the fastest-growing municipalities on the island, mainly because of new housing developments and an influx of *sanjuaneros*. Thankfully, Cidra still retains its small-town flavor. The road to Cidra is filled with

Pigging Out

*L*echón—*roast suckling pig cooked on a spit over coals outdoors— draws islanders to Guavate on weekends for an orgy of eating, drinking, and socializing. Although food is served at the numerous outdoor eateries every day of the week, Saturdays and Sundays are the most popular time to make the pilgrimage.*

*There are at least a dozen lechoneras on Route 184 in Guavate, a village that's technically part of Cayey. The highly recommended ones are those concentrated around km 27. Look for **Lechonera El Rancho Original,** located here for more than thirty years and claiming to be the first of its kind. **La Reliquia, El Monte, El Mojito, Los Piños,** and **El Rancho Numero Uno** all get good reviews. Many of these have indoor space or roofed patios for eating and dancing.*

Beginning Friday night, live music can be found in many of the establishments. Saturdays have the more traditional jíbaro music; Sundays have more salsa and merengue. Breakfast begins daily between 7:00 and 8:00 A.M., and places stay

open Friday through Sunday until 11:00 P.M. and weekdays until 8:00 P.M.

Most folks load up their plates with slices of lechón, juicy pork marinated for days before being slow-roasted. It's basted with orange juice, leaving a golden, crispy-skinned and smoky meat. Watch how deftly the meat is sliced with a swinging machete.

You can add vegetables such as yautia, yuca, or plantains, and arroz con gandules (rice with pigeon peas) or red beans with calabaza (pumpkin). Vegetarians will find plenty of options. For voracious carnivores, morcilla (blood sausage), longaniza (chicken and pork sausage), or pollo asado (roasted chicken) could be on the side. Cost is determined by the weight of your plate; a hearty meal can be had for $10. Good food, cold beer or piña coladas, and lively island music combine for a festive atmosphere and happy crowd.

The local roads are extremely winding and narrow, so drive carefully. Late in the afternoon temperatures begin to drop, so you may need a sweater or jacket.

Folk Music

*T*he mountain region and the jíbaro gave birth to Puerto Rican folk music, décima.

Based on the old Spanish seis, it is called the décima because it is sung in ten-line rhyming cadences, in an expression of either great joy or sorrow. Verbal improvisation is key to this music, and often a group of singers will perform the décima, each taking a line and trying to outdo those who came before. Today this music, which makes use of guitars of various strings (including the cuatro, the Puerto Rican version of a Spanish guitar, which can use a gourd for its body), maracas, güiro, and other gourd percussion instruments, informs the ballads and protest songs of singer Andrés Jiménez, who is known as "El Jíbaro."

vegetable, fruit, and flower vendors, and its central plaza is charming with its historic buildings and many trees. Five-mile-long *Lago Cidra* is a reservoir with good fishing.

Cayey is the next major mountain town you'll encounter on a southern route from San Juan. It's located on the northern slope of the Cordillera Central near its summit in the *Sierra de Cayey*, Puerto Rico's central mountain range in this area.

A *University of Puerto Rico* campus is located here, which lends this mountain town a larger cultural life than many of its neighbors. A permanent art collection features the work of Ramón Fraube (1865–1954), a Cayey painter whose realistic works depict everyday scenes of Puerto Rican mountain life.

Outside of the town center, on the road to *Jájome,* you'll find *The Sand and the Sea* (Route 714, km 5.2; 787–738–9086), a charming out-of-the-way restaurant serving local cuisine staples in an inventive way. A few minutes on the restaurant's back terrace is all it takes to realize that the drive here is worth it. The view extends down to the south coast and the sparkling Caribbean. Some rooms are available for overnight stays.

Another nice restaurant in a rural setting is the *Jájome Terrace* (Route 15, km 18.6; 787–738–4016). Flower gardens surround this mountain perch with views of the distant sea. French-influenced local dishes are served on an open-air terrace. Also in this area, on Route 15, is one of the beautiful official vacation residences of the Puerto Rican governor (not open to the public).

From either Cayey or Guavate, Route 14 picks up the baton of the Panoramic Route and takes you to the mountain town of *Aibonito.*

The best time to visit the town is during the annual Flower Festival (June) or the local festival run by chicken producer To-Rico (August). While flowers and food are the main attractions, respectively, like most Puerto Rican parties, there's also live music and a lot of dancing.

Aibonito is a must-stop, even though the Panoramic Route doesn't come directly here. At 2,500 feet, this is the highest town in Puerto Rico, a place where temperatures have been known to plummet to 40 degrees Fahrenheit. The town's name apparently stems from an account of a hapless seventeenth-century wanderer who stumbled on the town and remarked, *"¡Ai, que bonito!"* ("Oh, how pretty!") For a time, the town also served as Puerto Rico's capital, when Spanish troops moved here from San Juan to squelch an *independentista* uprising circa 1867.

Aibonito is surrounded by hills, chicken farms, and flower nurseries. It was once a summer retreat for the wealthy, and many stately residences remain. The plaza, with a movie theater and diner, has a nice lived-in air about it. One of the best establishments in town is **La Piedra Restaurant** (Route 7718, km 0.8; 787–735–1034), a mountaintop restaurant with a view. Much of the produce and many of the herbs used in the restaurant are grown on the premises. This is healthy *comida criolla* with a gourmet touch. *Mofongo* is a specialty. The owners suggest you bring a sweater.

The Central Mountains

The **San Cristóbal Canyon,** Puerto Rico's deepest gorge, lies between Aibonito and Barranquitas. The canyon, with sheer walls that shoot up 700 feet, was formed by the raging **Río Usabon,** a giant gash in this mountainous terrain. Route 725 gets you closest to the canyon. You'll know you're getting close because of the great number of businesses with *El Cañon* in their names. **Bar El Cañon** (Route 725, km 4) has cold cheap beer and a good jukebox. A trail from here leads to the canyon floor, but it's a rough hike. Farther along the road, at km 5.5, a narrow side road takes you closer to the top of the canyon. From here it's a much shorter hike to the bottom, which features a 100-foot waterfall.

The area surrounding the canyon was recently bought by the Puerto Rico Conservation Trust, which has started a clean-up and tree-planting campaign here. There are hundreds of plant species and about seventy-five bird species that claim this as their habitat, which is much drier than many mountain forests. To protect the ecosystem, the non-profit group wants to eventually limit canyon use to only guided tours.

Barranquitas, which overlooks the San Cristóbal Canyon, has the look of a European town, with closely built houses and narrow winding streets surrounded by hills. The focal point of the town's plaza is the white, red-roofed church, *Parroquia San Antonio de Padua,* that rises above the townscape. Barranquitas is set at an elevation of 1,800 feet and is just as cool and refreshing as Aibonito. It is best known as the birthplace of Luis Muñoz Rivera, who struggled for Puerto Rico's autonomy from Spain. It is also the final resting place of his son Luis Muñoz Marín, the governor of Puerto Rico from 1948 to 1964 and the seminal Puerto Rican political figure of the twentieth century.

The birthplace of Luis Muñoz Rivera is now the *Museo Casa Natal de Luis Muñoz Rivera* (10 Muñoz Rivera between Tonia Vélez and Padre Berríos Streets; 787–857–0230), located one block west of the town's

Luis Muñoz Marín

*B*orn in 1898, the year the American troops landed at Guánica, **Luis Muñoz Marín** literally mirrored the life of modern Puerto Rico. In fact, no single person has had as much of an effect on modern Puerto Rico.

The son of Luis Muñoz Rivera, the top Puerto Rican leader at the end of the nineteenth century, Muñoz Marín was well suited for the role. In his youth he traveled in bohemian circles in his adopted home of New York City. Urbane and proficient in English and Spanish, he also proved a deft politician who easily mixed with jíbaros in rural Puerto Rico.

At the age of forty, Muñoz and a group of liberal colleagues created the Popular Democratic Party in his father's birthplace of Barranquitas. The party controlled Puerto Rico for

decades under Muñoz's leadership with their slogan of "Bread, Land and Freedom." Rather than concentrating on resolving Puerto Rico's political status question, the new party focused its energy on improving economic and social conditions.

This effort reached its apex in the advent of Puerto Rico's current commonwealth status, called Estado Libre Asociado (free associated state), which was established on July 25, 1952, the anniversary of the U. S. invasion of Puerto Rico.

Muñoz reigned as top Puerto Rican leader for twenty-four years. During this time, Puerto Rico went from being "the poorhouse of the Caribbean" to the "showcase of the Caribbean."

plaza. The library's contents belonged to Muñoz Rivera, and the house provides a glimpse into life among Puerto Rico's elite at midcentury. There's also much here about his son, Muñoz Marín. Open Tuesday through Friday 8:00 A.M. to 3:30 P.M., Saturday 8:00 A.M. to noon.

Just around the corner is the mausoleum where Muñoz Rivera, his son, and their wives are buried (Padre Berríos Street). Open daily 8:00 A.M. to noon and 1:00 to 3:30 P.M.

Every year a huge three-day craft fair takes place around Muñoz Rivera's July 17 birthdate. It's one of the biggest fairs on the island and draws more than 200 artisans from across the island who set up their wares in the town's shaded plaza.

A bit northwest of Barranquitas lies *Orocovis,* probably the most isolated town on the island, located dead center in the island's mountain-

An Art with Attributes

*S*antos, *sculptures of saints in the Catholic religion, carved in wood by* santeros, *are thought by many to be the finest form of Puerto Rican folk art. The tradition of making these small, colorfully painted statues began when Catholic clergy, accompanying the Spanish in the colonizing of the island, taught Indians how to carve the figures as part of their conversion to Christianity, providing lessons in their new religion. Some attribute the* popularity santos-*making had with the Taínos to their own tradition of representing their gods as cemís, the wood, stone or pottery images used in religious practices.*

Puerto Rican santeros *have added to the Catholic lexicon uniquely Puerto Rican saints with local significance, existing outside the Church's sanction. Examples include the Miracle of Hormigueros, the Virgin of the Kings, and the Virgen del Pozo. The Tres Reyes (Three Magi, Kings, or Wise-*

men) is perhaps the most popular on the island, as well as Saint Anthony and Our Lady of Mount Carmel. Other common santos include the Holy Trinity, the Virgin of Monserrate, Saint Barbara, Saint Joseph, the Holy Family and La Mano Poderosa (The All-Powerful Hand). Even if contemporary santos are more an expression of art and less of religion, they continue to represent spirituality for Puerto Ricans and provide insight into the culture.

With a revival of interest in santos, both women and men carve in workshops in homes across the island. Santos are sold as an island craft and, like other fine works of art, can cost many hundreds of dollars. Interesting santos displays with both historic and contemporary works can be found in museums in San Juan and Ponce, as well as in smaller exhibits around the island. Santos are truly the art of making miracles appear possible.

Return to Roots

*A*grotourism is becoming a trend on the island. Visitors can now spend a day on a coffee plantation, sampling different brews and learning about life in the mountains. One company offering a bus tour out of San Juan is **Legends of Puerto Rico** *(787–605–9060; www.legendsofpr.com).*

ous middle. Many artisans have come from this area. To the south is **Villaba,** which can be reached most directly from Route 149, which travels south to Highway 52 near Ponce at Juana Díaz. Both towns have spectacular views extending to the coasts.

The Panoramic Route goes west along Route 143 from Barranquitas, passing through the Corozal mountain range and dissecting the awesome **Toro Negro Forest.** This 30-mile stretch between Barranquitas and Adjuntas to the west is the longest on the Panoramic Route and among the most beautiful. Traveling along the mountainous backbone of the *Cordillera Central,* it's possible to see both the north and the south coasts. Looking north, the mountains fall off into the tightly formed karst hills just before the Atlantic. Vast plains stretch south of the mountain range to the distant Caribbean. You can even see offshore islands, such as Ponce's Caja de Muertos, from here. Often, however, this mountainous road is draped in mist, and one gets the impression of traveling through a vast, impenetrable cloud forest.

Sandwiched between the mountain towns of Villaba and Jayuya, and Adjuntas and Orocovis, the **Toro Negro Forest Reserve** encompasses 7,000 acres in the heart of Puerto Rico. The reserve is every bit as impressive as the more famous El Yunque (Caribbean National Forest) in Río Grande–Luquillo. It, too, has some characteristics of the rain forest, but its junglelike vegetation is at higher elevations. Multitudes of mountain streams, with names like Salto de Inabón, Indalecia, Guayo, and Matrullas, lace the reserve. Adjacent narrow footpaths offer hikers a quick way to get off the beaten path. Bamboo, giant ferns, *tabonuco,* trumpet trees, and towering royal palms fill the forest.

The main entrance to the forest is at the **Doña Juana Recreational Area** (Route 143, km 32.4), which features a picnic area and an S-shaped swimming pool filled by the cold mountain streams. The area, which is the starting place of many trails in the reserve, also has a campground, with wooden lean-tos for protection from the rain. Stop by the Ranger Station (787–844–4051) for orientation and a trail map.

The Ranger Station is open most predictably during the summer from 8:00 A.M. to noon and 1:00 to 4:00 P.M. on weekdays.

Just outside the recreational area is *Las Cabañas de Doña Juana* (Route 143), a rustic, friendly place offering tasty mountain barbecue and other fare. The ribs are recommended. Also try the side dish of rice with white beans, unique in Puerto Rico, where most people prefer pink beans. Food can be eaten under the small *cabañas* that give the place its name.

The recreational area looks like a final outpost of civilization, with the dense forest looming at all turns. From here it's about a 2-mile hike to a lookout tower and the nearby *Doña Juana Falls,* which come crashing down 200 feet over a cliffside. The half-paved trail is a pretty easy hike, but take care: The constant rain makes for a slippery surface.

West of the recreation area, Route 143 passes *Lago Guineo* (Banana Lake), Puerto Rico's highest. This round lake, created by damming the Toro Negro River, is almost completely hidden by dense forest growth, notably towering bamboo, and is ringed by steep, slippery, red-clay banks. Those who come here will be greeted by fresh mountain air, the singing of the *coquí,* and little else.

Farther west lies *Cerro de Punta* (Route 143, km 16.5), Puerto Rico's tallest peak at 4,398 feet. It's possible to drive to the top on an extremely steep, 10-mile-long, single-lane gravel road, but most visitors will prefer to hoof it. However you get there, the view is worth it. Up top you can see all the way over to the capital city of San Juan and most of the Atlantic Coast. At other times the peak is wrapped in swirling mist, giving it an otherworldly, lunar quality.

North of the Toro Negro area are several towns and other attractions that are definitely worth a visit. Continue west along Route 143 beyond the cutoff to Ponce at Route 139. The next exit to the north will be Route 140, which leads to a mountain crossroads. Turn right on Route 144 to get to *Jayuya,* a mountain town resting in a valley beneath the imposing Cerro de Punta and surrounding mountains. Route 144 is the only way into Jayuya from either the west or the east. The town is surrounded by a lush valley, which in turn is circled by many of the highest peaks in the Cordillera Central. The town is filled with old coffee estates, as well as Taíno ruins and artifacts.

Parador Hacienda Gripiñas (Route 527, km 2.5; 787–828–1717 or 800–981–7575), built on the grounds of an old coffee plantation, is one of the best places to stay in Puerto Rico's interior. Built in 1853 by coffee baron and Spanish nobleman Eusebio Pérez del Castillo, the former plantation home was turned into an inn in 1975, and it retains the elegance and grandeur of its past. A wide porch, gorgeous gardens, and twenty acres of coffee fields surround it. Ceiling fans and hammocks point the way to laze away a few days here, and the chorus of chanting *coquís* lulls you further into relaxation. There is also a pool and an excellent restaurant. A small 2-mile trail from here leads to the summit of Cerro de Punta.

Jayuya is known for the Taíno relics found here. The **Cemí Museum** (787–828–5000) in town has a collection of Taíno pottery and the largest collection of *cemís*, Taíno ceremonial statues, on the island. Off Route 144 is **La Piedra Escrita** (The Written Rock), a huge boulder with Taíno petroglyphs. Located next to a stream, it's a wonderful picnic spot. In November the town hosts an annual **Indigenous Festival**, which combines native crafts with music and food. With the spirit of the *jíbaros* infusing this place, it's no surprise that in 1950 a one-day uprising by *independentistas* attempted to ignite a revolution here. Nearby Lares had, in 1868, been the location for a similar attempt.

North of here lies **Utuado** (take Route 140 to Route 111). The town is the unofficial center of the mountain district. Now that Highway 22 has been completed, it's also one of the most accessible towns in the region. Eventually, the highway will cut completely across the *Cordillera Central* and connect with the south coast at Ponce.

The place to stay in Utuado is **Casa Grande Mountain Retreat** (Route 612, km 0.3; 787–894–3939 or 888–343–2272; www.hotelcasagrande. com), located just off Route 140 in the town's lake district. The hotel is set on a very private 107 acres of tropical forest. Another former coffee plantation, the hotel has twenty rustic rooms, each with private bath, balcony, and hammock. There's also a restaurant, **Jungle Jane's** (featuring local and international dishes), and a bar. Yoga classes are offered. If you're exhausted, stressed out, or burned out, this is the place for you. Some might panic and feel it's sensory deprivation (no TV, no radio, no nightclub), but there are low-key pleasures to enjoy: good food, interesting people, a beautiful pool, and trails for hiking and horseback riding. Kids might be bored here; it really does feel like you are lost in the middle of nowhere. Across the road from Casa Grande, **Rancho de Caballos de Utuado** (Route 612, km 0.4; 787–894–9526) can provide horses for local rides.

Casa Grande is close to both **Lago Dos Bocas** and **Lago Caonillas,** two artifical lakes built as part of the same system. (In all, there are about six lakes making up this system.) Route 10 swings to the shore of **Lago Dos Bocas,** a popular, U-shaped lake ringed by restaurants. Small ferry

OFF THE BEATEN PATH

El Jíbaro

L *arger than life, the statue of a jíbaro by Highway 52 in the Cordillera Central represents the iconic importance in Puerto Rican culture of this character. "El Jíbaro" has come to stand for a rural, simple, hardworking, "salt of the earth" person, and a way of life disappearing in the urbanized landscape of modern Puerto Rico.*

Originally, Taínos had created settlements in the central mountains. During the Spanish conquest, those who could escape their enslavement came to hide and take refuge. They were joined by renegade Spaniards looking for their freedom as well. Because the rich soil permitted a range of crops to be grown, life in the mountains was comfortably self-sufficient, although isolated from the rest of the island. Certain characteristics developed, defining those living here: fierce pride in their hard work, a love of the land, and a local independence they cherished.

By the twentieth century, life had changed. The economic dominance of sugar in island agriculture and the immense growth of coastal plantations pressured farmers to give up their local work. Markets for mountain-grown products such as coffee and tobacco disappeared. Jíbaros—the "country folk"—unhappily looked for menial work in urban areas, forced to relocate. Looking out of place in the city, they were an easy target for ridicule. Other islanders, disconnected from their own rural roots, showed no appreciation or compassion for these people whose lives had been stripped of meaning once they left their beloved hills.

Today, however, the jíbaro enjoys more respect. As people realize what can be lost in their culture, they have a new appreciation of island history and traditions. There is pride in their national identity and the strengths shaping it. Puerto Ricans share a passion for their homeland and deep appreciation for the life it sustains.

boats take visitors on rides around the lake, and fishing is also a favorite pastime here. Call Cesar at (787) 894–9488 for a fishing expedition and Jenaro at (787) 878–1809 to rent kayaks.

Utuado makes a good base to explore many of the attractions in the interior of Karst Country and its mountainous adjacent regions (these are described in more detail in the North Coast and West chapter).

The Western Mountains

*C*offee country actually starts in Jayuya, but it flourishes in the western **Cordillera Central**. After passing the Toro Negro Forest Reserve, the Panoramic Route (now called Route 143) continues on to **Adjuntas**, known as the "town of the sleeping giant," as its silhouette

Fact

*Puerto Rico's own **Rita Moreno** was the first actress to win all four of the entertainment industry's highest awards: the Oscar, Emmy, Grammy, and Tony.*

suggests that illusion. Here the majestic peaks of the central mountain range give way to more roughly formed mountains and hills.

Adjuntas is an agricultural town surrounded by coffee fields, but citron, an ingredient processed from citrus fruits that is used in cakes, is by far the biggest crop here. In fact, the town is one of the world's leading producers of it.

West of Adjuntas, the Panoramic Route continues on Route 518. You'll pass by several private farms before reaching **Guilarte Forest Reserve,** which has a beautiful picnic area beside a eucalyptus grove. Five cabins are available for overnight rentals; call the Department of Natural Resources (787–724–3724) for reservations. The cabins are in the eucalyptus forest, providing a scenic setting. Within the reserve is the 3,950-foot-tall **Monte Guilarte,** one of the few peaks on the

Monument to the Puerto Rican *jíbaro*

How Taíno Is Boricua?

Conventional wisdom reckons that approximately 30,000 Taínos were living in what is now known as Puerto Rico when the Spanish arrived here on September 12, 1508. At that time Ponce de León, who would become Puerto Rico's first governor, peacefully exchanged greetings with Agüeybaña the Elder, the Taíno's head chief.

Just twenty-two years later, in 1530, a Spanish census reported a mere 1,200 Taínos left. Although many uncounted Taínos presumably fled to the mountains, today there is a widespread belief that the number of Taíno survivors may have been greater than what was originally reported.

In 1998 a group of professors from the University of Puerto Rico went to the isolated Maricao community of Indieras, one of the last reported hold-outs of the Taíno. There the researchers searched for subjects with the dark skin, long, straight black hair, and high cheekbones typical of the Taíno. Testing only subjects whose mothers also had similar characteristics, researchers found that 70 percent showed traces of an Amerindian DNA that may prove to be handed down from a Taíno ancestry. Intrigued, the researchers took a more general sample in the city of Mayagüez, using subjects regardless of features or mother's ancestry. There they found evidence of Amerindian DNA in 50 percent of the respondents.

Although more testing is needed, researchers believe that they might be able to prove that either there were many more Taínos than were originally thought to have existed or that the Taínos survived much longer than previously thought, even to the present.

island that isn't loaded down with serious media and telecommunications equipment. It's only 400 feet shorter than the island's highest point, and the lack of clutter makes a hike up here far more rewarding.

Just west of the forest reserve, the Panoramic Route passes the settlement of **Castañer,** one of the most remote parts of the town center and main settlement of Lares. This beautiful, one-road community is filled with friendly residents. Despite its isolation, there are some North American and other foreign settlers in the area.

Lares, an hour north along Route 128, is known as the birthplace of the largest uprising in Puerto Rican history. In 1868 Ramón Emeterio Betances, a distinguished physician and prominent voice in Puerto Rican politics, catalyzed the rebellion, which was dubbed *el grito de Lares,* literally "the shout of Lares." Although a republic of Puerto Rico was briefly declared, it was put down by the Spanish when the insurgents attempted to march on San Lorenzo.

Lares is a beautiful mountain town with a traditional Colonial Spanish central plaza, **La Plaza de la Revolución**, where thousands of *indepen- dentistas* gather each September 23 to celebrate the anniversary of *el grito*. As with most Puerto Rican political rallies, it's a surprisingly eas- ily digestible mix of political speeches, live music, and stimulating con- versation. There's plenty of beer and food, and scores of artisans come to sell their work. The town also jumps during its annual patron saint festival in early December.

The plaza's towering trees and scattered gardens obscure the view across the plaza but provide much-needed shade and fresh air. (If only San Juan plazas were the same.) Fronting the plaza is **Heladería Lares** (787-897-2062), a highly recommended ice-cream parlor that has dreamed up such unique ice cream flavors as *habichuelas* (bean), *plátano* (plantain), and *arroz* (rice).

Beyond Castañer, the Panoramic Route (now Route 128) continues past magnificent views and Lago Guayo. The road becomes Route 365 and then Route 366 before turning into Route 120 and the **Maricao Forest**. A 2,600-foot stone observation tower a half mile beyond the forest entrance affords great views of much of the island's western coast. Also in this area is the **Maricao Fish Hatchery** (Routes 105 and 444), where many freshwater fish species are raised to stock Puerto Rico's more than twenty island lakes. The hatchery is open weekdays 7:30 A.M. to noon and 1:00 to 4:00 P.M.; weekends 8:30 A.M. to 4:00 P.M. Free admission.

The town of **Maricao** is the smallest on the island in terms of popula- tion. A visit here will immerse you in a peaceful, isolated place that is lush in vegetation and blessed with dramatic vistas. Maricao is home to coffee plantations, including a former one now run as an inn, **Parador Hacienda Juanita** (Route 105, km 23.5; 787-838-2550; www.hacienda juanita.com). There are simple accommodations here, along with a game room, pool, and basketball and tennis courts. The resident chick- ens will scoot around you in the morning as you head to the veranda for breakfast; good coffee and local fruit are always available as well as heartier options. The restaurant, **La Casona de Juanita,** is a *mesóns gastronómicos* recognized for fine meals of *criollo* cuisine. Room rates include breakfast and dinner.

Another lodging option is to rent a cabin from the **Centro Vacacional Monte de Estado** (Route 120, km 131.1; 787-787-5632). It is necessary to reserve ahead (call 787-722-1771 or 888-767-4732). Cabins accom- modate six; the center has a pool, picnic area, observation tower, and basketball court.

Holidays bring more visitors to Maricao; Monte de Estado is its busiest when Puerto Ricans are vacationing. One event that always attracts a crowd is the coffee harvest festival in mid-February, with coffee and crafts featured, but plenty of music and dancing as well.

North of Maricao is *Las Marías,* another coffee-country town that offers more rural splendor for the traveler looking to get away from the hustle and bustle that informs much of Puerto Rican life. While Maricao feels like it's so far away from it all, it's actually quite close to Mayagüez—maybe a thirty- to forty-five-minute drive. The most pleasant route to Maricao is Route 120, which rises up into the mountains from Sabana Grande in the south.

Closing this book of possible adventures while in the mountains of Puerto Rico not only leaves it on a high note but in a special place of inspiration, awe, and majesty. Hopefully this book has shown you the wealth of choices and adventures that await you on *la isla.* Your visit can provide you with the experiences of new sights, sounds, and tastes as well as relaxation and a good time. You can feel challenged, enriched, and renewed from your time here. *Saludos y buen viaje*—have a great trip!

PLACES TO STAY IN THE CENTRAL CORRIDOR

THE EASTERN MOUNTAINS
Hampton Inn and Suites
Caguas
Perimeter Road off Highway 52, exit 23, Caguas
(787) 653-1111 or
(800) HAMPTON
www.hamptoninn.com

El Coquí Posada Familiar
Guest House
Route 722, km 7.3,
Aibonito
(787) 735-3150

Las Casas de la Selva
Route 184, Patillas
(787) 839-7318
www.ecotechnics.edu

Las Casitas Hotel
Route 162, km 4.8,
Aibonito
(787) 735-0180

Swiss Inn Guest House
and Hotel
Route 14, km 49.3,
Aibonito
(787) 735-8500

THE CENTRAL MOUNTAINS
Hacienda Margarita
Route 152, km 1.7,
Barranquitas
(787) 854-0414

Hotel Posada Jayuya
49 Guillermo Esteves,
Jayuya
(787) 828-7250

THE WESTERN MOUNTAINS
Gutierrez Guest House
Route 119, km 26.1, Las
Marias
(787) 827-2087

Lago Vista Hotel and
Restaurant
Lake Guajatca shorefront,
San Sebastián
(888) 779-3788

Monte Río Hotel
18 Cesar Gonzalez,
Adjuntas
(787) 829-3705

Villas de Sotomayor Resort
Hotel and Country Club
Route 123, km 36.8,
Adjuntas
(787) 829-1717
www.villasotomayor.com

PLACES TO EAT IN THE CENTRAL CORRIDOR

THE EASTERN MOUNTAINS

Chalet Jordano Ristorante
Route 172, km 4.9, Caguas
(787) 286-0085

El Cielito
Route 715, km 3, Cayey
(787) 738-1805

El Isleño-Caguas
Highway 1, km 27.4,
Caguas
(787) 653-9295

El Mesón de Jorge
Highway 1, km 57, Cayey
(787) 263-2800

El Mojíto
Route 184, km 27, Guavate
(787) 738-8888

El Panorámico
Route 173, km 2.1, Aguas
Buenas
(787) 732-6634

El Paraíso
Highway 1, km 29.1,
Caguas
(787) 747-2012

El Rancho Numero Uno
Route 184, km 27, Guavate
(787) 747-7296

El Sirimar
Route 156, km 45.2, Aguas
Buenas
(787) 732-6012

Ernesto's Restaurant
Route 156, Aguas Buenas
exit, Caguas
(787) 746-6260

La Cantara
D-6 Degetau, Caguas
(787) 743-0220

Los Olivos
Miguel Hernández, corner
of Safiro, Caguas
(787) 743-1020

Marcelo
Highway 1 at Mercado,
Caguas
(787) 743-8801

Marcos' Restaurant
3 Muñoz Rivera, Caguas
(787) 743-2306

Mexico Lindo
8 Muñoz Marín, Caguas
(787) 746-9066

Miramelinda
Road 7737, km 2.8, Cayey
(787) 738-0715

Mochomo's
162 Gautier Benitez
Avenue, Caguas
(787) 286-9181

Siempre Viva
Route 715, km 5.1, Cayey
(787) 738-0512

Tío Pepe
Route 723, km 0.3, Aibonito
(787) 735-9615

XabroXura
109 Degetau, Aibonito
(787) 991-0888

THE CENTRAL MOUNTAINS

Aquarium Sea Food
Restaurant
29 Esteves, Utuado
(787) 894-1500

Bar Plaza
21 Muñoz Rivera,
Barranquitas
(787) 857-4909

Café Tres Picachos
Route 144, km 2.5, Jayuya
(787) 828-2121

Doña Fela
Route 123, km 53.6, Utuado
(787) 894-2758

Don Pedro
Parador Hacienda
Gripiñas
Route 527, km 2.5, Jayuya
(787) 828-1717 or
(800) 981-7575

El Coquí Here
Route 152, km 3.6,
Baranquitas
(787) 857-3828

El Dujo
Route 140, km 8.2, Jayuya
(787) 828-1143

El Faro
Route 611, km 2.3, Utuado
(787) 894-3206

El Fogón de Abuela-Utuado
Route 612, km 7.3, Utuado
(787) 894-0470

El Mofongo Criollo
Route 152, Barranquitas
(787) 857-0480

Hacienda Margarita
Route 152, km 1.7,
Barranquitas
(787) 857-0414

La Estáncia Restaurant and
Inn
Route 615, km 4.5, Ciales
(787) 871-0518

La Llave de Oro
18 Cuatro de Julio,
Orocovis
(787) 867–3432

La Tosca Steak House
Route 152, km 8.9,
Barranquitas
(787) 857–4288

Mesón Don Alonso
Lago Dos Bocas dock
Route 612, km 3,
Utuado
(787) 894–0516

THE WESTERN MOUNTAINS
Criollo Buffet and
Salad Bar
Route 129, km 19.6, Lares
(787) 897–6463

El Taíno
Route 129, km 20, Lares
(787) 645–4591

La Casa de Los Tostones
Gigantes
Route 120, km 22.7,
Maricao
(787) 838–5572

Las Cavernas
Route 129, km 19.6, Lares
(787) 897–6463

Las Garzas
Villas de Sotomayor
Route 123, km 36, Adjuntas
(787) 829–1717

Terraza Tropical Restaurant
Route 123, km 24,
Adjuntas
(787) 829–0348

Villas de Sotomayor
Route 10, km 36.3,
Adjuntas
(787) 829–1717

Index

A

A La Banda, 66
Acua Expreso, 11
Adjuntas, 166
Aéropuerto Diego Jimenez Torres, 67
Aguada, 139–40
Aguadilla, 137
Aguas Buenas, 157
Aguas Buenas Caves, 157
Aguaviva, 10
Aguirre, 83–84
Aguirre Forest, 83
Aibonito, 159–60
Ají, 5
Ajili-Mójili, 34
Al Salám, 46
Albergue Olímpico, 91
Alcadía, 22
Aleli, 113
Alelí by the Sea, 34
Alpha Scuba, 65
Amadeus, 13
Amapola Inn & Tavern, 73
American Vegetable Gourmet Shop, 44
Añasco, 143–45
Anchor Inn, 67
Angel Ramos Foundation Visitors'
  Center, 134
Anticipation Harbor Cruises, 11
Antiqua Casa de Aduana, 82
Aquatica Dive Shop, 138
Aquatica Underwater Adventures, 149
Aqui Se Puede, 14
Archives and General Library of Puerto
  Rico, 32
Arecibo, 129–30
Arecibo Lighthouse and Historical
  Park, 129
Arecibo Observatory, 134
Arepas y Mucho Mas, 24
Arroyo, 81–82
Artesanías Ayala, 57
Atlantic Beach Hotel, 34
Atlas Art, 21
Attabeira Educative Travel, 149

Augusto's Cuisine, 41
Autoridad de Transportacíon Maritima
  ferry terminal, 66
Avenida Pedro Albizu Campos, 111
Aviones, 56

B

Babylon, 39
Bacardi Rum Factory, 10
Bahía Beach Plantation, 59
Bahía Las Croabas, 68
Bahia San Juan, 11
Baires, 13
Balneario Tres Hermanos, 143
balnearios (public beaches), x, xi,
  130, 144
Bananas, 73
Banco Popular, 4
Baños de Coamo, 92
Bar El Cañon, 160
Barbie Museum, The, 135
Barbosa Park, 37
Barrachina Village, 7
Barranquitas, 161
Barrio Guaypao, 110
Barrio Paris, 145
Barú, 14
baseball, 47
Basílica Nuestra Señora de la
  Monserrate, 146
beaches (balnearios), x, xi, 130, 144
Beaches, 32–40
Bebo's, 55
Belz Factory Outlet World, 58
Ben and Jerry's, 17
Benítez Fishing Charters, 40
Berwind Country Club, 60
Beside the Pointe Guest House, 141
Big Apple Deli, The, 36
Blue Caribe Dive Center, 74
Blue Macaw, The, 73
Blues Cafe, 112
Boquerón, 114–17
Boquerón Refugio de Ares, 114
Bossa Nova, 9

173

INDEX

Botanical Garden of the University of
  Puerto Rico, 49
Boveda, 21
Brass Cactus, 65
Bravos of Boston, 76
buses, xii
Butterfly People, 7

C

Cabañas de Yunque, 78
Cabo Rojo, 114
Cabo Rojo National Wildlife Refuge, 116
Café Berlin, 24
Café Bohemio, 18
Café la Violeta, 7
Cafe Manolin, 23
Café Puerto Rico, 10
Café Puertorriqueño, 93
Café San Sebastián, 13
Café Seda, 14
Café Tabac, 8
Café Zaguan, 11
Cafetería Los Amigos, 23
Cafetería Mallorca, 24
Caguana Indian Ceremonial Park, 133
Caja de Muertos, 99
Cambalache Forest, 133
Camp Alegre, 104
Caña Gorda, 106
Cancel Boats, 113
Candelero Resort at Palmas del Mar, 79
Canóvanas, 58
Caparra Ruins, 40
Capilla del Cristo, 21
Captain Freddie Rodriguez, 68
Caribbean National Forest, 61
Caribbean Paradise Hotel, 81
Caribbean Reef Dive Shop, 117
Caribbean Vacation Villa, 108
Caribe Cay, 66
Caribe Hilton, 29
Caribe Kayak, 69
Caribe Mountain Villas, 59
Caribe Playa, 81
Carite Lake, 157
Carli Cafe Concierto, 5
Carnegie Library, 32
Carnicería Restaurant Díaz, 44

Caruso Restaurant, 34
Casa Alcaldía, 96
Casa Armstrong-Poventud, 98
Casa Blanca, 16
Casa Cielo, 74
Casa Cubuy, 78
Casa Dante, 38
Casa de Callejón, 9
Casa de España, 32
Casa de Playa Beach Hotel, 38
Casa de Ramón Power y Giralt, 24
Casa del Caribe: A Tropical Bed and
  Breakfast, 35
Casa del Francés, 72
Casa del Libro, 21
Casa del Mar, 48
Casa Don Q, 3
Casa Flamboyant, 78
Casa Grande Mountain Retreat, 165
Casa Marshall, 78
Casa Morales, 120
Casa Roig, 80
Casa Salazar, 97
Casa Ulanga, 130
Casa Wiechers-Villaronga, 98
Castañer, 168
Castillo de San Cristóbal, 11
Castillo Serrallés, 98
Castillo Villa del Mar, 79
Catamaran Fun Cat, 67
Catamaran Getaway, 67
Catedral de San Germán de Auxerre, 120
Catedral de San Juan, 18
Cathedral of Our Lady of Guadalupe, 96
Cayey, 159
Ceiba, 77–78
Ceiba Country Inn, 78
Cementerio de San Juan, 12
Cemí Museum, 165
Central Mountains, The, 160–66
Central Park, 46
Central Roig, 80
Centro de Bellas Artes, 43, 83
Centro Vacacional de Boquerón, 115
Centro Vacacional Monte de Estado, 169
Centro Vacacional Villas de Anasco, 144
Cerro de Punta, 164
Cerro Gordo, 127

Chamonix Catamaran, 66
Charco Azul, 156
Chayote, 41
Che's Restaurante Argentino, 38
Cheers & Beers, 140
Chef Marisoll Creative Cuisine, 20
Chez Daniel, 79
Chez Shack, 74
Cidra, 158
Club de Artesanos, 110
Club Desportivo de Oeste, 117
Club Gallístico de Puerto Rico, 39
Club Lazer, 23
Club Náutico International, 67
Club Náutico of San Juan, 40
Club Seabourne, 76
Clubman, 8
Coamo Springs Golf and Tennis Club, 92
Coastal Highway, The, 111–14
Cobo Rojo Lighthouse, 116
Colonial Hotel, 145
Comfort Inn Tanama Princess, 34
Compay Cheo, 44
Complejo El Tuque, 101
Concepts, 46
Condado, 32–36
Condado Plaza Hotel and Casino, 33
Convento de los Dominicos, 15
Copamarina Hotel & Beach Resort, 106
Coral Princess Inn, 34
Costa del Mar Guest House, 80
Costa Dorado Beach Resort, 136
Costa Marina, 91
Covadonga, 3
Cristo Street, 17–22
Cronopolis Bookstore, 23
Crow's Nest, 74
Cueva Clara de Empalme, 131
Cueva de Doña Geña, 149
Cueva del Indio, 129
Culebra, 69–70, 75–77
Culebra Leatherback Project, 75
Culebrita, 77

D

Daniel's Seafood, 79
Desecho Dive and Surf Shop, 149
Dewey, 76

Diamond Palace Hotel & Casino, 35
Dinghy Dock, The, 76
Divers Outlet, 65
Divino Bacadito, 23
DMR Gallery, 23
Domes Beach, 142
Domínguez Pharmacy, 120
Don Pablo's, 17
Doña Juana Falls, 164
Doña Juana Recreational Area, 163
Dorado, 125
Dorado City Hall, 127
Dragonfly, 10
Dumas Restaurant, 30
Dunbar's Pub, 36

E

East Wind II Catamaran, 66
Eastern Mountains, The, 155–60
Eclipse, 137
Eco Xcursion Aquatica, 60, 69
El Arsenal, 4
El Batey, 17, 76
El Boquerón, 13
El Buen Café, 134
El Cairo, 46
El Canario by the Lagoon, 35
El Canario by the Sea, 35
El Canario Inn, 35
El Capitolio, 31
El Casino, 11
El Castillo San Felipe del Morro, 13
El Cocal, 80
El Comandante Hipódromo, 58
El Convento de Fátima, 106
El Faro, 69
El Galpón, 20
El Hamburger, 31
El Malecón, 127
El Merendero Sport Center, 45
El Mojito, 158
El Molino, 83
El Monte, 158
El Morro, 13
El Nuevo Horizonte, 80
El Patio Colonial, 99
El Patio de Sam, 13
El Pescador, 44, 113

INDEX

El Picazo, 68
El Picoteo Tapas Bar, 18
El Popular, 44
El Portal Tropical Forest Center, 62
El Quíinque, 13
El Quijote Beach Cabañas, 142
El Rancho Numbero Uno, 158
El Ricón Surf/Beach Shop, 138
El Teatro de Puerta Rico, 42
El Tivoli, 80
El Túnel Pizzeria, 139
El Túnel, 135, 136
El Tuque, 101
El Vigía Observation Tower, 99
El Yunque, 61–64
El Zipperle, 46
Ensenada, 110
Ensenada Honda, 76
Erin Go Bragh Charters, 66
Escambrón Beach Club & Restaurant, 30
Escuela de Artes Plasticas, 16
Esperanza, 72

F

Fajardo, 66–68
Fajardo Inn, 67
Fajardo Tours, 67
Ferries Del Caribe, 146
Festival del Tejído, 138
Fine Arts Cinema, 41
Fishes and Crabs, 48
Florida, 74
Ford Conde de Mirasol Museum, 72
Fortaleza, 3–11
fortresses, 11–17
Fox Delicias Mall, 96
Frank Meisler Sculptures, 7
Frida's, 46

G

Galería Arte Espinal, 24
Galería Arte Luna, 23
Galería Botello, 47
Galería Fosil Arte, 20
Galería Moro, 23
Galería Palomas, 21
Galeria Raices, 43
Galería Wilfredo Labiosa, 24

Gallery Cafe, 8
Gallery Inn, The, 11
Galloway's Bar & Restaurant, 117
Godfather's, 41
Gopal, 24
Great Lady, 127
Green Isle Inn, 39
Guajataca Beach, 135
Guajataca Forest, 133
Guánica, 104–111
Guánica Bay, 106
Guánica Forest Reserve, 108
Guavate, 157
Guayama, 82–83
Guaypao, 110
guest houses, xii
Guilarte Forest Reserve, 167
Guillermo's Econdite Pub, 116

H

Hacienda Buena Vista, 101
Hacienda Caribaldí, 65
Hacienda Enrique, 139
Hacienda La Esperanza, 129
Hacienda Lucía, 80
Hacienda Restaurant, 104
Hacienda Tamarindo, 73
Haitian Gallery, 10
Hang Loose Surf Shop, 137
Happy Belly's on the Beach, 137
Hatillo, 134
Hato Rey, 11, 45–48
Hecho a Mano, 23
Heladería Lares, 169
Hemingway's Place, 55
Hijos de Borinquén, 13
Hiram Bithorn Stadium, 47
Hix Island House, 74
Holiday Inn Mayagüez, 145
Hollywood Café, 99
Hormigueros, 146
Horned Dorset Primavera Hotel, 142
Hostal Colegial, 146
Hostería del Mar, 37
Hotel Cielo Mar, 138
Hotel Delicias, 67
Hotel El Convento, 17
Hotel El Tuque, 101

Hotel Hacienda El Pedregal, 138
Hotel La Playa, 39
Hotel Meliá, 96
Hotel Milano, 8
Hotel Parador Oasis, 119
Hotel Parador Palmas de Lucía, 80
Hotel Plaza de Armas, 22
Hotel Villa Forín, 138
Humacao, 79–80
Humacao Wildlife Refuge, 79
Hungry Sailor, 38
Hyatt Dorado Beach Resort and Country
    Club, 127

I

Iglesia del Espíritu Santo y San
    Patricio, 58
Iglesia de San José, 14
Iglesía San Francisco de Asís, 139
Il Grottino, 35
Il Perugino, 17
Inches Beach, 81
Indigenous Festival, 165
Inn on the Blue Horizon, 73
inns, xii
Instituto de Cultura Puertorriquena, 16
Interamerican University, 119
Inter-Continental San Juan Resort and
    Casino, 38
Isabela, 135
Isabel Segunda, 70
Isla de Cordona, 100
Isla de Magueyes, 113
Isla Desecheo, 142, 149
Isla Mata de Gata, 111, 113
Isla Mona, 147
Isla Nena, 67
Isla Verde, 38–40
Island Adventures, 74
Island Ventures, 100

J

Jah Rastafari Store, 24
Jájome, 159
Jájome Terrace, 159
Jayuya, 164
Jerusalem Restaurant, 46
Jobos Bay, 83

Joyuda Beach, 117
Juan A. Palerm Transportation Center, 49
Jungle Jane's, 165

K

Kaipo Kayak Rentals, 117
Kamel Art Gallery, 20
Karst Country, 130–34
Kasalta's Bakery, 36
King's Cream, 96
Krugger's, 13

L

L'Habitation, 36
La Alcadía, 145
La Bandera, 143
La Bodega del Hipopótamo, 49
La Bombanera, 23
La Cadena Hills, 140
La Caleta, 19
La Calle, 7
La Casa de las Casitas and Handcraft, 21
La Casa del Peru, 23
La Cascada, 117
La Casita Blanca, 42
La Casita Restaurant, 113
La Casona de Guavate, 157
La Casona de Juanita, 169
La Cava, 100
La Chaumiere, 11
La Cima Burger, 143
La Cima Hotel, 138
La Cruz de Colón, 138
La Cubanita, 13
La Cueva de Maria la Cruz, 58
La Cueva del Chicken Inn, 46
La Familia, 68
La Finca el Caribe, 74
La Fonda de Angelo, 92
La Fonda El Jibarito, 23
La Fortaleza, 6
La Guancha, 99
La Guardarraya, 104
La Mallorquina, 22
La Ostra Cosa, 20
La Parguera, 107, 111
La Piedra Escrita, 165
La Piedra Resturant, 160

INDEX

La Plaza de la Revolución, 169
La Pocita #2, 55
La Querencia, 9
La Reliquia, 158
La Rogativa, 18
La Rumba, 11
La Rumba, 14
La Selva Surf Shop, 65
La Soleil Beach Club, 55
La Terraza, 55
La Vereda, 55
Lago Caonillas, 165
Lago Cidra, 159
Lago Dos Bocas, 165
Lago Guineo, 164
Laguna Grande, 69
Laguna Tortuguero Nature Reserve, 128
Lajas, 114
Landing, The, 141
Lares, 168
Las Cabañas de Doña Juana, 164
Las Cabezas de San Juan, 68–69
Las Casas de la Selva, 155
Las Casitas Village, 68
Las Colinas, 140
Las Cucharas, 102
Las Marías, 170
Las Tortugas Adventures, 100
Lazy Parrot Inn & Restaurant, The, 141
Le Petit Chalet, 65
Lechonera Carmelo, 59
Lechonera El Rancho Original, 158
Legends of Puerto Rico, 163
Leonides, 139
Lion Fountain, 95
Liquid, 38
Lis A. Ferré Performing Arts Center, 43
Loíza Aldea, 56
Loquillo, 65
Los Castillos Meléndez, 139
Los Piños, 158
Lost Tubos, 128
Luchetti Lake, 104
Luis A. Ferré Science Park, 125
Lupi's Mexican Grill and Sports
    Cantina, 5
Luquillo, 64–66
Luquillo Beach Inn, 65

M

Majimo, 113
Mamacita's, 76
Mango's Café, 37
Mar & Tierra Restaurant and Bar, 112
Maria's, 21
Maricao, 169–70
Maricao Fish Hatchery, 169
Maricao Forest, 169
Marina de Salinas, 83
Marina de Salinas and Posada El
    Náutico, 91
Marina Puerto Chico, 67
Mark's at the Meliá, 96
Martí Coll Linear Park, 46
Martini's, 39
Martino's, 35
Mary Lee's by the Sea, 108
Máscaras de Puerto Rico, 7
Maunabo, 80–81
Mayagüez, 144–47
Mayagüez Resort & Casino, 145
Mayagüez Zoo, 146
Mercado de Río Piedras, 48
Metropol Restaurant, 39
Mi Coquí, 98
Mi Pequeño San Juan, 17
Miguelito's Pinchos, 110
Miramar, 40–41
Moca, 139
Mona Aquatics, 149
Mona Island Museum, 149
Monolo Diaz, 17
Monte Guilarte, 167
Moondance, 8
Mosquito Bay, 74
Mount Pirata, 75
Mount Resaca, 77
Municipal Vacation Center Luis Muñoz
    Marín, 134
Muñoz Marin Park, 48
Museo Casa Cautiño
Museo Casa Natal de Luis Muñoz
    Rivera, 161
Museo de Aguadia, 139
Museo de Arte de Puerto Rico, 45
Museo de la Familia del Siglo XIX, 9

Museo de la Farmacia, 9
Museo de las Américas, 16
Museo de Nuestra Raíz Africana, 14
Museo del Niño, 18
Museo Felisa Rincón de Gautier, 18
Museo Historico de Coamo, 94
Museo Pablo Casals, 14
Museum of Anthropology, History and
    Art, 48
Museum of Contemporary Puerto Rican
    Art, 42
Museum of Puerto Rican Music, 97
Museum of the History of Ponce, The, 97
Music People, 43

N
Naguabo, 78–79
National Wildlife Refuge, 75
Natural Islands, The, 147–49
Nono's, 13
North Coast, The, 134–34
Norzagaray, 11–17
Numero Uno Guest House, 37
Nuyorican Café, 9

O
Ocean Front Hotel and Restaurant, 137
Ocean Park, 36–38
Ocean Park Beach Inn, 36
Ocean Villas, 60
Ocean Walk Guesthouse, The, 36
Old San Juan, 1–25
Olé, 7
Orocovis, 162

P
Palacete Los Moreau, 139
Palomino Island Divers, 68
Pamela's Caribbean Cuisine, 37
Panorama Terrace Bar and Latin Grill, 8
Panoramic Route, 153
Papi's Pinchos, 111
Paradise Scuba Center, 113
Paradisus Puerto Rico, 60
Parador Baños de Coamo, 93
Parador Boquemar, 117
Parador Borinquén, 138
Parador El Faro, 138

Parador El Guajataca, 134
Parador Hacienda Gripiñas, 164
Parador Hacienda Juanita, 169
Parador Hotel El Sol, 145
Parador JB Hidden Village, 140
Parador Pichi's, 102
Parador Posada Porlamar, 113
Parador Villa Parguera, 113
Parador Vistamar, 135
Pareo, 7
Parguera Fishing Charters, 113
Park Plaza Normandic Hotel, 29
Parking Ballajá, 16
Parque Acuatico Las Cascadas, 138
Parque de Bombas, 96
Parque de Colón, 139
Parque de Las Flores, 110
Parque de las Monjas, 18
Parque de las Palomas, 21
Parroquia San Antonio de Padua, 161
Parrot Club, The, 9
Paseo Arias, 96
Paseo Atocha, 97
Paseo de Diego, 49
Paseo de la Princesa, 5
Paseo de Piñones, 56
Patillas, 81
Patio del Níspero, 18
Pedro Albizu Campos Recreation
    Area, 135
Peña Pará, 31
Phosphorescent Bay, 113
Pichi's Steakhouse and Seafood, 102
Pico Atalaya, 143,
Pikayo, 45
Pilón, 74
Piñones, 53–59
Piñones Ecotours, 56
Pirate's Cay, 76
Pirichi's, 117
Pito's Seafood Café, 102
Playa Boquerón, 114
Playa de Emajaguas, 81
Playa de Guayanilla, 102
Playa de Naguabo, 78
Playa de Ponce, 99
Playa del Dorado, 127
Playa Escondido, 68

INDEX

Playa Flamenco, 77
Playa Húcares, 79
Playa Humacao, 79
Playa Jauca, 92
Playa Jobos, 135, 136
Playa Joyuda, 117
Playa Larga, 80
Playa Lucía, 80
Playa Luquillo, 64
Playa Mar Chiquita, 128
Playa Montones, 136
Playa Santa, 110
Playa Santa Isabel, 92
Playa Sardinera, 148
Playa Seven Seas, 66, 68
Playa 79, 55
Playa Shacks, 137
Playa Tortuguero, 128
Playa Uvero, 149
Playa Zoni, 77
Playita Rosada, 113
Plaza Colón, 10, 145
Plaza de Armas, 22–24
Plaza de Hostos, 4
Plaza de San José, 14
Plaza del Mercado, 97
Plaza del Quinto Centenario, 16
Plaza las Américas, 47
Plaza Las Delicias, 95
Plaza Santo Domingo, 120
Plazoleta Rafael Carrión Pacheco, 4
Plazuela de la Rogativa, 18
Pleasure, 42
Ponce, 94–104
Ponce Hilton, 100
Ponce Museum of Art, The, 100
Ponce Yacht Club, 99
Porta Coeli Church, 119
Portofino, 66
Posada La Hamaca, 76
Proyecto Peces, 79
public thermal pools, 93
Pueblo, 22
Puerta de San Juan, 6
Puerta de Tierra, 29–32
Puerta La Bahía Hotel and Restaurant, 91
Puerto del Rey Marina, 66
Puerto Maunabo, 80

Puerto Real Bay, 117
Puerto Rican Art and Crafts, 8
Puerto Rico International Film
    Festival, 45
Puerto Rico International Speedway, 91
Pulpo Loco, 55
Punta Borinquen Golf, 137
Punta Guilarte, 81
Punta Higuera Lighthouse, 141
Punta Mar, 141
Punta Santiago, 79
Punta Tuna, 80
Punta Vacía Talega, 56

Q
Quebradillas, 134

R
Rafael Hernandez Airport, 137
Raíces, 5
Ramiro's, 34
Rancho de Caballos de Utuado, 165
Recinto Universitario Mayagüez, 145
Reef Bar and Grill, 53
Regency Hotel, 33
Reserva Forestal Carite, 156
Restaurant Croabas, 68
Restaurant Don Telfo, 44
Restaurant Siglo XX, 9
Restaurante El Mar de la
    Tranquilidad, 81
Restaurante Tantra, 9
Rincón, 140–43
Rincón Beach Resort, 143
Rincón Surf & Board Caribbean Surfari
    Guest House, 141
Río Abajo Forest, 133
Río Camuy Cave Park, 131, 133
Río Grande, 59–60
Río Grande de Loíza, 56
Río Grande Plantation Resort, 60
Río Piedras, 48–49
Río Usabon, 160
Ritz-Carlton San Juan Hotel and Casino,
    The, 39
Roberto Clemente Coliseum, 47
Rocar Seafood, 68
Roosevelt Roads, 68

Rosa's Sea Food Restaurant, 67
Ruta Panorámica, 80
Ruth's Chris Steak House, 39

S

Sabana Grande, 118
Sabores Al Natural, 45
Sacred Heart University, 42
Sala, 8
Salud, 35
Saminá, 8
Samuel Lind, 58
San Cristóbal Canyon, 160
San Germán Region, The, 117–20
San Gerónimo Bridge, 32
San Jacinto, 108
San Jacinto Restaurant, 108
San Juan, Metopolitan, 27–52
San Juan, Old, 1–25
San Juan Bay Marina, 40
San Juan Cinemafest, 45
San Juan Marriott Hotel & Stellaris
   Casino, 35
San Juan Symphony Orchestra, 43
San Sebastián, 11–17
Sand and the Sea, The, 159
Sandy Beach, 141
Sangria Coño, 112
Santa Ana Chapel, 24
Santuario de la Virgen del Pozo, 118
Santurce, 41–45
Santurce Marketplace, 44
Scenic Inn, 67
Sea Lovers Marina, 67
Sea Ventures Pro Dive Center, 66
Shamar Bar, 116
Shannon's, 49
Sharkey's Beach, 80
Sierra de Cayey, 159
Sin Titulo Galería de Arte
   Contemporaneo, 23
spelunking, 133
Spicy Caribee, 20
Spread Eagle, 67
St. Mick's Irish Pub and Restaurant, 37
St. Moritz, 33
Steam Works, The, 23
Sun Bay, 70

Sunset Beach Village, 81
surfing, 56

T

Taíno Divers, 149
Taller Galería En Blanco, 23
Tamarindo Estates, 76
tangerine, 38
taxis, xii, 7
Teatro La Perla, 96
Teatro Metro, 45
Teatro Tapia, 10
Teatro Yagücz, 145
13 Calle Dr. Santiago Veve, 120
Tibes Indian Ceremonial Center, 100
Tienda Bazaar Maria Lasalle, 139
Tierra Santa, 46
Toro Negro Forest, 163
Toro Negro Forest Reserve, 163
Torres de la Parguera, 113
Trade Winds, 73
Traditions, 8
travel information, xiv
Traveler, 67
Tree House Studio, 60
Tren del Sur de Arroyo, 82
Tres Pueblos Sinkhole, 131
Trinidad Gust House, 65
Trois Cent Onze, 8
Tropical Agriculture Research
   Station, 146
Tropical Fishing Charters, 68
Tropical Paradise Horseback Riding, 127
Tropical Trail Rides, 137
Tulio's Seafood, 79

U

Ultimate Trolley Beach, 37
University of Puerto Rico, 48, 159
Unplugged Café, The, 43
Urdin, 34
Utopia, 98
Utuado, 165

V

vacation centers, xii
Vega Alta Forest, 133
Ventajero Sailing Charters, 66

INDEX

Via Appia, 35
Vieques, 69–75
Vieques Air Link, 67
Viet Nam Palace Seafood Restaurant, 5
Villa de Carmen, 81
Villa Marina Yacht Harbor, 67
Villa Montaña, 137
Villaba, 163
Villas del Faro, 81
Villas Del Mar Hau, 136
Vista de Lago, 133

W
Warehouse, 42
Water Club, The, 38
Waterfront, The, 3–11
Wenchy's, 135
Western Mountains, The, 166–70
Westin Río Mar Beach Resort and
    Country Club, 60

Wheels for Fun, 10
Wildflowers Antiques, Cafe & Inn, 116
Wyndham El Conquistador Resort and
    Country Club, 67
Wyndham El San Juan Hotel & casino, 39
Wyndham Martineau Bay Resort and
    Spa, 75

Y
Yabacoa, 80
Yabucoa, 155
Yauco, 103
Yokahu Kayak Trips, 68
Yuan, 46
Yukiyu Sushi Bar and Teppan-Yaki, 5
Yum Yum Tree, The, 46

Z
Zabó Cocina Creativa, 36

About the Authors

Tina Cohen travels to Spanish-speaking countries and spends time on islands as often as possible. She writes about Latin America, art, and her favorite islands: Puerto Rico and off the coast of Maine. Being both a high school librarian and adventuress, she has discovered that research and road trips go together.

John Marino is city editor at the *San Juan Star*. He writes frequently about Puerto Rico and the Caribbean for the *New York Times*, Reuters news agency, *Newsday*, the *Economist Intelligence Unit*, and other publications.